What
JESUS
SAID ABOUT THE
HOLY SPIRIT

What

JESUS

SAID ABOUT THE

HOLY SPIRIT

AND HOW IT APPLIES TO

YOUR LIFE

TIM WOODROOF

LEAFWOOD
PUBLISHERS

Abilene, Texas

What Jesus Said about the Holy Spirit
and How It Applies to Your Life

Copyright 2010 by Tim Woodroof

ISBN 978-0-89112-647-8
LCCN 2010023112

Printed in the United States of America

Scripture quotations in this book, unless otherwise noted, are from The Holy
Bible, New International Version. Copyright 1984, International Bible Society.
Used by permission of Zondervan Publishers.

LIBRARY OF CONGRESS CATALOGING-IN-PUBLICATION DATA
Woodroof, Tim, 1955-
  What Jesus said about the Holy Spirit and how it applies to your life / Tim
Woodroof.
      p. cm.
  Includes bibliographical references (p.   ).
  ISBN 978-0-89112-647-8
  1. Jesus Christ--Teachings. 2. Holy Spirit--Biblical teaching. 3. Spiritual life--
Christianity. 4. Holy Spirit. I. Title.
  BS2417.H65W66 2010
  248.4--dc22
                                                    2010023112

Cover design by Marc Whitaker
Interior text design by Sandy Armstrong

Leafwood Publishers
1626 Campus Court
Abilene, Texas 79601

1-877-816-4455 toll free
For current information about all Leafwood titles, visit our Web site:
www.leafwoodpublishers.com

10 11 12 13 14 15 / 7 6 5 4 3 2 1

CONTENTS

Acknowledgements

Please allow me to thank several people for their kindnesses to me during the writing of the book.

I initially thought through this material while preaching for the Otter Creek Church in Nashville, Tennessee. I am grateful for their patience and for the freedom they gave me to color outside the lines. The writing of this book was also made possible by their financial support as I transitioned out of a preaching role to a new work as writer and church consultant.

I also worked through these ideas at the Abilene Christian University lectureships, the Christian Educators' Conference (a dedicated group of ministers—I appreciate you), and churches in Louisville, Kentucky, and Wichita, Kansas. My thanks to each audience for careful listening and enthusiastic response.

Writing requires quiet and privacy. Lee and Kelley Beaman and Rex and Cathy Harrison provided guest houses for me. And, increasingly, writing requires technological support: my grateful thanks to Kirk Davidson and his computer wizardry.

Several readers made comments on the manuscript—always supportive, often helpful, and sometimes vital. I am grateful to Grady King, Brad Sullivan, Benjamin Neeley, Curt Sparks, and—especially—Jerry Neill, Edward Fudge, Mom, Dad, David, and my sweet Julie. The book wouldn't be the same without your encouraging and insightful partnership.

As I write this, I'm preparing to travel to Beaverton, Oregon, to preach the funeral of a man whose friendship and mentoring have meant the world to me—Ron Stump. He was a great man in God's Kingdom, a greatness measured not in acclaim or wealth but in the pleasure of the Father. I miss you already, Ron.

Finally, a word of thanks to Leonard Allen: for seeing the great need to talk about the Spirit, for his encouragement of this project, and for his sensitive editing.

Chapter One

JESUS, THE SPIRIT, AND THE FINAL DISCOURSE

No wonder they are frightened. Something awful is about to happen. They don't know what. They don't know when. But soon. And terrible.

They can see it written on their Master's face, bearing down on his shoulders. They can smell it in the air, the sour stench of danger. They can feel the pressure of its coming—like a storm approaching.

So they gather this night in dread. It's hard for them to meet each other's eyes. Conversations are subdued. A meal is prepared but no one has much appetite. They pick at their food. They pick at each other. There are no jokes, no lighthearted banter. Their Master is "troubled in spirit," and the disciples match his mood.

Everything is about to change. And none of them wants that.

None but he. He wants it. In ways, he welcomes it. He knows exactly what is about to happen and when. He's known all his life. On this evening, no doubt, he has his own fears to wrestle with, his own dread. After all, the blood to be spilled will be his. The agony endured will be his.

But it is *their* agony that consumes him this evening, their fears and uncertainties. Everything is about to change. And he wants their faith to survive the storm.

He's tried to warn them that this would not end well. Cryptically at first ("The Son of Man must suffer many things"); more bluntly later ("I lay down my life"). And they see glimmers of the dangers he faces; they know about the threats and the plots. The anxieties and sense of dread they bring to this final supper indicate they sense something awful will happen and soon.

Yet still they seem confused by it all, stunned, like witnesses to a senseless tragedy. They don't understand Mary's anointing and its appropriateness to the moment. They don't understand the meaning of the triumphant crowds and how they will force the Pharisees' hands. They don't understand about Judas.

They don't get it. Even this close to the end, they don't get it. Perhaps they can't *afford* to get it. They have too much at stake.

Addicted to His Presence

They left everything to follow him—families, friends, houses, businesses. They trudged after him for three long years, sharing the fatigues of the road and the poverty of nomads, the conflicts in the synagogues, the successes and failures with the crowds. They saw wondrous things in that time: water to wine, temples cleansed, the lame healed, the blind given sight, a dead man called from the tomb. They *heard* wondrous things as well: "I am the bread of life," "I am the resurrection and the life," "I am the way, the truth, and the life."

What they saw and heard changed them. They are different men now, unfitted for fishing boats and tax tables. Their lives have been turned upside down. Jesus has done his damage. They've followed him and cannot turn back. "You don't want to leave too, do you?" Jesus asked them once as the fickle crowd leaked away. Peter's reply—"Lord, to whom shall we go?"—is part confession of faith and part lament. They believe Jesus has "words of eternal life." But he has also ruined them for ordinary living. That's what happens when you grow accustomed to the company of the Holy One of God.

And Jesus knows that also. He intended it. It was the reason he came, the reason he called them. All along, he planned to bind them to himself, addict them to his presence, and create a dependency on him from which they will never recover. Not just a need for his words or his wisdom or his wonders—a need for Jesus himself, his closeness, his intimate imminence.

Jesus taught them that being with him was better than families and friends. He showed them that being with him was better than Torah and Temple and tradition. He proved that when they were with him, they need not go hungry ("I am the bread of life"), they need not fear thief or robber ("I am the good shepherd"), they need not dread death ("I am the resurrection and the life"). They have learned that, so long as Jesus is in the boat, winds and waves cannot prevail.

They count on him. They rely on him. They depend on him.

"I Will Come to You"

But all that is about to change. On this last night—as Jesus washes their feet, as he breaks bread with them, as he sends Judas off to do his treacherous business—he understands that he has only a few hours to prepare them for life in his *absence* after spending three years persuading them that life in his *presence* is the only life worth living.

He is leaving them. And he has this last conversation—the "Final Discourse," recorded in John 13-16—to help them come to grips with that terrible truth.

> My children, I will be with you only a little longer. You will look for me, and just as I told the Jews, so I tell you now: Where I am going, you cannot come. (John 13:33)
>
> I am going to the Father, where you can see me no longer. (John 16:10)
>
> I came from the Father and entered the world; now I am leaving the world and going back to the Father. (John 16:28)[1]

Over and over. Repeatedly. Without relent. Ten times in the span of four chapters—"I am going away." This is Jesus the truth-teller, stubbornly stabbing a hard truth home. This is Jesus the bad-news prophet, predicting their biggest fear. Things are about to change. Jesus is leaving. And they can't stop him, they can't change his mind, they can't go with him.

No wonder they are "troubled" and afraid. No wonder they share such foreboding. They are right to be anxious. After all they'd been through, after all they'd sacrificed, Jesus is leaving them. And now they must contemplate a life without his voice, without his touch, without his face.

But that's not the whole story. Not by a long shot. As determined as Jesus is to tell his disciples he is going away, he is equally determined to tell them that he is *not* going away, that he will *never* leave them. After the leaving, he wants them to know there is a "coming again":

> I will not leave you as orphans; I will come to you. Before long, the world will not see me anymore, but you will see me. (John 14:18-19)
>
> I am going away and I am coming back to you. (John 14:28)
>
> I will see you again and you will rejoice, and no one will take away your joy. (John 16:22)[2]

Ten times in the same span of chapters. Ten antidotes to the toxic news of his departure—"I shall return." We hear this promise and immediately think of the resurrection. But Jesus has another "return" in mind. Or perhaps we hear this promise and think of Jesus coming on the clouds to gather us home. But that's not what he's talking about either. What Jesus has in mind on this last night is another sort of return entirely—a return we will spend this book exploring.

We can excuse the disciples, this difficult evening, for hearing the word "leaving" and listening to nothing else. But for Jesus, the "leaving" is not the point. It's the "coming back" that is important.

This is the overriding message of the Final Discourse. *This* is the fundamental point of everything Jesus has to say. Jesus is steeling his disciples for his departure with the repeated and emphatic promise that he is not abandoning them. It will seem that way, no doubt. It will *feel* as if he is dead and gone. But the reality will be very different.

Jesus has a plan for them—a plan to remain present with them beyond the grave.

The Spirit

It is in the Final Discourse that Jesus introduces his disciples (and us) to the *Paraclete*—the Holy Spirit the Father is about to send. He's already said important things about the Spirit in John's Gospel (e.g., the Spirit's role in new birth and true worship and full life). But he's never used this name before: *Paraclete*. Nor has he ever spoken as frankly and fully on the role of the Spirit in the lives of believers as here, on the eve of his exit.

He knows his time is short. He knows the disciples need something to sustain them in the days ahead, something to fill the vacuum of his imminent absence. Of the many things Jesus *could* have spoken about to prepare his disciples for his leaving, it is the Holy Spirit he chooses to focus on. In five sublime *Paraclete Passages* (John 14:16-21, 25-27; 15:26-27; 16:7-11, 12-16), Jesus introduces them to the "Companion," the "Comforter," the "Guide," explaining when the Spirit will come, what the Spirit will do, how the Spirit will help, and why the Spirit will be their sustaining strength for the remainder of their lives.

Although Jesus mentions other subjects in the Final Discourse, the promise of the *Paraclete* is his dominant theme. He talks about the *Paraclete* repeatedly. He keeps coming back to the subject. He never really leaves it. The *Paraclete* as his presence when he is gone. The *Paraclete* living in them and walking with them. The *Paraclete* teaching them what they need to know. The *Paraclete* calming their troubled hearts and giving them peace. The *Paraclete* testifying to the world and encouraging their testimony. The *Paraclete* convicting the world of guilt. The *Paraclete* continuing to reveal the Father.

Jesus says more about the Spirit in the course of this one conversation than in all his other teachings combined. With his last words, he throws the disciples the Spirit, a life-preserver to keep them afloat on the rough seas to come.

He doesn't offer them Torah or the Psalms. He doesn't point them to the faith of people in the past to bolster their faith in the future. He doesn't draw a parallel between Moses (stuck in the wilderness between Egypt and the Promised Land) and themselves (caught between incarnation and second coming).

He doesn't shore up their self-esteem. He doesn't tell them they have what it takes to tough out the hard days to come. He doesn't ask them to be brave or keep their eye on the ball. He doesn't encourage them to think positively.

Nor does he point them to each other, suggesting they draw strength and courage from intimate fellowship to survive the coming years. Love each other, yes. Wash each other's feet, certainly. But as Jesus prepares to leave them, he knows it will take something stronger than affection and mutual support if they are to persevere and carry on his mission.

He doesn't give them the sacraments or the church as the sustaining force of their lives in the future. He doesn't tell them that the New Testament will be their guide, if only they can hang on for thirty or forty years. He mentions only briefly and cryptically his second coming ("I will come back and take you to be with me"—John 14:3), but he doesn't suggest that the hope of his return will uphold them with the vigor they'll require.

What he offers his disciples on the cusp of his departure is a relationship with a living, indwelling, empowering, equipping, convicting, and revealing Spirit; someone who will be for them in the future what he has been for them in the past; someone who will continue his presence and mission forever; someone who will transform ninety-eight-pound spiritual weaklings into heroes of God's kingdom.

Of all the things Jesus could have talked about this final night, it is the Holy Spirit of God who dominates the conversation. And the time has come for disciples like us to ask the question, "Why?"

A Good Beginning

There is a crucial moment in the ministry of John the Baptist when he knew his work was coming to an end. He had accomplished the mission God had given him to do. He'd gone into the wilderness preaching. He'd announced the coming Messiah. He'd identified the "Lamb of God" and baptized him in the Jordan River. He'd pointed his disciples towards "the one who comes after me."

Already his influence was waning. Soon he would be in Herod's prison, baring his neck to the executioner's sword.

But John was at peace. His work was finished. Jesus' work was beginning. And that was as it should be. When a few remaining disciples complained that Jesus was preaching and baptizing and "everyone is going to him" (John 3:26), John just smiled and uttered the classic line, "He must become greater; I must become less" (John 3:30).

Something very similar is happening in the Final Discourse. Jesus understands that his ministry is coming to an end, that he has done what his Father has sent him to do. Just a cross and a tomb remain. But he understands also that *Another* is coming, with a new mission and a vital work. Like John before him, Jesus announces the "one who comes after me" and then points the disciples in his direction. All the talk Jesus does about the *Paraclete* during these final hours, all the promises he makes about the Spirit are—in essence—Jesus smiling and telling the Twelve, "I must become less; He must become greater."

Not "less" and "greater" in the sense of importance or significance. It is, rather, a matter of timing and emphasis. Jesus and his work have been the focus of the disciples up to this last night. Now, Jesus tells them, their focus must shift and broaden.

Jesus knew his life and ministry, his teachings and his imminent death, were a good beginning for the kingdom. But that's all they were: a beginning. That's all he ever meant them to be. Jesus never thought of his life-on-earth, his death-on-a-cross as the closing chapter in God's salvation book. There were more chapters yet to be written about the kingdom of God breaking into the world. And those final chapters would be authored by the Holy Spirit.

In the Final Discourse, we see Jesus marking that crucial moment when his work ends and the Spirit's work begins. His calling, teaching, healing, dying, and rising work was necessary to accomplish God's will. But so, too, was the work the Spirit was about to undertake—a maturing, transforming, guiding, revealing, encouraging, emboldening, convicting, sustaining work. All Jesus had achieved through his ministry and in the lives of his disciples would have no sustainable life, no persistent power and effect, without the subsequent ministry of the Spirit. Without the Spirit, his disciples would founder. They would lose hope and lack power. How long after the last of his resurrection appearances would their commitment last? Without the Spirit's ministry, Peter and the others were likely to give up and go fishing (John 21:3).

Jesus knew as much. He knew that, with his leaving, it was only a matter of time before these men left as well—back to their boats and their families, dead dreams discarded.

Jesus, however, had something much better in mind. He knew the Spirit was on the way. He knew the Spirit's work would sustain and equip these men for the mission ahead. He was counting on the Spirit "becoming greater."

That's why he talked at such length about the Spirit that last night. He needed his disciples to know there was *another* coming. He needed them to understand what that *other* would do for them. And he needed them to shift their dependence on his physical presence to an unwavering dependence on the Spirit who would be present with them forever.

Their dreams depended on this. His mission depended on it. The hope of the world hung upon it.

The Spirit and Us

Most believers today haven't recognized the Final Discourse as a primary resource for understanding the role of the Holy Spirit in our lives. We haven't taken seriously what Jesus says here about the *Paraclete*. Which is odd, given that our circumstance as believers today is so similar to the situation faced by the Twelve as Jesus prepares to leave. They were wondering what becomes of disciples who can no longer see, hear, and touch their Master. We wonder the same thing. The remainder of their lives, the rest of their ministries, will play out in the context of Jesus' departure and absence. Our lives and ministries are shaped by that same reality. For us, as for them, the struggle to follow a missing Lord is real and wracking. Like them, we yearn for and need a relationship with Jesus more tangible than the memory of his words and deeds.

So when Jesus promises them he is coming back, you'd think we would crowd around the Twelve to ask if Jesus is talking to us as well. When Jesus offers them a Spirit by which he intends to be present again, you'd expect us to ask whether that Spirit is for the rest of us. When he tells them about an indwelling, empowering, equipping Spirit available for disciples, we should be straining to hear every word.

But we're not.

It's odd, too, that we tend to overlook this section of John when it speaks to such a critical handoff (from Jesus to the Spirit) that has such significance for our lives and discipleship. If Jesus intended for the Spirit to take up the care and feeding of his followers after he left, shouldn't we be curious about that? If Jesus counted on the Spirit's work to sustain and equip his disciples, shouldn't we know about that and depend on it?

Apparently not. For many of us have been deaf to Jesus' promises about the Spirit in John's Final Discourse. For some, this deafness stems from an assumption that his words are not relevant to us. They were for the Twelve alone: special men, specially chosen and commissioned, with special powers and privileges. Disciples today can *eavesdrop* on this conversation and *overhear* what Jesus tells the Apostles about the Spirit. But these words weren't meant for us. Jesus never intended for us to take these Spirit-promises personally.

For others, this deafness can only be explained by a consuming focus on the Spirit in other parts of Scripture. There are those who run right past the Spirit in the Final Discourse in their eagerness to get to the Spirit in Acts. Better to marvel over the Spirit's dramatic work in the first-century church (and yearn for a similar experience) than to dwell on the details of this difficult discussion about someone named "the *Paraclete*."

Either way, we haven't really lingered with Jesus in the Upper Room and given serious attention to his teaching about the Spirit's nature and mission. Which is a shame. Because what Jesus says in the Final Discourse about the *Paraclete* provides compelling reasons for rethinking what we believe about the Spirit and his work.

First, Jesus himself is our guide to the Spirit in this section of John. In other parts of the New Testament, where other words are spoken about the Spirit, it is Luke or Paul or Peter who does the talking. I certainly believe these writers are inspired and speak with Jesus' voice. I do not think their words about the Spirit are in any way "secondary" or "once removed" from Jesus himself. But I do find it compelling when Jesus is directly quoted on any subject—especially when he has something to say about a matter as important as the Holy Spirit. He mentions the Spirit rarely in the other Gospels. In John, however, Jesus speaks directly and at length about the Spirit *fifteen* times. And that's important for people who are hungry to hear from Jesus himself on this subject.

Second, the Final Discourse places great emphasis on *who* the Spirit is, not just what the Spirit does. He is a Companion, a Helper, a Teacher, and a Comforter. More than that, as we will see, he is *Jesus* present again and forever in the world. His work is Jesus' work. His name is Jesus' name. He shares Jesus' heart and priorities and character. The Holy Spirit is no stranger, with an odd agenda and an unknown nature. Jesus tells us, in the *Paraclete* Passages, that we can trust the Spirit because we know the Spirit. He is Jesus in other form.

Third, what Jesus says in the Final Discourse about the work of the Spirit has little to do with miracles and much to do with making us spiritual. Although Jesus talks about the Spirit at great length in this passage, he never mentions tongues or healing or prophecy or any other supernatural manifestations of the Spirit's gifts. Let me hasten to add that this is not because Jesus disdains such gifts. He is, in fact, the author of them all, blessing his church with every good gift that comes from his Father. But Jesus never mentions miraculous gifts in the *Paraclete* Passages. He has other Spirit-filled matters he wants to discuss with his distraught disciples.

For that reason, while learning about the Spirit from the lips of Jesus, we don't have to wade through the *charismata* to get at the work of the Spirit we value most—transformation, wisdom, Christ-like character, courage—a work of the Spirit (in other words) that can make us *spiritual*. It is that "greater work" of the Spirit Jesus addresses in the Final Discourse. That work is still *supernatural*: the Holy Spirit of God offering us companionship, teaching, peace, courage, conviction, and revelation that no physics can explain. It is still God breaking miraculously into our lives and our world to accomplish his sovereign purposes. But (at least in the Final Discourse) that "in-breaking" happens in our hearts and results in maturity and transformation rather than signs and wonders.

Finally, the Spirit Jesus describes and promises in the Final Discourse is so winsome, so fit for our present need, that pursuing him is worth whatever effort and re-evaluation may be involved. If you read carefully what Jesus says about the Spirit in the Final Discourse, you cannot help but hope for such a Spirit in your own life.

I believe that this *Paraclete* is not a limited-time offer or a temporary measure or a phase the church grows out of or something the birth of the New Testament makes redundant. He is the birthright of all those who leave everything to follow Jesus. He is the inheritance, security, and hope of all who dare to become Christ's disciples. He is the necessary power made available by our Lord to all those who must soldier on in his absence.

A life without the Spirit, a life without his transforming presence, is not the life God intends for us. He never meant for those who love him—then or now—to live in abandonment and absence. He has something far better in store.

Chapter Two

WHY BOTHER WITH
THE SPIRIT?

The subject of the Holy Spirit is difficult for many of us. Truth be told, it's been a difficult subject for most people at most times, beginning with Paul's labored attempts to talk about the Spirit with the Corinthians and running all the way to modern musings about whether and how the Holy Spirit works in our lives today.

It is an emotional subject—threatening, subjective, and intensely personal. It opens old wounds. It awakens old fears. It calls into question long-held assumptions and long-lived conclusions. It makes some of us ask whether there has been too little Spirit in our particular religious heritage. It makes others of us wonder whether, in our tradition, there may have been too *much* Spirit or a skewed view of the Spirit.

It is a subject that, necessarily, drives us back to our Bibles and forces us to ask difficult questions about how we understand Scripture and how (or whether) the horizon of the first-century world intersects with our world today. It raises scholarly issues, involving large words like "hermeneutics" and "pneumatology," that have most of us reaching for aspirin as soon as the dialogue begins.

It is a subject that, unfortunately, has proven divisive over the long history of the church. How ironic that unity and peace, which are the Spirit's gift to the Body (Eph 4:3), should so often be the first casualties when the Holy Spirit comes up for debate.

So why open this can of worms all over again? Why should we bother with the Spirit?

There are many ways to answer that question, to justify yet another look at the role of the Spirit in the life of God's people. I will content myself with just two reasons—the two reasons that go to the heart of my motives for writing this book. One of them has to do with the church at large: the deep divide in the church over the Spirit and his work; the consistent "missing the point" to which the church is prone when it comes to the Spirit's agenda; and the vulnerability of the church when it gets the Spirit wrong. I'm reserving this larger issue for the close of the book (Chapter Sixteen), after we've grappled with Jesus' teachings on the Spirit in the Final Discourse and are better equipped to have that difficult discussion.

For now, let's focus on the second reason—a far more personal reason—for bothering with the Spirit all over again. There is a condition, common to all disciples, that only an authentic relationship with the Spirit can remedy. Contrary to what you may have heard in the current rash of positive-thinking, health-and-wealth, blissed-out preaching so popular these days, following Jesus is messy. It raises all kinds of doubts about God and about ourselves. It confronts us with difficult challenges and difficult people. It is often stressful and pain-filled. It is not—in a word—*easy*. If we are to deal honestly with our calling, we can't avoid the prickly parts of discipleship. The Apostles were facing that very prickliness on the night Jesus announced he was leaving. And the solution he offered them to help blunt the barbs—the *Paraclete*—is the same solution we need to survive the stings and stabs of being disciples in this broken world.

A Confession

Faith is a fight for me.

Perhaps you come to faith more naturally, less awkwardly. There are those who are blessed with the "gift of faith" (1 Cor 12:9). If you are that kind of Christian, please accept my congratulations and forgive my envy. But faith has always been a struggle for me. I wake up every day to wrestle once again with the commitment I have made. It is something I question and worry over and constantly reassess.

It's not the big questions that keep me up at night: questions about the existence of God or his purposes in this world. It is, rather, the smaller, more practical questions that cause me bother. Questions like: Do people really change? Is personal transformation possible? What can God possibly do through someone as limited as myself? Where is the power to live in Christ-like ways, to overcome sin, to be holy? Why does church have to be so difficult? When will God's people start living up to their potential and mission? Why is the world so allergic to good news?

Wrestling with questions like these leaves me feeling certain things about my discipleship and my walk of faith. I'm not particularly proud of these feelings. I'm not offering them to anyone as a model to emulate. I'm *confessing* rather than *boasting*. See if you can relate.

I often feel *lonely* in my faith. Not that I don't enjoy the relationships I have with brothers and sisters. Not that I don't appreciate the companionship I've found in the church. But I miss my Master. I wish I had a relationship with him that was more personal, more intimate. I'd like to hear his voice, feel his touch, and sit at his feet. I wish I could take him to Starbucks and share a cup of coffee. When others speak of a "personal relationship with Jesus Christ," something stirs within me. That's exactly what I long for.

I often feel *overwhelmed*. I know Jesus has left his kingdom business for disciples to finish. But frankly, there are times when I know I don't measure up, when I feel Jesus has given me a job that is larger than I can wrap my arms around. His mission is so important, so vital, but I am so weak and inadequate. It overwhelms me that Jesus has left his work in my hands.

I often feel *afraid*. I understand that I need to testify to the truth I've found in Jesus Christ. I understand God expects me to go into "all the world and preach the gospel." But there are times I resist that commission. The hostility of the world frightens me. I know what the world does to truth-tellers. Frequently, I'm tempted to be timid when I want to be bold.

I often feel *powerless*. It's not just that the mission is difficult. There are parts of the mission I simply *can't* accomplish. I don't have the power! I can't make people love the light. I can't break hearts or create a hunger for truth. I can't open blind spiritual eyes. Those feats are beyond me. Yet I know God's work in this world cannot be done without such things happening. How can I change a world when I can't even change a single heart?

Finally, there are often times I feel *small*. It's not just the mission that's too big for me. It's the God I serve, the Master I follow, the gospel I preach. They are all larger-than-life. They show up my puniness in comparison. I can't understand them, much less contain them. Yet that is precisely what God has called me to do: contain his image; shine with his light; become the fullness of his Son; reflect his glory. God is a fire hydrant, gushing his truth at me. But I am a straw, capable only of sips and trickles. He is too much for me. He is more than I can bear.

Anyone Else Feel This Way?

I don't think I'm the only follower of Jesus to experience this. As I speak at various events around the world and talk about these feelings, I see heads shaking in every audience: "Yes, I feel the same way." The fact that other Christians empathize doesn't surprise me. I'm not all that different from my fellow believers. Truth be told, I'm not all that different from the first disciples . . . and neither are you.

Disciples have always felt such things. Even the disciples who walked and talked with Jesus. *Especially* the disciples who walked and talked with Jesus. They struggled with loneliness and inadequacy and timidity and limitations and incapacity as they stumbled after Jesus. Read the Gospels again. Their struggle is written large on every page.

But there was one particular evening when they felt these things intensely, with a strength that must have made them wonder whether they would ever recover. It was the night Jesus gathered them in an upper room and washed their feet . . . the night he gave them his flesh to eat and his blood to drink . . . the night when he broke the news he was leaving them and returning to the Father.

"I am going away, and where I am going you cannot come . . . I am leaving; you must stay behind . . . I am returning to the Father, but you must remain to fight the good fight and carry on the mission." Jesus pulls the rug out from under his disciples this final night and unleashes in them a flood of emotions.

In the shock of this announcement, the Apostles were feeling precisely what I have been describing, the emotions that are so characteristic of my own walk.

They felt *abandoned*. Jesus was leaving them behind. They'd spent the last three and a half years walking and talking with him. He had always been there for them, just ahead of them on the road. They loved being with him. They found hope in being with him. They needed Jesus. And now he was bowing out.

They felt *inadequate*. Not that the Twelve were ever very good disciples, mind you. They didn't understand Jesus' teaching. They couldn't muster much faith. They argued and bickered and missed the point. They didn't know what to do or say. So long as Jesus was leading, they managed to bumble along behind. But, especially on that final night, they knew they could not carry on the mission alone.

And they were *frightened*. They'd seen, in the last three years, how Jesus was treated when he spoke the truth. They were about to see—in graphic detail—what the world would do to truth-tellers who won't shut up. Jesus warns them this evening: "Now *you* are the truth-tellers. I am leaving my words to you and you must speak them. The world will hate you for that. They will persecute you and kill you." You can almost touch the fear radiating from the Apostles.

They certainly felt *powerless*. They realized specific things had to happen to make God's kingdom come, God's will be done. But *they* didn't know what to do. They only knew they were incapable of doing what was necessary. Heart surgery? Mind change? Character transformation? If *Jesus* couldn't make people believe, what hope did mere *Apostles* have?

Mostly, they felt *small*. They were just tax collectors and fishermen, after all. They were immature and selfish and unlearned. They were, quite frankly, in over their heads . . . way out of their depth. They were trying to understand the nature of God. They were attempting to grasp the love, the gospel, the purposes of God. They were striving to live out the life of God. And they just weren't big enough to hold his fullness and glory.

The Final Discourse

These are the difficult feelings that consume Jesus on this final evening: the fears and uncertainties, the loneliness and doubts of his closest companions. Everything is about to change. And he wants their faith to survive the storm.

On this last night, spent with the men he loved most, Jesus washes their feet and urges them to wash one another's feet. He commands them to love each other in the future as he as loved them in the past. He begs them, "Don't be afraid . . . don't let your hearts be troubled."

But mostly what Jesus does as he prepares his disciples for his departure is talk to them about the Holy Spirit. There is a Spirit coming, a Spirit named "The *Paraclete*." Jesus keeps referring and returning to him—time and again. Just when you think he's moved on to the next topic, he circles round to the *Paraclete* once more and says something new and hopeful about him.

The overriding theme Jesus presses home in this final conversation is that, when the *Paraclete* comes, he will be for the Apostles what Jesus has been for them. More to the point, Jesus tries to make it clear that the *Paraclete* will fill the gaps left behind by Jesus' departure. All the prickly questions and difficult emotions stirred up in the Apostles by their Master's exit will be remedied by the *Paraclete's* advent. He is the cure for what ails them this night—and on every other occasion when discipleship gets difficult.

Do the disciples feel abandoned? Because of the Spirit's presence, Jesus will be present with the disciples once again. "I will ask the Father, and he will give you another Paraclete to be with you forever—the Spirit of truth. The world cannot accept him, because it neither sees him nor knows him. But you know him, for he lives with you and will be in you. I will not leave you as orphans; I will come to you" (John 14:16-18).

"I know you'll miss having me walk and talk with you as I do now," Jesus tells these men. "But when the Spirit comes, he will live with you. He will live *in* you. And you will discover that *he* is *me* in forever form." (This "Promise of Presence" is the subject of Chapter Eight.)

Do they feel inadequate? When the Spirit comes, he will equip disciples for the mission Jesus has entrusted to them. "The Paraclete, the Holy Spirit, whom the Father will send in my name, will teach you all things and will remind you of everything I have said to you. Peace I leave with you; my peace I give you. I do not give to you as the world gives. Do not let your hearts be troubled and do not be afraid" (John 14:26-27).

"I know you are overwhelmed by the mission and worry about your effectiveness," Jesus tells the Twelve. "But the Spirit will teach you everything you need to know to do my work. He'll equip you. He'll make you competent for changing the world." (This "Promise of Teaching" is the subject of Chapter Nine.)

Are they frightened and tongue-tied? When the Spirit comes, he will testify about Jesus to the world and give disciples the courage to testify. "When the Paraclete comes, whom I will send to you from the Father, the Spirit of truth who goes out from the Father, he will testify about me. And you also must testify, for you have been with me from the beginning" (John 15:26-27).

"I know your fear will tempt you to keep quiet," Jesus sympathizes. "But the Spirit will speak up for me with a witness no threat or torture can silence. And the Spirit will help you testify . . . he will give you words and courage." (This "Promise of Testimony" is the subject of Chapter Ten.)

Do the disciples feel powerless? The Spirit will accomplish things mere disciples cannot do.

> I tell you the truth: It is for your good that I am going away. Unless I go away, the Paraclete will not come to you; but if I go, I will send him to you. When he comes, he will convict the world of guilt in regard to sin and righteousness and judgment: in regard to sin, because men do not believe in me; in regard to righteousness, because I am going to the Father, where you can see me no longer; and in regard to judgment, because the prince of this world now stands condemned. (John 16:7-11)

"When he comes," Jesus assures them, "he will convict the world of guilt. He will confront the world's resistance. He will harrow hearts in preparation for the seed of the gospel." The salvation of the world is not all on the shoulders of the Twelve (or us!). Jesus promises the Spirit will forge a partnership with them and do the kingdom work they don't have the power to accomplish. (This "Promise of Conviction" is the subject of Chapter Eleven.)

Do they feel small? When the Spirit comes, he will increase the capacity of disciples . . . making them larger souls.

I have much more to say to you, more than you can now bear. But when he, the Spirit of truth, comes, he will guide you into all truth. He will not speak on his own; he will speak only what he hears, and he will tell you what is yet to come. He will bring glory to me by taking from what is mine and making it known to you. All that belongs to the Father is mine. That is why I said the Spirit will take from what is mine and make it known to you. (John 16:12-15)

On this night, Jesus has given them more than they could bear; their tiny cups overflow! But in the future, the Spirit will enlarge the disciples, mature them, and make them more capable of bearing the glory of God. He will turn spiritual thimbles into buckets into barrels so that even puny disciples can contain the fullness of God. (This "Promise of Revelation" is the subject of Chapter Twelve.)

On this final night, as Jesus prepares the disciples for his leaving and addresses all the fears and doubts that arise as a result, he offers them the Spirit. The solution to their fear and insufficiency is the Spirit. It is the Spirit—alive, indwelling, powerful, wise, courageous, equipping, and tangible—who will make these disciples sufficient for what is yet to come.

The Apostles did not yet understand what he was offering. But, at this point, they must have been grateful for any attempt at comfort. Drowning men clinging to a timber. Starving men gnawing a bone.

Are These Promises for Us?

Is the conversation between Jesus and the Twelve that last night meant to be overheard by disciples like us? Does it have any relevance to our lives?

It would be nice to think so because the Spirit we discover in the Final Discourse so perfectly fills the gaps we experience in our own lives.

Those who are willing to answer that question with "Yes" are often unwilling to apply the salve of the Spirit to the particular hurts Jesus is addressing with the Twelve. "Yes, the promise of the Spirit applies to us!" they insist, and then rush off to other parts of the New Testament to see what signs and wonders might be in store for us as a result. Wait! Slow down! Can't we pause with Jesus, here in the Upper Room, long enough to realize he is revealing a ministry of the Spirit far more intimate than any miracle or sign? There is a heart-work the Spirit wants to do in disciples that is more desperately needed (then and now) than quaking buildings and prophetic utterances. If Jesus' promise of the Spirit is relevant to disciples today, it needs to be relevant *in the same way*—a promise of a Spirit who will live in us and transform us from the inside out. That promise deserves a pause, and some of our time and attention.

Those who insist on answering the question with "No," who are unwilling to apply Jesus' promise of the Spirit to modern-day disciples, have the burden of explaining why the Apostles were offered the Holy Spirit to fill the gaps of Jesus' absence while we, who struggle with the same gaps, are not offered the same remedy. They got the promised and potent Spirit; we get a pew. Hardly seems fair, does it? Truth is, there are just some gaps only a tangible Spirit can fill . . . some needs only an indwelling Spirit can supply . . . some works only a living Spirit can perform. That contribution of the Spirit to our lives is more desperately needed by disciples today than better worship practices or intimate small groups. If Jesus' promise of the Spirit is *not* relevant to us, we are in deep trouble. For we cannot fix what ails us by our own power. And not even the church, not even the Bible, can sooth every prickly barb raised by serving a Master no longer here.

I believe the same promises made to the Twelve that last night are meant for us as well. The same presence made available to the first Apostles is the presence we can enjoy—through the Spirit. The same competence for ministry offered to them is the competence and equipping offered to us—by the Spirit. The same boldness in testimony, the same courage in the face of opposition, can be ours today—because of the Spirit. The same partnership, working with God to win the world, is available to us—in the Spirit. The same deepening and maturing that allowed those disciples to bear more and understand more and *be* more, can take place in us—by God's Spirit.

As with the Twelve, Jesus still breathes on believers today and says, "Receive the Holy Spirit" (John 20:22). And it's a good thing, too. Jesus has been gone a long time. Our lives have frayed from constant contact with the world. Our churches have forgotten their true business. No longer are we ambitious to "turn the world upside down"; we've settled instead for "hanging on" until the Lord comes again. Our testimony is muted. Our courage has waned. We're tired and confused and uncertain. It's tough being a disciple in this cold world.

That's why it is so important for us to re-hear what Jesus says about the Spirit in John's gospel, to recover the indwelling Spirit we find there. It's time to reclaim the promises Jesus made about the *Paraclete*. It's time to repair and refurbish a relationship with the Spirit who, alone, has the power to lift our lives and our churches to a world-changing level once again.

That's what this book is about. Welcome to the journey!

THE SPIRIT IN SCRIPTURE

This section provides a survey of what the Bible says about the Spirit. Those with little patience for thoroughness may want to skip this section and go straight to the heart of the book—Section Two. But those who appreciate the broad understanding that only perspective brings and crave the confidence that only thought-rooted-in-Scripture can give will value this overview.

You might wonder how this kind of survey helps with our narrower focus on the Spirit in John's Gospel. Actually, it contributes in three ways. First, it provides a context for Jesus' teachings about the Spirit that allows us to hear in the Final Discourse both echoes of and contrasts to teachings about the Spirit in other biblical books. Second, it highlights the fact that the Bible's treatment of the Spirit is not uniform—different writers have different interests when it comes to the Spirit—which suggests Jesus (in John) may speak to the subject of the Spirit with a unique voice that requires our focused attention. Third, it raises a handful of questions that tend to come up consistently in the Bible's witness to the Spirit and go to the heart of how we understand the Spirit and his work.

We start (in Chapter Three) with the surprisingly robust treatment of the Holy Spirit in the Old Testament. How did the Spirit work before Christ appeared? What was the experience of Israel with the Spirit?

Chapter Four gives a quick survey of teaching on the Spirit in the Synoptic Gospels (Matthew, Mark, and Luke) and in Acts. You may be surprised (as I was) to discover what is *not* said about the Spirit in these books.

In Chapter Five we walk through the letters of Paul. Paul has a unique contribution to make to our understanding of the Spirit's work, including most of what we know about an *indwelling* Spirit.

Chapter Six zooms in on the Gospel of John—our ultimate destination—by reviewing what is said by Jesus in that Gospel about the Spirit and, particularly, about the *Paraclete*.

Finally, in Chapter Seven, I reproduce for you the text of the Final Discourse (John 13-16) and draw special attention to the *Paraclete* passages.

Chapter Three

THE SPIRIT IN THE OLD TESTAMENT

You only get two verses into the Bible before the Spirit shows up. "In the beginning God created the heavens and the earth. Now the earth was formless and empty, darkness was over the surface of the deep, and the Spirit of God was hovering over the waters" (Gen 1:1-2).

God and the heavens, the formless earth and the dark deep, are the only things to precede the Spirit in Scripture. The reference to the Spirit is simple and enigmatic. No explanation. No development. It's as if the writer mentions the Spirit "for the record," wanting his presence noted before the world came into existence. "God was there. The Spirit of God was there. In the beginning."

He was there again when God created man (breathing into him "the breath of life," a phrase commonly associated with the Spirit—see Job 33:4) and when, later, God pondered what to do with his fallen creatures: "Then the LORD said, 'My Spirit will not contend with man forever, for he is mortal; his days will be a hundred and twenty years'" (Gen 6:3).

The Spirit was present during the days of the Exodus. We see him (symbolically) in the flames of the burning bush (Ex 3:1-6) and in the pillar of cloud and fire (Ex 13:21-22). But he is mentioned explicitly in the ministry of Moses: "I will come down and speak with you there, and I will take of the Spirit that is on you and put the Spirit on them" (Num 11:17).

This is the first reference in Scripture to the Spirit being "on" a specific individual. That the individual is Moses, the most significant figure in the Old Testament, does not surprise us. It does, however, lend weight to the importance of the Spirit's presence in accomplishing God's work.

This Spirit on Moses marks him. The evidence is as plain as the radiance on his face. In the book of Exodus, we learn that "the Lord would speak to Moses face to face" (33:11). Such close communion with God sets Moses aglow:

> When Moses came down from Mount Sinai with the two tablets
> of the Testimony in his hands, he was not aware that his face was
> radiant because he had spoken with the LORD. When Aaron
> and all the Israelites saw Moses, his face was radiant, and they
> were afraid to come near him. . . . When Moses finished speak-
> ing to them, he put a veil over his face. But whenever he entered
> the LORD's presence to speak with him, he removed the veil
> until he came out. And when he came out and told the Israelites
> what he had been commanded, they saw that his face was radi-
> ant. Then Moses would put the veil back over his face until he
> went in to speak with the LORD. (Ex 34:29-35)

This "radiance" reappears as the "glory" that descends on Sinai and later fills both the Tabernacle and the Temple. It is a frequent sign of God's presence and a common symbol for God's Spirit.[1]

Like Moses, Joshua was anointed with the Spirit (Num 27:18; Deut 34:9). So were the Judges: "the Spirit of the Lord came on Othniel" (Judg 3:10); "Then the Spirit of the Lord came upon Gideon" (Judg 6:34); "Then the Spirit of the Lord came upon Jephthah" (Judg 11:29); and—especially—"the Spirit of the Lord came upon Samson in power" (Judg 14:6).

The first kings of Israel were anointed, not just with oil, but with the Spirit. It happened with Saul ("the Spirit of God came upon him in power"–1 Sam 10:6) and with David ("So Samuel took the horn of oil and anointed David in the presence of his brothers, and from that day on the Spirit of the Lord came upon David in power"–1 Sam 16:13). King David was especially conscious of the Spirit's presence in his life. On his deathbed, David rejoiced that "the Spirit of the Lord spoke through me;

his word was on my tongue" (2 Sam 23:2). He credited the Spirit with inspiring him with "the plans of all that the Spirit had put in his mind for the courts of the temple of the LORD and all the surrounding rooms, for the treasuries of the temple of God and for the treasuries for the dedicated things" (1 Chron 28:12).

David depended on God's Spirit to lead him (Ps 143:10); marveled that God's Spirit was everywhere (Ps 139:7); and begged God never to take his Holy Spirit away (Ps 51:11).

The Prophets experienced the presence of God's Spirit. Elijah (1 Kgs 18:12), Isaiah (Isa 48:16), Ezekiel ("the Spirit came into me and raised me to my feet, and I heard him speaking to me," Ezek 2:2), and Micah ("I am filled with power, with the Spirit of the Lord," Mic 3:8)—all felt the quickening and empowering of the Spirit. The author of Nehemiah attributed the work of the prophets (admonishing Israel) to "your Spirit" (Neh 9:30).

But it wasn't just Israel's leaders and holy men who experienced the Spirit's presence. All Israel remembered a God who "set his Holy Spirit among them" (Isa 63:11). All Israel received God's "good Spirit to instruct them" (Neh 9:20) and "were given rest by the Spirit of the Lord" (Isa 63:14). All Israel "rebelled against the Spirit of God" (Ps 106:33) and "grieved his Holy Spirit" (Isa 63:10). And "the whole house of Israel"— dry bones though they were—experienced a national renewal and return because of an encounter with the Spirit: "I will make breath enter you, and you will come to life. I will attach tendons to you and make flesh come upon you and cover you with skin; I will put breath in you, and you will come to life. . . . I will put my Spirit in you and you will live, and I will settle you in your own land" (Ezek 37:5-6, 14).

Many of us have no idea there is so much Spirit in the Old Testament. But there he is when we finally look . . . everywhere: in the beginning, through the Exodus, with every form of leadership in Israel's history, and experienced palpably and profoundly by Israel as a whole. According to the prophets, however, the best was yet to come.

The Spirit in the Messianic Age

According to the Old Testament writers, a widespread and radical experience of the Spirit would be the distinguishing characteristic of the

Messianic Age—that much-anticipated time when God planned to pour out his Spirit in special measure. The Spirit who had been present for God's people since the beginning would be extraordinarily, dramatically present when the "Anointed One" came.

Yes, "the Spirit of the Lord" was to rest on the Messiah himself to an exceptional degree:

the Spirit of wisdom and of understanding,
the Spirit of counsel and of power,
the Spirit of knowledge and of the fear of the LORD. (Isa 11:2)

And, yes, God did promise to "put my Spirit on" his Messiah so justice could be established upon the earth (Isa 42:1-4) and the "year of the Lord's favor" proclaimed (Isa 61:1ff).

But the defining mark of the Messianic Age would be the availability of the Spirit to *all* people—everyone who put their hope in the Lord and his Anointed. Isaiah, with his grand visions of the Messianic Kingdom, attests to this spate of the Spirit again and again. He looks forward to a time when "the Spirit is poured upon us from on high" (32:15), when God will "pour water on the thirsty land, and streams on the dry ground . . . and my Spirit on your offspring" (44:3). On that day, the Spirit of God will gather the messianic people together (34:16) and gush forth upon them like streams in the desert (35:1-10). Joel echoes Isaiah's proclamation of a Spirit for "all people." Sons and daughters, male and female, old and young will be filled: everyone who calls upon the name of the Lord—2:28-32.

And this presence of the Spirit, this watering of the dry land, is to be "forever": for the Messiah's people, their children, and "their descendants from this time on" (Isa 59:21).

Taken as a whole, the witness of the Old Testament is that the Spirit has *always* been present—with God, with God's creation, and with God's people. From the beginning to the Messianic Age. And not just present: *actively* present, *vigorously* present. The Spirit creates, gives life, accompanies, anoints, leads, empowers, grants prophetic visions and utterances, and vivifies dry spiritual bones. The withdrawal of that Presence is a dreaded prospect for ancient Israel. The demonstration of that Presence is a comfort to and affirmation of ancient Israel. And the promise of a greater Presence, the prospect of the Spirit poured out in the Messianic Era, is a hope that fuels Israel through the dark days of the Exile and the lean times of Second Temple Judaism.

Observations on the Spirit in the Old Testament

With this brief summary behind us, a few observations are in order. First, and to repeat, *the Old Testament portrays an ever-present Spirit*. The significance of this for us is the recognition that the Holy Spirit is not a "first-century" phenomena, an artifact of apostolic Christianity. He is, rather, a "constant." Wherever and whenever God encounters his people, the Spirit has always been there.

Christians at both ends of the Spirit-spectrum today have been quite willing, in their eagerness to showcase the Spirit in the first century, to downplay the role of the Spirit prior to Christ's coming. Those who emphasize the Pentecost outpouring and see Acts 2 as a dividing line in faith history separating the Spirit-haves from the Spirit-have-nots don't always appreciate an active, present, hard-working Spirit in the world before Pentecost. An anemic Spirit, maybe. A Spirit with one hand tied behind his back. But surely not the powerful, sovereign, boundless Spirit found in Acts (and experienced now).

Those at the other extreme (who downplay the role of the Spirit for discipleship today) want to emphasize that the time of Jesus and the Apostles was unique in regard to the Spirit. Nothing like it before or since. The Spirit was present and vigorously active during the lifespan of the Apostles. But only then. In order to cut the Spirit off from our present, this viewpoint has largely cut the Spirit off from Israel's past.

Both positions largely ignore an essential commonality between experiences of the Spirit in both Testaments: common vocabulary like "power," "poured out," "glory," and "filling," and common manifestations like prophecy and visions. They largely ignore any evidence suggesting the Spirit conducted God's business with Israel in much the same manner as he did later with the first-century church.

Even a cursory look at the Old Testament evidence, however, leads us to recognize that the Spirit played a far larger role in ancient Israel than most of us have realized.

A second observation: Even in the Old Testament, we begin to get an inkling of a *distinction between the Spirit's miraculous work and his transformative work*. Certainly, the presence of the Spirit is closely linked to supernatural manifestations like prophecy and revelation—manifestations where people are *conduits* for the Spirit's power and God's words. Yet there are also hints of a *transformative* work of the Spirit, a work done in hearts and character.

The Spirit, for instance, is closely connected by Old Testament writers with the giving of the Law and the words of the prophets. Both were intended to cause a "change of heart" in Israel, to produce repentance and righteousness. (David, as an example, speaks of the Spirit leading him "to do your will," Ps 143:10). To the degree that revelation was able to accomplish this heart-change in Israel, the change should be seen as a work of God's Spirit.

Ezekiel foresees a day when God will put his Spirit directly into the hearts of Israel—a Spirit who needs no mediation of words and law—and transform them. He laments an Israel who has abandoned God's commands and followed the ways of the surrounding nations. He confesses Israel's sins and offenses. But he then envisions God showing mercy to his people and bringing them back to the Promised Land where, once again, "they will be my people, and I will be their God" (Ezek 11:20). This restoration is only possible, however, because of an outpouring of the Spirit:

> I will sprinkle clean water on you, and you will be clean; I will cleanse you from all your impurities and from all your idols. I will give you a new heart and put a new spirit in you; I will remove from you your heart of stone and give you a heart of flesh. And I will put my Spirit in you and move you to follow my decrees and be careful to keep my laws. (Ezek 36:25-27)

This Spirit "in you" will do something more wondrous than making the sun stand still—he will empower Israel for obedience. He will cleanse and soften and motivate. He will change Israel's heart and stimulate a hunger for the holy.

A third observation: In the Old Testament, *the transformative is always miraculous but the miraculous is not always transformative*. David's

penitence over Bathsheba was only made possible by God's interven-
tion. Jonah's change of heart came about because God "swallowed him
up." Whenever Israel is faithful or penitent or lives righteously, the
Spirit of God has to be moving powerfully behind the scenes. In the
Old Testament, people mature or repent or seek God or experience a
change of heart, not because of their own stellar qualities and self-control, but because God moves miraculously to touch the hearts of men
and women.

But the miraculous does not always prompt transformation. Consider
the seventy elders of Israel who saw the plagues, walked through the Red
Sea, and ate the manna and quail; the elders who, in addition, personally experienced a powerful, miraculous filling of the Spirit: "Then the
Lord came down in the cloud and spoke with [Moses], and he took of
the Spirit that was on him and put the Spirit on the seventy elders. When
the Spirit rested on them, they prophesied . . ." (Num 11:25).

That extraordinary experience of the Spirit, however, did little to
soften hearts or encourage obedience. Not long after, these same elders
led a rebellion against Moses (Num 14), threatening to stone him and
take the people back to Egypt. It was these elders (among others) God
condemned when he said: "Not one of the men who saw my glory and
the miraculous signs I performed in Egypt and in the desert but who
disobeyed me and tested me ten times—not one of them will ever see
the land I promised . . . . No one who has treated me with contempt will
ever see it" (Num 14:22-23). These same men defied Moses again with
Korah. They were among the 250 supporters of Korah's attempted coup,
the "well-known community leaders who had been appointed members
of the council" (Num 16:2). In his anger, God devoured them with fire
(Num 16:15).

This is but one instance where people experienced the Spirit's miraculous work yet were not changed. These men actually prophesied by the
Spirit's power. But they were not transformed as a result.

The troubling case of Samson presents us with the same paradox.
His birth was announced by an angel and accompanied by wonders and
signs (Judg 13). More than any of the other judges (in fact, more than all
the other judges combined), Samson is described in Scripture as a man
who experiences the Spirit of the Lord "in power" (Judg 13:25; 14:6,

19; 15:14). Yet that power is mostly a matter of biceps and pectorals, manifested in feats of physical strength. Samson tears a lion apart with his bare hands. He breaks bonds with ease. He kills enemies by the hundreds. He topples a temple.

The Spirit falls on Samson and the result is superhuman physical strength. But Samson is not transformed because of it. To the contrary, he rivals Ahab as the wickedest character in the Bible. There is not a single redemptive quality mentioned in the four chapters devoted to his life (Judg 13-16). Samson is relentlessly portrayed as rebellious, violent, lustful, greedy, vindictive, foolish, and whinny. In the end, he dies by his own hand.

Once again, in the life of Samson, we have wonders without transformation, marvels without character. As we will see, this same disconnect between the miraculous and the transformative repeats itself in the New Testament.

The Spirit, then, is alive and well in the witness of the Old Testament. His fingerprints are all over creation and covenant, Tabernacle and Torah, prophets and kings. He cannot change every heart but, whenever heart-change happens, you can be sure the Spirit has been working. The Spirit is an integral and indispensible part of the life of Israel.

With the coming of the Messiah, however, the Spirit will have an even larger role to play. He will be poured out in fullness. And once he is unleashed into the world, there will be no return to dry ground.

Chapter Four

THE SPIRIT IN THE SYNOPTIC GOSPELS AND ACTS

As you might expect of a collection of books describing the Messianic Age, the Spirit plays a prominent role in the New Testament. The word "spirit" (*pneuma*) occurs over 350 times. Twenty-three out of twenty-seven New Testament books raise the subject of God's Spirit (only Philemon, 2 and 3 John—exempted by reason of brevity—and James omit any reference). Some New Testament writers seem obsessed with the subject: the word "spirit" occurs over seventy times in Acts!

The New Testament's witness to the Spirit, then, is broad and strong. But, as we will see, it is not always or equally *deep*. This becomes evident when we turn to the Synoptic Gospels—Matthew, Mark, and Luke.

The Witness of the Synoptic Gospels

The word "spirit" occurs some seventy-five times in the Synoptic Gospels (so called because they tend to see—"optic"—things similarly). At first blush, this abundance of references promises a wealth of information for people who want to understand the Spirit better. When you look more closely, however, you discover that precious little of what is said about "spirit" in the Synoptics has much direct application to the lives of disciples.

For one thing, almost half of spirit references in the Synoptics are to *evil* spirits (fifteen in Mark alone!). Jesus drives them out, rebukes them, gives his disciples authority over them, teaches parables including them, and is accused of being possessed by one himself. Another nine times, the word "spirit" is used to mean *personal attitude* or the *interior self* (e.g., "the spirit is willing, but the body is weak," Matt 26:41).

That leaves only thirty-three direct references to the *Holy* Spirit in the Synoptics. Yet even the majority of those speak to the Spirit and the *Messiah* rather than the Spirit and *disciples*. We learn, for instance, that the Messiah is predicted by the Spirit (Matt 22:43; Mark 12:36; Luke 4;18); that he and his forerunner will be filled with the Spirit (Matt 3:16; 4:1; 12:18; Luke 1:15-17, 80; 4:14, 18); that the arrival of the Messiah is prompted by the Spirit (who impregnates Mary—Matt 1:18—and inspires various people to announce the coming birth—Luke 1:41; 2:25); and that Jesus will be proved the Messiah by baptizing with the Holy Spirit (Matt 3:11 and parallels).

What do we actually glean from the Synoptics that might be pertinent to *disciples*? It's good to know that the Spirit can conceive a child in a woman. But since few of us are planning a virgin birth, such information has limited relevance. And it's important to know that the Spirit predicted Jesus' coming and descended on him at baptism. But these were *distinguishing marks* by which the Messiah would be recognized, not experiences offered to every disciple.

When it all boils down, there is relatively little found here about how the Spirit works in the hearts and lives of disciples. This is what we *can* say:

First and foremost, the Synoptics proclaim that disciples have access to the Spirit because of Jesus Christ. He baptizes them with the Spirit, *in* the Spirit. "John answered them all, 'I baptize you with water. But one more powerful than I will come, the thongs of whose sandals I am not worthy to untie. *He will baptize you with the Holy Spirit* and with fire'" (Luke 3:16 and parallels, emphasis mine).

John the Baptist, eager to say "I am not the one," points to Jesus and claims for him the power of Spirit baptism. John can get people wet. But Jesus can bathe people in the Holy Spirit. We may argue about what, exactly, this means and to whom, specifically, it applies. But this power to baptize with the Spirit is a defining mark of the Messiah's ministry. It is the line in the sand that distinguishes the limits of the Spirit prior to the

Messiah from the fullness of the Spirit after the Messiah. The Messiah, dripping with the Spirit, immerses all who come to him with that Spirit. This is certainly true for his first disciples. Is it true for all disciples? For us? That is not a question the Synoptics address.

They do tell us, however, of a God who wants to give his Spirit to those who ask:

"If you then, though you are evil, know how to give good gifts to your children, how much more will your Father in heaven give the Holy Spirit to those who ask him!" (Luke 11:13). Jesus portrays here a Heavenly Father who is ready, willing, and eager to pour out his Spirit. He describes God as a gift-giver anxious to bestow his Spirit-gift on those he loves. In this word picture, God does not give grudgingly or against his better judgment. He gives with all the love and generosity a good father feels for his cherished children.

All that remains in the Synoptic gospels, after these meager morsels about the Spirit's interaction with disciples, are a few interesting details. We learn, for instance, that the Spirit can put words in the mouths of disciples when words come hard. In all three Synoptics, Jesus tells the Twelve: "Whenever you are arrested and brought to trial, do not worry beforehand about what to say. Just say whatever is given you at the time, for it is not you speaking, but the Holy Spirit" (Mark 13:11 and parallels).

Again, who this promise applies to (only the Twelve or others?) is not a question addressed by the Synoptics. (Although the fact that this offer of the Spirit's help is written to Christians who are themselves under attack and subject to persecution may suggest the promise extended at least to them.)

Another detail: we are warned in the Synoptics about the dangers of blaspheming the Holy Spirit—the unforgiveable sin. "And so I tell you, every sin and blasphemy will be forgiven men, but the blasphemy against the Spirit will not be forgiven. Anyone who speaks a word against the Son of Man will be forgiven, but anyone who speaks against the Holy Spirit will not be forgiven, either in this age or in the age to come" (Matt 12:31-32 and parallels). We may not know what such "blasphemy" looks like or how it is accomplished. But we're quite certain we don't want to be guilty of it.

Finally, Mark mentions that "signs" will accompany disciples in their ministry (Mark 16:17-18). Though the Spirit is not mentioned in this passage, it is clear these signs anticipate a Spirit-filled future.

That's the sum and total of what we learn about the Holy Spirit and believers from the Synoptics: the Spirit is available because of the Messiah; God wants to give him to disciples; he can speak through disciples in trying times; we mustn't speak against him; and signs (prompted by the Spirit?) will go hand-in-hand with discipleship in times to come.

The Witness of Acts

Acts has more to say about *spirit* than any other book in the New Testament canon. Like the Synoptics, there are references here to *evil spirits* or an individual's *inner spirit*. But these are rare. Most references—fifty-five specific passages—point directly to the *Holy* Spirit. His footprints are all over Luke's story of the earliest church. Unlike the Synoptics, however, and as you would expect given the different focus of this book, Acts testifies to the work of the Spirit in the *lives of believers* rather than in the ministry of Jesus.

Listen, for instance, to the variety of ways Luke (the author of Acts) describes the advent of the Spirit for disciples. Disciples are *baptized in* the Spirit (Acts 1:5, 8; 2:4ff; 11:15-16) and *filled with* the Spirit (2:38; 4:31; 9:17; 13:9). They *receive* the Spirit (1:8; 2:38; 8:15, 17; 10:47) and are *given* the Spirit (5:32; 8:18; 15:8). The Spirit *comes on* disciples (1:8; 10:44; 11:15; 19:6) and is *poured out* upon them (2:17; 10:45). The breadth of vocabulary is striking.

Luke uses this vocabulary of fullness some thirty times in Acts, repeatedly and emphatically proclaiming that these first Christians were Spirit-endowed. He may not tell us much about individual disciples like Stephen, Philip, Cornelius, Barnabas, or Agabus, but he wants us to know they were all filled with the Holy Spirit. He may not spend time describing the first church's worship liturgy or sacramental practices, but he goes into long and loving detail about the Spirit falling at Pentecost, and again at Cornelius' house, and repeatedly as the Apostles go out to "the ends of the earth."

The result of this fullness was a very tangible experience of the Spirit for the disciples. They *saw* the Spirit's presence (Acts 2:3, 33), *felt* his power (4:31), and *heard* his voice (8:29; 10:19; 13:2; 21:11). They could recognize him in others (6:3-5), sense his encouragement and support (4:8, 31; 9:31; 13:9), and listen to his specific guidance and commissioning (8:29; 13:2-4; 16:6-7).

And, also as a result of this fullness, the first believers enjoyed a consistent experience of the miraculous. The testimony throughout Acts to this close connection between the Spirit and the supernatural is frequent and unambiguous.

At Pentecost, there was a loud sound "from heaven," the Spirit fell, tongues of flame appeared, believers spoke in other languages, and Peter bore witness to a crucified man brought back to life. The church witnessed "many wonders and miraculous signs" (2:43). No wonder they were all "filled with awe."

A cripple was healed at the temple gate, Peter preached the Messiah to the gathered crowd, the Council of Elders were "astonished" at the courage and boldness of the Apostles, the church gathered to pray and felt the building shake as they were filled with the Spirit (3:1ff, 11ff; 4:13, 31). No wonder "much grace was upon them all."

Ananias and Sapphira were accused of lying to the Holy Spirit and struck dead for their deception (5:1ff). No wonder "great fear seized the whole church."

"The apostles performed many miraculous signs and wonders among the people" (5:12). The sick were healed and evil spirits cast out (5:15-16). Angels appeared to release the Apostles from jail (5:17ff). Of course "they never stopped teaching and proclaiming the good news." With all these wonders taking place, would you?

Philip performed miraculous signs in Samaria (including exorcisms and healings). When the crowds saw the miracles, "there was great joy in the city" (8:5-8). I understand why. Later, the Spirit directed Philip to meet a man on a desert road. He preached to and baptized the Eunuch. And then he was (suddenly) "beamed" to a city fifteen miles away. No wonder he "traveled about, preaching the gospel," thrilled to be part of something so . . . well . . . thrilling (8:36-40).

Paul received a vision on the Damascus Road (Acts 9). He heard the divine voice. He was told to go into the city and wait. His sight was taken away. Ananias was also given a vision and specifically instructed to find Paul and heal his blindness. It doesn't surprise me that, in such a context, Ananias did as he was told, or that Paul was marked by the vision and subsequent healing, or that he accepted Christ's commission to the Gentiles.

Do I need to remind you of Tabitha raised from the dead (9:40), or Peter's vision of the sheet and the unclean animals (10:9ff), or the falling of the Spirit on Cornelius (10:44-46), or Peter's release from prison by an angel (12:6-10), or Herod struck dead by God (12:23)? Do we need to revisit the Spirit "calling" Barnabas and Saul to mission work (13:2), or Saul's blinding of Elymas the sorcerer (13:11), or the healing of the cripple at Lystra (14:10), or the vision of the Macedonian Man (16:6ff) and the exorcism of the slave girl at Philippi (16:18), or the miracles in Ephesus (19:11-12), or the rescue from the shipwreck (27:9ff)?

Wherever the Spirit shows up in Acts, something supernatural breaks out. The Spirit falls and people speak in tongues. The Spirit enters and people prophesy. The Spirit empowers healings, physically "teleports" disciples, grants visions, speaks directly and directively to the church, and "compels" or "prevents" specific actions (Acts 16:6-7; 20:22). In the most extreme (and disturbing) case recorded by Luke, the Spirit strikes people dead.

In Acts, the Spirit is persistently, relentlessly miraculous.

That is the extent of what we learn about the Holy Spirit and believers from Acts: the Spirit is poured out on followers of Jesus Messiah; they experience the Spirit in very tangible ways; the Spirit works miracles for and through them.

Observations on the Spirit in the Synoptics and Acts

In light of this review, a few observations can be made about the witness of the Synoptics and Acts to the Spirit.

Observation #1: Acts would seem to be a more relevant source of information about the *Spirit and disciples* than the Synoptics. There simply isn't much said by Matthew, Mark, and Luke on the subject of the Spirit's role in believers' lives. Certainly we should glean what *is* there. But a theology of the Spirit's work in God's people based solely on the Synoptics would be a very slim volume.

Acts, on the other hand, speaks to the subject of the Spirit and disciples with great frequency. There is a Spirit-seam here that should be mined afresh: a fullness of the Spirit available for disciples; a tangible Spirit who can be readily experienced; and a miraculous Spirit who works through disciples. Whether this Spirit *remains* available in this way is not a question Luke addresses directly in his account of the early church. It is, in fact, a question that has provoked considerable controversy through the centuries, including our own time. The power of Luke's story demands that we ask and continue to ask this question, even if the answer proves difficult or elusive.

Observation #2: There is a great deal we *don't* learn about the Spirit from the Synoptics and Acts. There is nothing in these writings about who the Spirit is or his indwelling presence in believers. Nothing about the Spirit's transforming or sanctifying work. Nothing about the Spirit's forming of character or changing of hearts. Nothing about killing the sinful nature and prompting new life or shaping morality, relationships, and communion with God.

The Synoptics hardly address the Spirit's interaction with disciples at all. The disciples watch the Spirit work through Jesus. They receive an offer of the Spirit for the future. But the Synoptics say nothing about how the disciples experienced the Spirit for themselves. (John insists, in fact, that the disciples could not receive the Spirit until after the death and resurrection of Jesus—7:39; 20:22.)

It is not unfair to state, then, that—in the Synoptics—disciples were *witnesses* to the Spirit, even *students* of the Spirit. But the Spirit had no *presence* in the disciples and left behind no *residue* in their lives. He was promised to them in the Synoptics, but not delivered.

Acts is a different matter. The promised Spirit comes. He baptizes the disciples. He works on and through them. The Spirit in Acts changes what disciples *do*, what they *decide* about certain matters, and how they *act* in particular situations. The Spirit empowers believers to speak boldly and well, causes them to heal and prophesy, and calls them to certain ministries or places.

And yet, it must be noted that Acts says little about the Spirit maturing disciples or convicting them of sin or teaching them to love holiness.

The Spirit themes so prominent in Paul's letters are largely absent in Acts. No words about the Spirit's role in putting to death the old man, controlling the minds and appetites of believers, or prompting growth into the likeness of Christ. I am not suggesting hearts do not change in Acts or people don't deepen in the Lord. They do. Saul becomes Paul, after all! I am simply saying that Acts never portrays the Spirit in such a way that we would *expect* character changes as the natural and intended effect of the Spirit's presence in the lives of believers. If all we had was Acts, we would know much about the Spirit's signs and wonders but little about the Spirit's work of maturing and sanctifying.

Thus, the same thing can be said of Acts as was said of the Synoptics: disciples are *witnesses* to the Spirit and *students* of the Spirit. Even more in Acts, they are also *conduits* for the Spirit, *channels* through whom the Spirit demonstrates his presence and power and to whom he communicates his will. But Acts simply does not address an *interior* work of the Spirit, breaking the power of sin and creating new, Christ-like lives. The book is focused on the church and its beginnings, not individuals and their spiritual development.

Observation #3: As in the Old Testament, so in the Synoptics and Acts, we trip over the truth that an experience of the miraculous is not always transformative. The Pharisees witnessed Jesus' miracles, but refused to come to faith (Matt 9:32-34). Capernaum saw miracles that would have made Sodom weep, yet remained unmoved (Matt 11:23). Jesus went home to people who knew his life and heard reports about his miracles, and discovered a lynch mob (Luke 4:14ff). And, of course, there is the troubling case of Judas, who witnessed all the healings and wonders, who—presumably—cast out a demon or two himself on Jesus' authority. But his heart remained hard. The signs made no dent in him. In the end, he decided it was better to have betrayed and lost than never to have betrayed at all.

We find the same truth in Acts. The Pharisees continue their resistance in spite of more healings. Ananias and Sapphira saw the signs and wonders performed by the Apostles; but it did not cure their greed or prevent them from lying to the Holy Spirit (Acts 5:1ff). Simon was "astonished by the great signs and miracles he saw" (Acts 8:13), but he still tried to buy spiritual power with filthy mammon. Paul visited Corinth and established his most charismatic church; but spiritual gifts did not translate there into spiritual people. Miracles don't necessarily change hearts.

Observation #4: There are obvious differences between the experience of the Spirit by disciples in the Synoptics and Acts and the experience of the Spirit that is my common lot. These differences may limit how teachings about the Spirit found there apply to my life now.

"Hold on a minute," some will say. "Our contemporary experience of the Spirit should be the same as the ancients. The Spirit should be just as present, just as vigorous and miraculously active, now as then!" they tell us. "The problem is *us*. We must be quenching the Spirit, preventing the Spirit, in some way. We need to repent and redouble our efforts to experience the wonders of Acts for ourselves."

That may be true. But I still insist there are obvious differences between now and then when it comes to the sphere of the Spirit.

Take the matter of evil spirits, for instance. In the Synoptics, they were so thick that even confused, doubting, "little faith" disciples stumbled over them at every turn. They inhabited children, raving lunatics, and helpless women. They spoke out loud, witnessing and begging for mercy. They fled their preferred, human victims and entered animal hosts. On almost every page of the Synoptics, Jesus meets and casts out an evil spirit.

But that's not my common experience of the spiritual world. I can't remember the last time I ran into an evil spirit—and I think I would remember something like that. Perhaps I am so spiritually blind that I can't see an evil spirit when it's staring me right in the face. Maybe I have quenched the Spirit so thoroughly that I am oblivious to obvious spiritual forces and entities. Before I succumb to spiritual self-contempt, however, it's at least worth asking whether there might be an actual and significant difference between Jesus' day and my own (or, for that matter, between Palestine and other places in the first century world where the gospel took root without mention of evil spirits). Could it be that a different worldview, a different understanding of causality, or a different level of access by the forces of evil to other times and places explains the absence of evil spirits in our present experience? Must we insist, since evil spirits were a reality then and there, they must be a reality here and now?

If this difference is a function of changing times rather than stubborn hearts, we have to read the Synoptics and Acts differently. What they tell us about spiritual realities during the ministries of Jesus and the earliest church may spark our curiosity but may not prove much help for handling spiritual realities of our own.

I raise this example about evil spirits to segue into another, more troubling problem. I find a similar "difference" in the way the Holy Spirit behaves then and now. There is an "intrusiveness" to the Spirit in Acts that seems thoroughly alien to us. These days we struggle mightily to seek the Spirit, find the Spirit, and engage the Spirit. But in Acts, the Spirit is inescapable. Disciples are baptized in, filled up with, or overcome by the Spirit at every turn. They bump into the Spirit unexpectedly, without request, in surprising and unanticipated ways. The Spirit simply and sovereignly falls, pours, fills, directs, prevents, and warns—without the early Christians so much as lifting a spiritual finger!

Far from requiring invitation, the Spirit in Acts operates in invasive and irresistible[1] ways. He needs neither permission nor encouragement. He is *there*, a fact of first-century Christian life, whether invited or not. In truth, his presence is often inconvenient (his "falling" on Cornelius posed significant challenges for the Jerusalem church—Acts 11:2-3), sometimes scandalizing ("These men are not drunk, as you suppose . . ."—Acts 2:15), and, on occasion, dreaded ("Great fear seized the whole church" after the Spirit's handling of Ananias and Sapphira—Acts 5:11). The Spirit described in Acts seems little concerned with whether disciples *want* his presence. He never asks them. Rather, his concern is to *be present*, whether wanted or not.

This difference between the first-century experience of the Spirit and our own has been the source of much puzzlement. Even the most charismatic streams of modern Christianity must prescribe specific, intensive regimens in order to induce a discernable experience of the Spirit: cleansing rituals, prayer, fasting, reading, extensive instruction, prolonged meditation, and torturous "seeking." It seems the Spirit must be *cajoled* into appearing, *coerced* into a tangible presence, in these latter days. But in the first century, the Spirit was aggressively seeking out Christians, not the other way around.

I can't explain this difference, but I can recognize it. The disciples of Acts are ambushed by the Spirit while I am left to chase after him, pleading for the least little blessing. Why? I don't know. But surely it's worth considering that, to the extent such differences are real, Acts may not be the best yardstick for measuring an experience of the Spirit today. Instead of pining for the Jerusalem Spirit—constantly disappointed with ourselves and baffled by God when tongues of flame do not anoint us— perhaps we would do better to ask how God's Spirit wants to work with us today, stubbornly believing that he still does. He may not act now in precisely the same manner as he did then. But perhaps he has a plan to accomplish his ultimate purposes differently.

The presence of these obvious differences between the first-century world and my own gives me the courage to question whether there might be one more significant difference. The Spirit in the Synoptics and Acts is always miraculous. Matthew, Mark, and Luke know no other "working" of the Spirit than the supernatural. Whether it is visions and voices or healings and tongues, the Spirit we see in these books always makes his presence known in extraordinary ways.

But that, once again, is not my common experience—or the experience of the people I go to church with. Perhaps it should be. One day it may be. But for now, it is not. I know there are Christians and churches for whom an experience of the miraculous is commonplace, whose witness to the Spirit includes more wonders than mine. I do not question their experiences or doubt the validity of their Christian walk.

Of course, they can and do question mine. Some use my lack of the experience of the miraculous to discount my relationship with the Spirit. Under the glare of their criticism, I am tempted to spiritual insecurity. Hearing their stories, I sometimes suffer from Spirit-envy. But in spite of this, I cling to the hope that, while my experience of the Spirit is different, it is neither invalid nor (ultimately) lacking.

I see the fruit of God's Spirit evident in the lives of those who have never performed or witnessed a miraculous healing. I see cross-formed lives and Christ-shaped character in people who don't speak in tongues or utter prophecies. And there is something in me that believes spiritual fruit and cross-formed lives is, in the end, the point of the Spirit's work.

So I ask: Is the Spirit *always* and *inevitably* accompanied by miraculous manifestations (as Acts suggests)? Does the absence of the miraculous *necessarily* mean the absence of the Spirit? Is the presence of the miraculous the *exclusive* measure of a valid spiritual experience?

Or does God have something else, something other, for his people to experience as a result of the Spirit's work? To get at that "other," we'll have to leave the Synoptics and Acts to sift through what remains in Scripture to be said about Spirit. We're going to land, eventually, in the Gospel of John and look at what Jesus teaches about the Spirit. Before John, however, we will make one more stop . . . a brief detour into the letters of Paul. I think you will be encouraged by what we find there.

Chapter Five

The Spirit in the Writings of Paul

Paul uses the word "Spirit" more than any other New Testament writer—125 times in the thirteen letters attributed to him. Unlike the Synoptics, almost all of Paul's Spirit references are to the work of the Spirit in the lives of believers. And unlike either the Synoptics or Acts, Paul moves beyond noting the Spirit's miraculous manifestations to offering an understanding of the Spirit as the transformer of human hearts.

Without question, Paul does witness to the miraculous. He insists, for instance, that his preaching and teaching were not only accompanied but made effective by "a demonstration of the Spirit's power" (1 Cor 2:4).

> I will not venture to speak of anything except what Christ has accomplished through me in leading the Gentiles to obey God by what I have said and done—by the power of signs and miracles, through the power of the Spirit. So from Jerusalem all the way around to Illyricum, I have fully proclaimed the gospel of Christ. (Rom 15:18-19)

> For we know, brothers loved by God, that he has chosen you, because our gospel came to you not simply with words, but also with power, with the Holy Spirit and with deep conviction. (1 Thess 1:4-5)

The things that mark an apostle—signs, wonders and miracles—were done among you [by me] with great perseverance. (2 Cor 12:12)

In these verses, Paul reminds his readers (and informs us) that he came preaching not just with Spirit-words but with Spirit-signs.

Paul is charismatically gifted. He speaks in tongues ("more than all of you," 1 Cor 14:18), heals (e.g., Acts 14:8-10), casts out demons (Acts 16:16-18), prophesies (Acts 27:21-26), and sees visions (2 Cor 12:1-4). He is adamant that his commission to the Gentiles and the gospel he preached were conveyed by supernatural, not natural, means (Gal 1:11-17). Where he goes on mission journeys, what he does, even how long he stays are all dictated by direct revelation of God's Spirit (Acts 13:2; 16:6-7; 18:9-11; 20:22).

Moreover, Paul ministers and writes to Christians who themselves are charismatically gifted. The Corinthians (of course) experience a wide range of miraculous spiritual gifts (tongues, healing, prophecy, and words of "wisdom" and "knowledge," to name but a few). Writing to the Galatians, Paul recognizes that "God gives you his Spirit and works miracles among you" (3:5). Timothy has a "gift of God" which Paul forbids him to "neglect" but, rather, urges him to "fan into flame" (1 Tim 4:14; 2 Tim 1:6). When disciples lack charismatic gifts, Paul lays hands on them to correct the deficiency (Acts 19:6; 2 Tim 1:6). He does not want his converts to "be ignorant" of the Spirit's gifts (1 Cor 12:1). To the contrary, he encourages them to "eagerly desire spiritual gifts" and to "excel in gifts" (1 Cor 14:1, 12).

So far, Paul is another example of the sort of Apostle we've already met in Acts: preaching accompanied by signs; exercising charismatic gifts; and encouraging those gifts in others. Where Paul goes next, however, treads new ground. A *sign-producing-Spirit* is as far as the Synoptics and Acts venture. But not Paul. There is a great deal more on the subject of the Spirit Paul wants to talk about. When he's done with miracles, he's only getting warmed up. And it is to that "more" we now turn.

The Spirit "in you"

Paul introduces a preposition into his discussion of the Spirit that is absent in the writings we've already surveyed: "in." Paul does talk about *receiving* the Spirit and *being given* the Spirit and having the Spirit *poured out*—just as Acts and the Synoptics do. But while these other writings describe the Spirit "on" believers and "with" believers, and believers acting "by" and "through" the Spirit, they never speak of the Spirit "in" believers.

Yet this particular preposition is the one Paul characteristically uses when writing about the Spirit and disciples:

> You, however, are controlled not by the sinful nature but by the Spirit, if *the Spirit of God lives in you*. And if anyone does not have the Spirit of Christ, he does not belong to Christ. But if *Christ is in you*, your body is dead because of sin, yet your spirit is alive because of righteousness. And if the Spirit of him who raised Jesus from the dead *is living in you*, he who raised Christ from the dead will also give life to your mortal bodies through *his Spirit, who lives in you*. (Rom 8:9-11, emphasis mine)

> Do you not know that your body is a temple of the *Holy Spirit, who is in you*, whom you have received from God? (1 Cor 6:19, emphasis mine)

> Now it is God who makes both us and you stand firm in Christ. He anointed us, set his seal of ownership on us, and put *his Spirit in our hearts* . . . . (2 Cor 1:21-22, emphasis mine)

> Because you are sons, God sent *the Spirit of his Son into our hearts* . . . . (Gal 4:6, emphasis mine)

> I pray that out of his glorious riches he may strengthen you with power through *his Spirit in your inner being*, so that *Christ may dwell in your hearts* through faith. (Eph 3:16, emphasis mine)

> Guard the good deposit that was entrusted to you—guard it with the help of *the Holy Spirit who lives in us*. (2 Tim 1:14, emphasis mine)

This Spirit "in you," "living in you," "in your hearts," "in your inner being," resident in the bodies and minds of disciples, is a radical development from the signs-oriented Spirit of the Synoptics and Acts. Yes, Paul experiences the supernatural gifting of the Spirit. But he also experiences something else—an indwelling Spirit who is shaping his heart. Yes, the Spirit prompts tongues and prophecies. But he prompts something more—the mind of Christ and the life of God.

With this tiny preposition "in," Paul introduces the possibility of a Spirit so intimate, so personal, that disciples are touched at the level of heart and soul, mind and character, traits and personality. Whatever else the Spirit may do, Paul understands that the Spirit has an *internal* work to accomplish, a work that takes place *inside* disciples, in their "nature," affecting their appetites and desires, shaping their attitudes and emotions.

This understanding of the Spirit living "in" disciples is foundational for Paul. It colors almost everything he says—from his teachings on gifts, through his instructions about ethical living, to his views of the church.[1] The Spirit indwells. And for Paul this is a difference that makes all the difference.

Take, for instance, what Paul has to say about the *teaching role* of the Spirit. One of the prime functions of the Spirit (in Paul's mind) is to instruct believers: revealing God's will, teaching God's way, and training God's life. But the Spirit doesn't teach in ordinary ways. He isn't confined to words and PowerPoint presentations. Because the Spirit *indwells* us, he has access not just to our eyes and ears, but to our thoughts and motives, our temptations and emotions. His teaching is "deeper" than any other we have ever experienced. And that makes his instruction uniquely powerful and transformative.

Paul prays, for example, that God will give the Ephesians "the Spirit of wisdom and revelation, so that you may know him better" (Eph 1:17). But his prayer is not for a lecturing Spirit who inculcates systematic theology or more facts about the faith. Rather, the prayer is for a revealing Spirit who enlightens "the eyes of your heart" and fosters hope and power (1:18-19). Precisely because this Spirit indwells, his teaching impact is greater than merely informing the mind. He guides the way to intimacy with God. He reveals spiritual perspectives and forms a godly mindset. He turns facts into wisdom. He teaches head and heart, soul and spirit. He mentors motives and desires. He can do this because he indwells and has direct access to our "inner being."

A second passage making the same point is that cryptic, strangely compelling paragraph in which Paul connects the Spirit's ability to teach "God's secret wisdom" and "the deep things of God" to the fact that he lives "in" believers. It is a passage worth quoting at length:

The Spirit searches all things, even the deep things of God. For who among men knows the thoughts of a man except the man's spirit within him? In the same way no one knows the thoughts of God except the Spirit of God. We have not received the spirit of the world but the Spirit who is from God, that we may understand what God has freely given us. This is what we speak, not in words taught us by human wisdom but in words taught by the Spirit, expressing spiritual truths in spiritual words. . . .

> "For who has known the mind of the Lord
>   that he may instruct him?"

But we have the mind of Christ. (1 Cor 2:10-16)

Only God's Spirit can know God's thoughts. To know God's thoughts requires an infusion of God's Spirit. And that is precisely what God has made available to believers: his Spirit in them, giving them access to his "deep things." Who has "known the mind of the Lord," Paul asks? We have! We do! God has put his Spirit in us. And because his Spirit indwells believers, we have "the mind of Christ," we can know "the deep things of God."

All this is good and needed: the Spirit "in" believers . . . the possibility of an intimate Spirit . . . the Spirit teaching and touching us in our "inner being." But it is what Paul does next with the Spirit "in you" that is truly revolutionary.

The Spirit and Transformation

Because the Spirit lives "in" us and has such intimate access to the deepest parts of our being, Paul believes the Spirit is able to perform a truly miraculous work: healing our broken lives and restoring in us the image of God. Paul directs most of his words about the Spirit to the Spirit's role in *changing hearts*. It is a subject he finds endlessly fascinating and ultimately important.

It is Paul who leads us beyond a *present* Spirit and a *supernatural* Spirit to a Spirit capable of *transforming* the "self." Certainly, there are hints of this capacity in the Old Testament writings (as we have noticed)—a Spirit who creates new hearts and prompts holy living. But it is left to Paul to develop what this transformational work actually looks like in the lives of God's people.

Paul understands (more than most) just how broken humanity is, how much damage sin has done to the children of Adam. He knows something more radical than a new law and more dramatic than new wonders is required to undo the curse of Adam. People need heart surgery; hearts healed from the hurts of Eden; new hearts with a fresh hunger for things that are holy.

Rules don't change hearts. Words—even God's words—can't accomplish what is most needed in us. Signs can lead the heart to water, but they cannot make it drink.

Enter the indwelling Spirit. According to Paul, healing the human heart and transforming our human natures is the Spirit's best and greatest work. Paul envisions an entirely new way of living made possible by the Spirit "in" us, a life radically different from the brokenness of life "in Adam" and the impotence of life "in the flesh." This new life is characterized by holiness, God-hunger, Christ-likeness, and true righteousness. It is the life God intended for us all along—the image-of-God-life he created us to live at the beginning. It is a life so different, so "other," it can only be fueled by the supernatural power of the Holy Spirit.

This Spirit-life begins when God saves us, "through the washing of rebirth and renewal by the Holy Spirit" (Titus 3:5). This washing leaves believers "sanctified," holy, and righteous before God; not because of anything we have done, but due entirely to the sovereign decision of God:

> From the beginning, God chose you to be saved through *the sanctifying work of the Spirit* . . . . (2 Thess 2:16, emphasis mine)
> [God made me a minister] so that the Gentiles might become an offering acceptable to God, *sanctified by the Holy Spirit.* (Rom 15:16, emphasis mine)
> You were washed, *you were sanctified*, you were justified in the name of the Lord Jesus Christ and *by the Spirit* of our God. (1 Cor 6:11, emphasis mine)

Already, though, Paul is pointing to something more—not just a change of our *status* in the mind of God, but a change of our *character*. Paul hints in these passages of an ongoing salvation—salvation from the penalty of sin, yes; but also salvation from the power of sin, the dominion of sin, the slavery of sin.

For a salvation *that* great, something more than an initial washing is required. Paul believes the Spirit to be a surgeon, cutting away at the old nature of sin and grafting into us a new nature, a new self. There is a "circumcision of the heart," he writes (Rom 2:29), that only the Spirit can perform. Not the law. Not religious ritual. Not our most determined efforts. Nothing less than the knife of God's Spirit, a circumcision of character performed by the Spirit, is required for heart-change to occur.

The notion of a cutting and killing work of God's Spirit appears repeatedly in Paul's letters. The Spirit sets believers "free from the law of sin and death" (Rom 8:2), puts "to death the misdeeds of the body" (Rom 8:13), and teaches disciples to "put off the old self" (Eph 4:22). Through the Spirit, we die to the "old way of the written code" (Rom 7:6) and the desires of the sinful nature (Gal 5:16-17).

But Paul's Spirit does not just "cut off"; he also grafts on. It is due to the power and teaching of the Spirit that we are able to put on "the new self, created to be like God in true righteousness and holiness" (Eph 4:24). It is because the Spirit has allowed us to "set our minds on things above" that we are empowered to "put on the new self, which is being renewed in knowledge in the image of its Creator" (Col 3:10). It is the Spirit's control that makes it possible for us to be "living sacrifices, holy and pleasing to God . . . transformed by the renewing of your mind" (Rom 12:1-2).

Paul's "Spirit in you" is thus a transforming Spirit, sanctifying believers first by washing them, then teaching them, and then cutting off the old self to make room for the new. Paul's "Spirit in you" changes our status with God, then our minds and attitudes, and then our very natures.

This transformative power is, for Paul, the Spirit's greatest and most miraculous ability. He talks about it—revels in it—in every one of his major letters. Consider the following examples.

The Spirit and Transformation in Paul's Writings

The Spirit who transforms is a major theme in the letter to the Romans, particularly in chapters 7 and 8. Paul, in chapter 7, thoroughly depresses us with his depiction of those who are left to their own devices for living holy lives. ("I am sold as a slave to sin . . . What I hate, I do . . .

Sin is living in me . . . I desire to do good, but I can't carry it out . . . I
keep doing evil . . . I am a most wretched man!"—Rom 7:14-19, 24)

But Paul does not intend to leave us to our own devices. His depiction of humanity-without-Spirit in chapter seven gives way to the depiction of humanity-with-Spirit in chapter eight. And what a difference!

> So now there is no condemnation for those who belong to
> Christ Jesus. And because you belong to him, the power of the
> life-giving Spirit has freed you from the power of sin that leads
> to death. . . . We no longer follow our sinful nature but instead
> follow the Spirit.
>
> Those who are dominated by the sinful nature think
> about sinful things, but those who are controlled by the Holy
> Spirit think about things that please the Spirit. So letting your
> sinful nature control your mind leads to death. But letting
> the Spirit control your mind leads to life and peace. . . . (Rom
> 8:1-6—NLT)

"Who will rescue me from this body of death?" Paul asks. Christ
will! How will he do this? Through the gift of his transforming Spirit! It is
the Spirit who sets us free from the law of sin and death. It is by the Spirit
we now live. Our minds are set on what the Spirit desires. The Spirit con-
trols us (8:9). The Spirit makes us alive to righteousness (8:10). We put
to death the misdeeds of the body by the power of the Spirit (8:13). We
are children of God, led by the Spirit of God (8:14).

Far from normalizing chapter seven as the sad but inevitable experience of Christian living in this broken world, Paul introduces us to
the "Spirit of life," inviting us to move into and live out of the spiritual
realities of chapter eight. The indwelling Spirit changes everything. And,
most of all, he changes *us*.

The transforming Spirit is also an important and recurring theme
in Paul's correspondence with the Corinthians. The Corinthians are
convinced they are spiritual (*pneumatikoi*) because they are gifted. They
believe they have arrived, spiritually, because they can speak in tongues.

Paul begs to differ. He points to a laundry list of problems in the
Corinthian church (like sexual immorality, factions, arrogance, lawsuits,
idolatry, divisions, and resurrection heresies—to name a few) and dares

to tell these spiritually gifted, miraculously endowed brothers: "I could not address you as spiritual but as worldly—mere infants in Christ. I gave you milk, not solid food, for you were not yet ready for it. Indeed, you are still not ready. You are still worldly. For since there is jealousy and quarreling among you, are you not still worldly: Are you not acting like mere men?" (1 Cor 3:1-3).

They ask him questions about spiritual gifts, eager to know more (1 Cor 12:1). Paul answers briefly (1 Cor 12:4-11), but he is far more interested in teaching them about a transforming Spirit whose gifts are meant to change their attitudes towards each other (1 Cor 12:12-31) and lead them on to the "greater gift" of love (1 Cor 12:31-13:3). What good are tongues and prophecy when the Corinthian church is fractured by factions and pride? What good are spiritual gifts that don't make you spiritual?

By the time he writes 2 Corinthians, Paul is at the end of a long and difficult struggle for the character of this church. The Corinthians are finally showing signs of coming around to Paul's point of view. Paul rejoices that, after hard letters and painful visits, comfort is finally breaking out in Corinth (2 Cor 1:3-7).

Barely past the greeting, Paul sets out to redefine what it means to be "spiritual." It means trusting Paul's motives, even when they do not understand his behavior (2 Cor 1:12-24). It means responding to his correction with penitence (2:1-4). It means forgiving those who have opposed Paul in the past (2:5-11). It means ministering to each other and the world with integrity and competence (2:14-3:6).

Most of all, though, it means *being transformed*. Paul explains that even the ministry of Moses—a ministry of condemnation and death— left a mark: it set Moses' face aglow (2 Cor 3:7). Our ministry—a ministry of the Spirit that brings life and righteousness—also leaves a mark, one that will never fade (see 2 Cor 3:8-11).

For the Lord is the Spirit, and wherever the Spirit of the Lord is, there is freedom. So all of us who have had that veil removed can see and reflect the glory of the Lord. And the Lord—who is the Spirit—makes us more and more like him as we are changed into his glorious image. (2 Cor 3:17-18—NLT)

This is not an easy passage, but the point seems clear enough. As we freely, boldly, fully gaze at the glory of Christ, the Spirit acts upon our hearts to transform us into the likeness of the One we worship. It may take some time. It may happen in stages. But transformation does happen. It is, according to Paul, the defining characteristic of the Spirit within us.

The subject of a transforming Spirit comes up yet again when Paul writes to the Galatians. He is afraid they have fallen for a "different gospel" (Gal 1:6). He is worried that, "after beginning with the Spirit," they have decided to rely on themselves instead (3:3).

For four chapters Paul wanders between expressions of astonishment, biographical testimony, and musings on Old Testament stories. By the fifth chapter, Paul decides to get down to business. In his best apostolic voice, he tells the Galatians that the salvation they seek doesn't come through getting it right but through Christ (5:2). Justification before God is rooted in grace, not their keeping of the law (5:4). And—especially—the righteousness they hope for can never be accomplished by circumcision, but only by waiting on the transforming Spirit (5:5).

At this point, Paul launches into ten verses that should be tattooed on the right forearm of every believer:

> So I say, live by the Spirit, and you will not gratify the desires of the sinful nature. For the sinful nature desires what is contrary to the Spirit, and the Spirit what is contrary to the sinful nature. They are in conflict with each other, so that you do not do what you want. But if you are led by the Spirit, you are not under law.
>
> The acts of the sinful nature are obvious: sexual immorality, impurity and debauchery; idolatry and witchcraft; hatred, discord, jealously, fits of rage, selfish ambition, dissensions, factions and envy, drunkenness, orgies, and the like. I warn you, as I did before, that those who live like this will not inherit the kingdom of God.
>
> But the fruit of the Spirit is love, joy, peace, patience, kindness, goodness, faithfulness, gentleness and self-control. Against such things there is no law. Those who belong to Christ Jesus have crucified the sinful nature with its passions and desires.

Since we live by the Spirit, let us keep in step with the Spirit. (Gal 5:16-25)

Okay. It would make a rather lengthy tattoo. But what themes! Here again are ideas raised in Romans: the tension between flesh and Spirit; the victory of Spirit over flesh; living by the Spirit, being led by the Spirit, acting under the Spirit's control. Here again is Paul's confidence that we can be transformed by the Spirit, freed from the desires of the sinful nature to follow the desires of the Spirit.

But there is something new here as well: the Spirit's fruit. Delectable evidence of the Spirit's presence in our lives. The transformative results of the Spirit within us. Paul expects that those who live by the Spirit, who are led by the Spirit, will behave in radically different ways: not lust but love; not rage but joy; not discord but peace; not selfish ambition but kindness; etc. He anticipates that believers will "keep in step with the Spirit" and that this lock-step has specific and powerful implications for the way believers live.

The Galatians want the right fruit. They just refuse to bark up the right tree. They keep climbing the bough of themselves, looking for fruit they are not capable of bearing. Paul assures them that, if only they will return to the Spirit and his transforming ways, they can find the "righteousness for which we hope."

All these passages attest to Paul's conviction that the Spirit dwells in believers and that his most important work is transforming our hearts. There are references in these letters to the Spirit's miraculous works. But they are relatively rare and brief. What Paul cannot stop talking about is the miracle of a Spirit who saves believers from the power of sin and empowers sinners to live faithful lives. Whatever else Paul's churches experience as Christians, Paul encourages them to encounter the Spirit who transforms.

Observations on the Spirit and Paul

Before we put aside Paul's teaching on the Spirit and move to John, a few observations are in order.

First, it is Paul who introduces us to an indwelling Spirit who transforms our hearts. Paul fills in what otherwise would be an incredibly broad and frustratingly deep gap between the Spirit's release into the world and disciples changed into the image of God. It is because of Paul's writings that we have some awareness of the Spirit "in" us, of the Spirit's ability to touch us intimately, of a transforming work that begins with washing and continues in "circumcision of the heart." It is due to Paul that we learn the Spirit gives power over sin, the ability to live righteously, and the capacity to bear the image of Christ. While the Synoptics focus on the ministry of Jesus, and Acts on the growth of the church, Paul focuses on the maturation of God's people into God's image. As a result, we find in Paul a treasure-store of teaching about the Spirit's transforming work.

Second, what we know of Paul reinforces the distinction between the miraculous and transformative works of the Spirit we've seen elsewhere. There are wonders and there are heart-changes, miracle gifts and the new self. Nor are these two works of the Spirit necessarily connected. Experiencing the miraculous does not always prompt transformation (the Corinthians are an example). Circumcision of the heart does not first require an encounter with signs and wonders (the Roman Christians seem to bear this out). What relationship these two spheres of the Spirit's work have to each other is not clear to me. Paul affirms them both as legitimate expressions of the Spirit's presence. But he also demonstrates a decided preference.

Third, it is the *transforming* part of the Spirit's work that most interests Paul. If you stripped Acts and 1 Corinthians out of the New Testament, we would know next to nothing about a charismatic Paul or charismatic churches. I do not say this to disparage or downplay the *charismata*. I say it only to point out that when Paul is speaking (rather than Luke) and when Paul is not correcting charismatic excesses in Corinth, he says little about miraculous manifestations and much about a Spirit who transforms. I suspect this is because, in Paul's thinking, Spirit-signs may be able to prompt faith but only the interior work of the Spirit matures it. And since his letters are primarily *maturing* documents, he places greater emphasis there on the heart-work of the Spirit.

Even when Paul does take up miraculous gifts (as in 1 Corinthians), he moves quickly to transformative matters. Not that the miraculous embarrasses Paul. But he is motivated to move beyond signs and wonders to the wonder of a Spirit who transforms the broken, stubborn, willful human heart.

Fourth, there is a clear pecking order to the spiritual gifts in Paul's writings. Tongues are for personal encouragement and have no place in the assembly unless there is an interpreter who can "edify the church" (1 Cor 14:5, 27-28). Prophecy, while better, must still be limited to "two or three" and should only be done "for the strengthening of the church" (1 Cor 14:26). Speaking in the context of spiritual gifts like tongues and prophecy, miracles and healings, Paul can still point to "greater gifts" and a more "excellent way" (1 Cor 12:31) made available by the Holy Spirit:

> If I speak in the tongues of men and of angels, but have not love, I am only a resounding gong or a clanging cymbal. . . . Love never fails. But where there are prophecies, they will cease; where there are tongues, they will be stilled; where there is knowledge it will pass away. For we know in part and we prophesy in part, but when perfection comes, the imperfect disappears. (1 Cor 13:1-10)

Paul is making a distinction here between gifts of limited (and temporary) importance and gifts of ultimate (and lasting) import. The Spirit who changes hearts makes it possible for us to *love* as Paul describes in this wonderful chapter—a Spirit-gift that never fails and always contributes to "the strengthening of the church." The ability to love in Christlike ways is the Spirit's *greatest* gift, his highest expression of spiritual maturity. Love makes gifts like tongues and prophecies pale in comparison. Paul encourages the Corinthians to "eagerly desire spiritual gifts." But he insists they "follow the way of love"—a spiritual state approaching "perfection"—whatever other gifting they may receive (1 Cor 14:1). For Paul, the miraculous gifts are optional to the Christian life; the transforming gift is not.

The Gospel of John echoes many of the themes about the Spirit found in the Old Testament, the Synoptics, and Acts of the Apostles. But what John says about the Spirit sounds most like Paul. As we will see, John is equally fascinated by a Spirit "in us," a Spirit who makes his home with us. Like Paul, John champions a Spirit who teaches and reveals and comforts. Most of all, John joins Paul in placing emphasis squarely on a Spirit who transforms. The Spirit who indwells makes a difference in our lives and in our walk as disciples—a needed and necessary difference.

It is to John's witness about the Spirit we turn now.

Chapter Six

The *Paraclete* in John

The Gospel of John provides a unique opportunity for us to learn about the Holy Spirit. John says things about the Spirit—and says them *in a way*—that can be heard and appreciated by people who are hungry for the Spirit but want to be discerning in their approach.

Not that John speaks frequently to the subject of the Spirit. There are only twenty one Spirit-references in the entire book (compared, remember, to some seventy in Acts). But, in this instance, we really do have a case of quality over quantity. The little John says is well-worth hearing.

It's worth hearing because, unlike the Synoptic Gospels, most of what is said about the Spirit in John is directly applicable to disciples. It's worth hearing because, unlike Acts and very like Paul, what is said about the Spirit is focused on the *transforming* work of God's Spirit in our lives. And most of all—as we will see—it is worth hearing because John directly quotes what Jesus says and thinks on the subject.

John strips the work of the Spirit down to bare essentials—who the Spirit is, what the Spirit does in the world, how the Spirit works on the hearts of believers—and places those essentials on the lips of Jesus. If we do not understand everything there is to know about the Spirit after reading his Gospel, we at least have a good foundation on which to build a relationship with the Spirit.

John and the Synoptics

A few of the Spirit references found in John are reminiscent of things we've already seen in the Synoptics.

There are a couple of instances, for example, where the word "spirit" is used to speak of a human rather than divine spirit, an inner being or "self." (John, for example, describes Jesus as "deeply moved in spirit.") This use of "spirit" (with a little "s") has its Synoptic equivalents.

John, like his fellow Gospel writers, stresses the importance of the Spirit at the beginning of Jesus' ministry. He has the Baptist report: "I saw the Spirit of God come down from heaven as a dove and remain on him. I would not have known him, except that the one who sent me to baptize with water told me, 'The man on whom you see the Spirit come down and remain is he who will baptize with the Holy Spirit.' I have seen and I testify that this is the Son of God" (John 1:32-34). This Spirit "coming down" was a critical part of identifying Jesus, singling out the "Lamb of God," the "Son of God," the One who "takes away the sins of the world," and the One who "will baptize with the Holy Spirit."

We also find in John (in one of only two comments made about the Spirit in John's voice) an assuring promise: "For the one whom God has sent speaks the words of God, for God gives the Spirit without limit" (John 3:34). Here, like the other Gospel writers, John connects Jesus to the Messianic Age—a time when God would pour out his Spirit on all flesh. It's easy to hear in this statement an echo of Luke's portrait of a Father "who gives the Holy Spirit to those who ask him" (Luke 11:13).

Finally, John (like the Synoptics) talks about the Spirit in the context of Jesus' miraculous ministry. John 1-12 is often titled "The Book of Signs." In these chapters, John builds his story of Jesus around seven miracles: water to wine, healing an official's son, healing a lame man, bread for the crowds, walking on water, opening the eyes of the blind man, and raising the dead.[1] Everything we learn about the Spirit in John is learned in the wider context of Jesus' miraculous ministry.

Thus, John does a few things we've seen the Synoptic writers do: begin Jesus' ministry with the Spirit; promise Jesus would baptize with the Spirit; assure readers God would be giving the Holy Spirit; and talk about the Spirit in the context of Jesus' miraculous and sign-filled ministry.

On the other hand, there are a few things the Synoptics talk about frequently that John entirely ignores. While they see evil spirits around every corner and under every rock, John says nothing on that subject at all. There are no exorcisms in John, no mandate given to the disciples to cast out demons. Nor does John, so intent on talking about signs in the ministry of Jesus, say anything about signs accompanying the disciples. Jesus performs wonders in this Gospel, but the disciples never do.

The Spirit in the Voice of Jesus

John testifies to signs throughout his Gospel as proof that Jesus is who he claims to be. But he also drops teachings about the Spirit like breadcrumbs—as though he wants his readers to follow him to some greater destination. That greater destination is somewhere readers of the Synoptic Gospels have never been before, for the rest of John's teaching on the Spirit leads in a different and strikingly original direction.

This may be due (in part) to the fact that John consistently places words about the Spirit on the lips of Jesus. In the Synoptics, Spirit sayings come from angels or Old Testament quotes or the Gospel writers themselves (reporting specific events). But Jesus says "Spirit" only five times in Matthew, three times in both Mark and Luke.[2]

In John, however, the great majority of times the Spirit is mentioned, Jesus is doing the mentioning. He speaks directly and personally about the Spirit fifteen times—often at great length and depth. In other words, when the Spirit comes up in John, the letters are likely to be in red. This is something unique to the Fourth Gospel . . . and uniquely precious.

The first time Jesus raises the subject of the Spirit is in his long conversation with Nicodemus. They have met "at night" and Nicodemus wants to talk about new birth:

In reply Jesus declared, "I tell you the truth, no one can see the kingdom of God unless he is born again."

"How can a man be born when he is old?" Nicodemus asked. "Surely he cannot enter a second time into his mother's womb to be born!"

Jesus answered, "I tell you the truth, no one can enter the kingdom of God unless he is born of water and the Spirit. Flesh gives birth to flesh, but the Spirit gives birth to spirit. You should not be surprised at my saying, 'You must be born again.' The wind blows wherever it pleases. You hear its sound, but you cannot tell where it comes from or where it is going. So it is with everyone born of the Spirit." (John 3:3-8)

There is a great deal to process here: "born again," the divide between flesh and Spirit, the mysterious and sovereign nature of the Spirit "blowing" where he pleases. Nicodemus has to work hard to keep up. What is striking for our purposes, however, is how different this is from anything we've heard in the Synoptics. Not contrary to Matthew, Mark, and Luke, but certainly novel and more detailed. And certainly important information for disciples as they learn to walk in the Spirit.

It is also striking how much more these ideas sound like Paul than the other Gospel writers. Paul draws a connection between the Spirit and new birth (Gal 4:29; Titus 3:5), a new "self" (Eph 4:23-24; Col 3:10-11), that sounds very much like "You must be born again." He makes the same distinction between flesh and Spirit (e.g., Rom 8). He also has a vast appreciation of the mysterious nature of the Spirit (Eph 3:2-5; Rom 8:26-27; 1 Cor 2:6ff). John's treatment of the Spirit has a lot more in common with Paul than with Luke and the others.

Jesus brings up the subject of the Spirit again while sitting with a woman by a well in Samaria.

You Samaritans don't really know the one you worship. But we Jews do know the God we worship, and by using us, God will save the world. But a time is coming, and it is already here! Even now the true worshipers are being led by the Spirit to worship the Father according to the truth. These are the ones the Father is seeking to worship him. God is Spirit, and those who worship God must be led by the Spirit to worship him according to the truth. (John 4:22-24—CEV)

She wants to talk about well water and buckets and worship traditions. Jesus prefers to talk about missing husbands and life-style and true worship. Worship, says Jesus to the woman, must be "led by the Spirit" and "according to the truth." It is not defined by place or tradition. It is a holy experience marked out and made possible by the Holy Spirit of God.[3]

Again, there is nothing like this in the Synoptic Gospels. And again, this sounds a great deal like Paul ("It is we who worship by the Spirit of God"—Phil 3:3).

When Jesus feeds the crowds (John 6:1-15), they clamor for more. But Jesus knows they want bread for their stomachs, not nourishment for their souls. They'll eat but they will not believe. They crave his loaves and fish but not his words. Jesus tells them what they should be hungry for: "The Spirit is the one who gives life! Human strength can do nothing. The words I have spoken to you are from that life-giving Spirit" (John 6:63—CEV). Like Nicodemus and the Samaritan woman, the crowds are stuck at the level of the flesh. Jesus keeps trying to lift their eyes to the Spirit plane. The Spirit is where eternal life is found, not lunch. "Live above this world," Jesus seems to say. "Live for more than this world."

The same plea is found in the Synoptic Gospels (e.g., "Store up for yourselves treasures in heaven"—Matt 6:19ff). But only in John's Gospel is this plea linked directly to the Spirit. And in Paul. "Those who live according the flesh have their minds set on what the flesh desires. Those who live according to the Spirit have their minds set on what the Spirit desires" (Rom 8:5).

The Spirit in the Final Discourse

Already, Jesus has said some wonderful and original things about the Spirit in John's Gospel: the Spirit "without limit"; the Spirit and new birth; the Spirit and worship; the Spirit and life.

But as the Gospel of John reaches its climax—and especially when we come to the Final Discourse—Jesus steps up to a whole new level. His teaching about the Spirit becomes frequent and compacted. In chapters 14-16 (the heart of the discourse), Jesus talks directly about the Spirit in five extended passages. Because the Spirit is named "the *Paraclete*" in these passages, they are known collectively as "the *Paraclete* Passages." Jesus says more about the Spirit here than in all the rest of his teaching combined.

If the first half of John provides breadcrumbs about the Spirit for us to follow, what Jesus says about the Spirit in "The Final Discourse" is surely the destination to which those crumbs lead.

The purpose of this book is to look at the *Paraclete* Passages in detail, to hear what Jesus promises to the disciples, and to consider what those promises might mean for us. Jesus says the Spirit is coming; the Spirit will live in the disciples and be Christ's presence for them; the Spirit will help the disciples live informed, obedient, well-equipped lives; the Spirit will witness to and help the disciples witness to the world; the Spirit will convict the world of guilt; and the Spirit will continue to reveal the Father to believers.

These are important promises, with important implications for all who want to follow Jesus. As we will see, what we find in the Final Discourse are teachings never broached in the Synoptic Gospels or Acts: a Spirit who indwells; a Spirit who transforms and matures; a Spirit who touches broken hearts and minds as well as ailing bodies. Jesus talks repeatedly in this discourse about the Spirit "in" you (just as Paul does).

As he talks, Jesus introduces us to a *person*. The Spirit is not just a force or a power. He has an identity, a personality.

And he has a name.

The Paraclete

"What's in a name?" asked Shakespeare. "That which we call a rose by any other name would smell as sweet."[4] Perhaps he is right. Still, names are important, even if they don't affect the way roses smell.

At the heart of the Final Discourse are five passages where Jesus speaks of the Holy Spirit. In each (each save the last), he calls the Spirit the *Paraclete*—the only instance in the New Testament when the Spirit is called this and the only place in the New Testament (except once in 1 John) where the word *Paraclete* occurs at all. Because the word is rare (even in secular Greek), it is hard to define precisely. Yet this is the particular word Jesus used when referring to the Spirit. This word had significance for Jesus. It is important to understand as best we can what the word means.

Jesus actually refers to the Spirit by other terms in these chapters—the Spirit of Truth, the Holy Spirit—and a variety of descriptors: the One the Father gives (or sends), the One Jesus sends, the One who will be with the disciples forever. But *Paraclete* is his most consistent and distinctive name for the Spirit.

A Spirit by any other name might also smell as sweet. Still, if Jesus thought enough of the name *Paraclete* to use it so persistently for the Spirit, I'd like to know more about what that name means.

The reason I am about to drag you, Dear Reader, through the etymological swamps is because I want you to know the name of the one Jesus has given us to be our Companion on life's journey. Enough of that depersonalizing "It." Enough of avoiding a living Spirit with talk about "influence" and "attitude" and "spiritual frame of mind." No more "Holy Ghost."

The Spirit is a being, a person.
And, according to Jesus, his name is *Paraclete*.

Para-who?

[Warning: technical jargon ahead!]

Paraclete is actually the anglicized form of the original Greek word *parakletos*. It is a *transliteration* (to use the formal term) rather than a *translation*. Because the meaning of this Greek word is obscure (and the focus of no little scholarly debate), some translations actually avoid the word entirely (by simply using the word "Spirit") rather than commit themselves to a particular English noun.[5]

Even when they decide to translate, however, there isn't much agreement among scholars as to which word renders the meaning best. In fact, translations are all over the map. The variety of options in English Bibles (Advocate,[6] Comforter,[7] Counselor,[8] Helper,[9] Friend,[10] Intercessor,[11] and—regrettably—Strengthener[12]) and the frequency of marginal notes suggesting even *more* alternatives, gives us some indication as to how long and hard translators have grappled with this term.

A clue to the meaning of *Paraclete* comes by looking at the two words from which it is formed: *para* and *kaleo*. *Para* is a preposition meaning "beside" or "along with." *Kaleo* means "to call." Putting these two words together suggests a meaning for *Paraclete* of "one who is called beside or summoned."

Using the constituent parts of a word to define the word is not always wise (try it with "butterfly"). As it turns out, however, the above definition for *Paraclete* has considerable merit. In secular Greek, the word

Paraclete most often takes this very sense when it shows up in legal contexts. When it does, it refers to what we moderns would call a "lawyer": a legal advocate who is asked to defend another.

Professional, paid lawyers did not exist at the time of the New Testament. (They were a later invention of the Romans—the same folks who brought us blood sports and world domination.) Instead, a family member or friend would be "called" to serve as spokesman, standing with the defendant to argue his case before a judge and jury. This "friend" was known as a *Paraclete*.

Is Jesus borrowing this term from the legal realm to describe the Spirit as one who stands beside us, who speaks up for and defends us, who vouches for us in the divine court? This is the background for the word *Paraclete* that recommends translations like "Advocate" and "Intercessor."

The problem with drawing a definition for *Paraclete* from a legal context is that there is nothing very "lawyerly" about the work of the Spirit described by Jesus in John's Final Discourse.[13] There is no hint of divine courts or judges and juries or the Spirit speaking up in the defense of believers in this passage.

The idea of the Spirit as someone who is "on our side," who "stands beside" us through thick and thin, is certainly appropriate—a conclusion that will grow stronger as we understand more of what Jesus says about the Spirit's work in the Final Discourse. But the legal context just doesn't work. Not in John. Thus, to use a translation like "Advocate" may push us too far in a direction John never intended.[14]

There is a verb form of this word (*parakaleo*) that is much more common in the New Testament and in the Greek world of the first century. Paul uses this word, for instance, when he wants to *urge* (Rom 12:1) or *encourage* (1 Thess 2:12) or even *plead with* (Phil 4:2) his readers. It is the word used in passages that speak of *comfort* ("who *comforts* us in all our troubles"—2 Cor 1:4) or *exhortation* ("Do not rebuke an older man harshly, but *exhort* him as if he were your father"—1 Tim 5:1).

The common thread between these various translations of *parakaleo* is of someone speaking into the lives of others—often powerfully—in order to achieve a positive effect. If you read this meaning back into the name Jesus uses for the Holy Spirit, it's easy to see how we got translations like "Comforter," "Helper," "Friend," or "Counselor." The *Paraclete* is the one who comes from the Father to encourage us, to comfort and console us, to advise and strengthen us. He speaks into our lives—often powerfully—in order to achieve a positive effect.

With this meaning, you still get overtones of someone who "is at our side," who stands up and speaks up for us (which is a good thing). But there is the added nuance of one who not only speaks *for* us, but one who speaks *to* us. Jesus may well be saying the Spirit is not just our "defender," he is also our supporter and advisor, someone who whispers wise counsel to us.

Regrettably, none of the English words that try to convey these ideas really seems up to the task. All are either lacking in breadth and power or carry significant baggage for English speakers. To translate *Paraclete* as "Helper" makes the Spirit sound like an errand boy and carries unfortunate overtones of servant status and lower class. "Friend" seems overly familiar (in the same category as calling God "Daddy"). "Counselor" brings up associations like "marriage counselor" or even "camp counselor," associations that contaminate rather than enlighten. D. A. Carson regrets that, "In today's ears, 'Comforter' sounds either like a quilt or like a do-gooder at a wake, and for most speakers of English should be abandoned."[15] "Strengthener" (shudder) reminds one of hair products.

Each of these terms reflects an aspect of the actual work of the *Paraclete* described in John.[16] Jesus paints the Spirit as someone who lives with and in disciples, teaching them who they are and what God wants them to do, revealing ever more of God to them. He portrays the Spirit—whatever we name him—as someone who helps, comes to aid and assist, offers encouragement and consolation, and gives guidance and wisdom. He is friend, mentor, parent, teacher, spouse, role-model, older and wiser sage, partner, workmate, and foxhole companion—all rolled into one.

It's just that no single English word seems capable of carrying the entire load.

Thus, Herman Ridderbos writes: "'Paraclete'—we may conclude—here has a specific meaning that can hardly be conveyed in one word in our language (and many others) but of which the dominant idea is of someone who offers assistance in a situation in which help is needed."[17]

And Andreas Köstenberger concludes: "Perhaps 'helping presence' captures the import of the term better than any other . . . for the following reasons: (1) this is what Jesus was while with the disciples; (2) this encompasses the various functions laid out for the Spirit in John 14-16; (3) this transcends (but may include) the legal context of the term. . . ."[18]

Here, then, are the meanings that lie behind the Greek word *Paraclete*:

Advocate	Counselor	Intercessor	Supporter
Comforter	Helper	Encourager	Advisor
Companion	Friend	Exhorter	Consoler
Guide	Helping Presence		

One who is called beside or summoned
One who speaks up for us
One who speaks into our lives to achieve a positive effect
One who offers assistance in a situation where help is needed

For purposes of this book, I cannot bring myself to settle for any one English term. So I will simply keep the original word *Paraclete* (italicized whenever it occurs) and ask you—the reader—to keep in mind the layers and nuances encompassed by the word.

The Name that Smells as Sweet

Jesus is leaving his disciples. He promises to send someone in his place, someone who will help his disciples *be* his disciples after he has gone.

Essentially, he promises himself in other form.

As we will see, the *Paraclete* will not be a "Jesus substitute," some kind of "Jesus lite." Rather, the *Paraclete* will be the hands and face and voice of Jesus, his actual presence, and the means by which he will continue to commune with the disciples.

The Final Discourse bears witness to this Helping Presence, available to all who love Jesus, sent by the Father to walk with believers along the way. According to Jesus, the *Paraclete* will keep the disciples alive to God. He will make them effective in their living and work. He will help them in their mission. And his presence, as we will see, will last "forever."

These promises raise all manner of questions, like: Why is this Spirit so necessary? How does he work? Is this same Spirit for us? We will spend the rest of this book pursuing such questions.

For the moment, I simply ask you to consider how the name we use for the Spirit will affect the way the Spirit smells to us. In a religious context where "Spirit" might as well be called "Bible Study" or "Careful Exegesis" or "Proper Hermeneutic," the bloom is certainly off the rose. Any discussion of the Spirit that bogs us down in historical-critical methodology and the conjugation of Greek verbs is bound to fail the sniff test.

At the other extreme, there are religious contexts where "Spirit" might as well be named "Stranger" or "Perpetrator of the Odd and Offbeat" or "Means of Getting My Own Way." Names like these will always smell fishy, no matter how much essence-of-rose you sprinkle on them!

When we talk, however, about a Spirit named *Paraclete*, there is a certain fragrance that fills the air. You catch a whiff of the aroma of Christ. You inhale the breath of God and smell the rich perfume of life.

The Spirit as *Paraclete* smells sweet indeed. I want to inhale that Spirit with every breath I take. I want his scent in my life and on my heart. I need his heady perfume.

I suspect you do too.

Chapter Seven

THE TEXT OF THE FINAL DISCOURSE

Below is the text of the Final Discourse from John. I include this passage in its entirety because I believe it is important for readers of this book to root their reading in the key text that forms the basis of the book. We will be wading in and out of this passage through the pages to follow.

There is debate in the literature about what verses actually constitute the Final Discourse. Some don't begin the Discourse until Judas leaves the room (13:30). Others want to extend the Discourse through the prayer recorded in John 17.

I have chosen to let the fundamental dynamics of this conversation—the Last Meal, the Upper Room, Jesus interacting with his disciples—set the boundaries for the Final Discourse. Thus, because the evening begins as chapter 13 opens, I start the discourse there. And because Jesus is addressing his Father rather than the disciples in chapter 17, I end the discourse before the High Priestly Prayer.

Please spend some time immersed in this passage. Wash yourself with its words. Scrub its themes and messages into the pores of your soul. Jesus has something important to say to the Twelve on this final night. If my reading is correct, he has something important to say to us as well. Imagine Jesus speaking over the heads of his Apostles to all the other disciples through all the ages to follow who listen to this conversation by means of John's testimony.

I've included the chapter and verse markings in this passage only to help you navigate more easily. And I've marked the *Paraclete* Passages so you cannot miss them: boldface and italics.

13 ¹It was just before the Passover Feast. Jesus knew that the time had come for him to leave this world and go to the Father. Having loved his own who were in the world, he now showed them the full extent of his love.

²The evening meal was being served, and the devil had already prompted Judas Iscariot, son of Simon, to betray Jesus. ³Jesus knew that the Father had put all things under his power, and that he had come from God and was returning to God; ⁴so he got up from the meal, took off his outer clothing, and wrapped a towel around his waist. ⁵After that, he poured water into a basin and began to wash his disciples' feet, drying them with the towel that was wrapped around him.

⁶He came to Simon Peter, who said to him, "Lord, are you going to wash my feet?"

⁷Jesus replied, "You do not realize now what I am doing, but later you will understand."

⁸"No," said Peter, "you shall never wash my feet.

Jesus answered, "Unless I wash you, you have no part with me."

⁹"Then, Lord," Simon Peter replied, "not just my feet but my hands and my head as well!"

¹⁰Jesus answered, "A person who has had a bath needs only to wash his feet; his whole body is clean. And you are clean, though not every one of you." ¹¹For he knew who was going to betray him, and that was why he said not everyone was clean.

¹²When he had finished washing their feet, he put on his clothes and returned to his place. "Do you understand what I have done for you?" he asked them. ¹³"You call me 'Teacher' and 'Lord,' and rightly so, for that is what I am. ¹⁴Now that I, your Lord and Teacher, have washed your feet, you also should wash one another's feet. ¹⁵I have set you an example that you should do as I have done for you. ¹⁶I tell you the truth, no servant is greater than his master, nor is a messenger greater than the one who sent him. ¹⁷Now that you know these things, you will be blessed if you do them.

¹⁸"I am not referring to all of you; I know those I have chosen. But this is to fulfill the scripture: 'He who shares my bread has lifted up his heel against me.'

¹⁹"I am telling you now before it happens, so that when it does happen you will believe that I am He. ²⁰I tell you the truth, whoever accepts anyone I send accepts me; and whoever accepts me accepts the one who sent me."

²¹After he had said this, Jesus was troubled in spirit and testified, "I tell you the truth, one of you is going to betray me."

²²His disciples stared at one another, at a loss to know which of them he meant. ²³One of them, the disciple whom Jesus loved, was reclining next to him. ²⁴Simon Peter motioned to this disciple and said, "Ask him which one he means."

²⁵Leaning back against Jesus, he asked him, "Lord, who is it?"

²⁶Jesus answered, "It is the one to whom I will give this piece of bread when I have dipped it in the dish." Then, dipping the piece of bread, he gave it to Judas Iscariot, son of Simon. ²⁷As soon as Judas took the bread, Satan entered into him.

"What you are about to do, do quickly," Jesus told him, ²⁸but no one at the meal understood why Jesus said this to him. ²⁹Since Judas had charge of the money, some thought Jesus was telling him to buy what was needed for the Feast, or to give something to the poor. ³⁰As soon as Judas had taken the bread, he went out. And it was night.

³¹When he was gone, Jesus said, "Now is the Son of Man glorified and God is glorified in him. ³²If God is glorified in him, God will glorify the Son in himself, and will glorify him at once.

³³"My children, I will be with you only a little longer. You will look for me, and just as I told the Jews, so I tell you now: Where I am going, you cannot come.

³⁴"A new command I give you: Love one another. As I have loved you, so you must love one another. ³⁵By this all men will know that you are my disciples, if you love one another."

³⁶Simon Peter asked him, "Lord, where are you going?" Jesus replied, "Where I am going, you cannot follow now, but you will follow later."

[37]Peter asked, "Lord, why can't I follow you now? I will lay down my life for you."

[38]Then Jesus answered, "Will you really lay down your life for me? I tell you the truth, before the rooster crows, you will disown me three times!

14 [1]"Do not let your hearts be troubled. Trust in God; trust also in me. [2]In my Father's house are many rooms; if it were not so, I would have told you. I am going there to prepare a place for you. [3]And if I go and prepare a place for you, I will come back and take you to be with me that you also may be where I am. [4]You know the way to the place where I am going."

[5]Thomas said to him, "Lord, we don't know where you are going, so how can we know the way?"

[6]Jesus answered, "I am the way and the truth and the life. No one comes to the Father except through me. [7]If you really knew me, you would know my Father as well. From now on, you do know him and have seen him."

[8]Philip said, "Lord, show us the Father and that will be enough for us."

[9]Jesus answered: "Don't you know me, Philip, even after I have been among you such a long time? Anyone who has seen me has seen the Father. How can you say, 'Show us the Father'? [10]Don't you believe that I am in the Father, and that the Father is in me? The words I say to you are not just my own. Rather, it is the Father, living in me, who is doing his work. [11]Believe me when I say that I am in the Father and the Father is in me; or at least believe on the evidence of the miracles themselves. [12]I tell you the truth, anyone who has faith in me will do what I have been doing. He will do even greater things than these, because I am going to the Father. [13]And I will do whatever you ask in my name, so that the Son may bring glory to the Father. [14]You may ask me for anything in my name, and I will do it.

[15]"If you love me, you will obey what I command. [16]*And I will ask the Father, and he will give you another Paraclete to be with you forever— [17]the Spirit of truth. The world cannot accept him, because it neither sees him nor knows him. But you know him, for he lives with you and will be in you.* [18]I will not leave you as orphans; I will come to you.

[19]Before long, the world will not see me anymore, but you will see me. Because I live, you also will live. [20]On that day you will realize that I am in my Father, and you are in me, and I am in you. [21]Whoever has my commands and obeys them, he is the one who loves me. He who loves me will be loved by my Father, and I too will love him and show myself to him."

[22]Then Judas (not Judas Iscariot) said, "But, Lord, why do you intend to show yourself to us and not to the world?"

[23]Jesus replied, "If anyone loves me, he will obey my teaching. My Father will love him, and we will come to him and make our home with him. [24]He who does not love me will not obey my teaching. These words you hear are not my own; they belong to the Father who sent me.

[25]"All this I have spoken while still with you. [26]*But the Paraclete, the Holy Spirit, whom the Father will send in my name, will teach you all things and will remind you of everything I have said to you.* [27]Peace I leave with you; my peace I give you. I do not give to you as the world gives. Do not let your hearts be troubled and do not be afraid.

[28]"You heard me say, 'I am going away and I am coming back to you.' If you loved me, you would be glad that I am going to the Father, for the Father is greater than I. [29]I have told you now before it happens, so that when it does happen you will believe. [30]I will not speak with you much longer, for the prince of this world is coming. He has no hold on me, [31]but the world must learn that I love the Father and that I do exactly what my Father has commanded me.

"Come now; let us leave.

15 [1]"I am the true vine, and my Father is the gardener. [2]He cuts off every branch in me that bears no fruit, while every branch that does bear fruit he prunes so that it will be even more fruitful. [3]You are already clean because of the word I have spoken to you. [4]Remain in me, and I will remain in you. No branch can bear fruit by itself; it must remain in the vine. Neither can you bear fruit unless you remain in me.

[5]"I am the vine; you are the branches. If a man remains in me and I in him, he will bear much fruit; apart from me you can do nothing. [6]If anyone does not remain in me, he is like a branch that is thrown away and withers; such branches are picked up, thrown into the fire and

burned. [7]If you remain in me and my words remain in you, ask whatever you wish, and it will be given you. [8]This is to my Father's glory, that you bear much fruit, showing yourselves to be my disciples.

[9]"As the Father has loved me, so have I loved you. Now remain in my love. [10]If you obey my commands, you will remain in my love, just as I have obeyed my Father's commands and remain in his love. [11]I have told you this so that my joy may be in you and that your joy may be complete. [12]My command is this: Love each other as I have loved you. [13]Greater love has no one than this, that he lay down his life for his friends. [14]You are my friends if you do what I command. [15]I no longer call you servants, because a servant does not know his master's business. Instead, I have called you friends, for everything that I learned from my Father I have made known to you. [16]You did not choose me, but I chose you and appointed you to go and bear fruit—fruit that will last. Then the Father will give you whatever you ask in my name. [17]This is my command: Love each other.

[18]"If the world hates you, keep in mind that it hated me first. [19]If you belonged to the world, it would love you as its own. As it is, you do not belong to the world, but I have chosen you out of the world. That is why the world hates you. [20]Remember the words I spoke to you: 'No servant is greater than his master.' If they persecuted me, they will persecute you also. If they obeyed my teaching, they will obey yours also. [21]They will treat you this way because of my name, for they do not know the One who sent me. [22]If I had not come and spoken to them, they would not be guilty of sin. Now, however, they have no excuse for their sin. [23]He who hates me hates my Father as well. [24]If I had not done among them what no one else did, they would not be guilty of sin. But now they have seen these miracles, and yet they have hated both me and my Father. [25]But this is to fulfill what is written in their Law: 'They hated me without reason.'

[26]*"When the Paraclete comes, whom I will send to you from the Father, the Spirit of truth who goes out from the Father, he will testify about me.* [27]*And you also must testify, for you have been with me from the beginning.*

16 [1]"All this I have told you so that you will not go astray. [2]They will put you out of the synagogue; in fact, a time is coming when anyone who kills you will think he is offering a service to God. [3]They will do such things because they have not known the Father or me. [4]I have told you this, so that when the time comes you will remember that I warned you. I did not tell you this at first because I was with you.

[5]"Now I am going to him who sent me, yet none of you asks me, 'Where are you going?' [6]Because I have said these things, you are filled with grief. *[7]But I tell you the truth: It is for your good that I am going away. Unless I go away, the Paraclete will not come to you; but if I go, I will send him to you. [8]When he comes, he will convict the world of guilt in regard to sin and righteousness and judgment: [9]in regard to sin, because men do not believe in me; [10]in regard to righteousness, because I am going to the Father, where you can see me no longer; [11]and in regard to judgment, because the prince of this world now stands condemned.*

[12]"I have much more to say to you, more than you can now bear. *[13]But when he, the Spirit of truth, comes, he will guide you into all truth. He will not speak on his own; he will speak only what he hears, and he will tell you what is yet to come. [14]He will bring glory to me by taking from what is mine and making it known to you. [15]All that belongs to the Father is mine. That is why I said the Spirit will take from what is mine and make it known to you.*

[16]"In a little while you will see me no more, and then after a little while you will see me."

[17]Some of his disciples said to one another, "What does he mean by saying, 'In a little while you will see me no more, and then after a little while you will see me,' and 'Because I am going to the Father'?" [18]They kept asking, "What does he mean by 'a little while'? We don't understand what he is saying."

[19]Jesus saw that they wanted to ask him about this, so he said to them, "Are you asking one another what I meant when I said, 'In a little while you will see me no more, and then after a little while you will see me'? [20]I tell you the truth, you will weep and mourn while the world rejoices. You will grieve, but your grief will turn to joy. [21]A woman giving birth to a child has pain because her time has come; but when her baby is born she forgets the anguish because of her joy that a child is born into the world. [22]So with you: Now is your time of grief, but I will see you again and you will rejoice, and no one will take away your joy. [23]In that day you will no longer ask me anything. I tell you the truth, my Father

will give you whatever you ask in my name. [24]Until now you have not asked for anything in my name. Ask and you will receive, and your joy will be complete.

[25]"Though I have been speaking figuratively, a time is coming when I will no longer use this kind of language but will tell you plainly about my Father. [26]In that day you will ask in my name. I am not saying that I will ask the Father on your behalf. [27]No, the Father himself loves you because you have loved me and have believed that I came from God. [28]I came from the Father and entered the world; now I am leaving the world and going back to the Father."

[29]Then Jesus' disciples said, "Now you are speaking clearly and without figures of speech. [30]Now we can see that you know all things and that you do not even need to have anyone ask you questions. This makes us believe that you came from God."

[31]"You believe at last!" Jesus answered. [32]"But a time is coming, and has come, when you will be scattered, each to his own home. You will leave me all alone. Yet I am not alone, for my Father is with me.

[33]"I have told you these things, so that in me you may have peace. In this world you will have trouble. But take heart! I have overcome the world."

THE SPIRIT IN THE FINAL DISCOURSE

From the moment Jesus called them from tax tables and fishing nets, the disciples stuck close to their Master. They were with him at the Wedding Feast, when he cleared the temple, as he talked with the Samaritan woman, in the wilderness with the crowds. They never ventured far from Jesus, nor he from them. There were rare occasions when he withdrew to pray. Once, he sent them out to preach on their own. But, for the most part, Master and followers were inseparable.

It was the one constant of Jesus' ministry. Whatever else happened, whatever uncertainties they had to navigate, the disciples knew Jesus was *there*. They steered by his Star. From the beginning, he was their fixed and certain point as they sailed the chartless seas of Messianic ministry and their own new calling.

But no more. On the night he is betrayed, Jesus has to watch his disciples run aground on the unexpected rock of his imminent departure.

It is at this point Jesus introduces his disciples to the *Paraclete*. In a series of five passages, Jesus equips his disciples for a life without his physical presence by pointing them to the ministry of the Spirit who will continue his work. The chapters of Section Two take up each of these passages in turn.

Chapter Eight looks at the first *Paraclete* Passage (John 14:16-17) and the "Promise of Presence" it contains. Through the Spirit, the disciples will continue to experience a relationship with Jesus. Because of the

Spirit, they will continue to "see" Jesus and "live" with him. The Spirit will become Jesus' forever presence with his disciples.

Chapter Nine focuses on the second *Paraclete* Passage (John 14:26) and its "Promise of Teaching." The disciples have a mission to accomplish. Jesus assures them the Spirit will guide and instruct them as they continue the vital work he began in the world.

Chapter Ten examines the third *Paraclete* Passage (John 15:26-27) and its "Promise of Testimony." Part of the mission given to the disciples involves testifying about Jesus before a hostile world. Jesus wants them to know they will not be alone in that work—the Spirit will testify with and through them.

In Chapter Eleven we look at the fourth *Paraclete* Passage (John 16:7-11) and its "Promise of Conviction." In a world so full of sin and rationalization, disciples can feel oh-so-powerless. There is no need. God is still at work in his world, acting through his Spirit to convict his broken creatures of their sin and their need for him.

Then in Chapter Twelve we study the fifth *Paraclete* Passage (John 16:12-15) and the "Promise of Revelation." Jesus has so much more to say about his Father. But the disciples cannot bear it. So he offers them the Spirit who will reveal the Father in portions they can swallow. The Spirit, knowing their limits, reveals what they need to know of God as they are capable of receiving it.

Section Two is the heart of this book. This is where we do the hard digging through John's Gospel to discover the treasure buried there: what Jesus has to say about the Holy Spirit. In the following section we'll spend some time learning how that applies to our lives and particular circumstances.

Chapter Eight

THE PROMISE OF PRESENCE

(JOHN 14:16-23)

No wonder they feel abandoned. Jesus is going away. He's just told them so. He is leaving and they cannot go with him.

Into their foreboding, Jesus pours every reassuring word he can lay his hands on. Many of these reassuring words point to the *Paraclete*. And the first of these reassuring *Paraclete*-words promises both a future for the disciples in the wake of the Cross and the presence of Jesus as they meet that future.

Jesus begins by talking to the Twelve about who the Spirit *is*, his nature and identity.

> 14:16And I will ask the Father, and he will give you another *Paraclete* to be with you forever—17the Spirit of truth. The world cannot accept him, because it neither sees him nor knows him. But you know him, for he lives with you and will be in you. 18I will not leave you as orphans; I will come to you.

Jesus is God

John 14, from beginning to end, addresses identity questions. It opens with the question, "Who is the Father?" Jesus answers by making an astounding claim: "I am the way and the truth and the life. No one comes to the Father except through me. If you really knew me, you would know my Father as well. From now on, you do know him and have seen him" (John 14:6-7). He has made such claims before. In fact, these claims have been a source of major conflict with the religious authorities. The Pharisees were driven to murderous rage when, early in his ministry, they heard him "calling God his own Father, making himself equal with God" (John 5:18). They picked up stones to throw at him again when he made the bald statement, "Before Abraham was born, I AM" (John 8:58—a clear echo of God's self-defining statement to Moses: "Tell the Israelites, 'I AM has sent me to you'"—Ex 3:14). Yet again, they reached for rocks when Jesus proclaimed, "I and the Father are one" (John 10:30).

But now, alone with his disciples, Jesus strings together a series of claims linking himself directly to God—not as a prophet or a teacher but as the living incarnation of Deity, God in the flesh, the visible revelation of the invisible God. Since he *is* God, to know Jesus is to know God; to see Jesus is to see God.

When Philip misses the point and asks Jesus to "show us the Father," Jesus repeats himself and elaborates on the theme just to be clear.

> Don't you know me, Philip, even after I have been among you such a long time? Anyone who has seen me has seen the Father. How can you say, 'Show us the Father'? Don't you believe that I am in the Father, and that the Father is in me? The words I say to you are not just my own. Rather, it is the Father, living in me, who is doing his work. Believe me when I say that I am in the Father and the Father is in me. . . . (John 14:9-11).

He *has* shown them the Father. He has revealed God by disclosing himself! Jesus is God in flesh-form. Jesus and the Father are living in each other; they are the same in nature and character. Jesus speaks the words of God and does the work of God. The Father and the Son are *one*.

Jesus answers Philip's request in a way that unmistakably identifies the Father with himself. God is no stranger to the disciples. He is not hidden and unknown. Jesus reveals God to the disciples by letting them get to know *him*.

Jesus Is Spirit

In a similar way John 14 also asks, "Who is the Spirit?" In answering that question, Jesus uses the same strategy, doing with the Spirit what he's done with the Father: pointing to himself. "And I will ask the Father, and he will give you another *Paraclete* to be with you forever—the Spirit of truth" (John 14:16-17a).

In this initial broaching of the Spirit subject, Jesus introduces the Spirit as the *Paraclete*. We've already looked at this term (in Chapter Six) and seen that it carries a number of different and important overtones. For now, remember the dominant idea behind *Paraclete* is "someone who offers assistance in a situation in which help is needed."[1]

Jesus promises that God will send "someone to help" the disciples as soon as he himself leaves. And a good thing too. For if ever a group of men needed help, it was the disciples on the eve of Calvary. They needed help coping with and understanding the cross. They needed help wrapping their minds around resurrection. They needed help knowing what to do next and how to continue their mission and where to find courage and power. In truth, the disciples have needed help from the first moment they met Jesus. All along, they required constant and tangible assistance: to make sense of what they saw and heard, to understand the parables, to rescue them and encourage them and empower them, to grasp who Jesus was and what they'd gotten themselves into.

For the past three years, Jesus himself has provided that assistance. *He* has been their *Paraclete*, their Helper and Companion. Now, however, Jesus points to "*another*" *Paraclete*: someone who will provide practical assistance for the disciples in the future just as Jesus has provided it in the past.[2]

This is the first hint in John's Gospel as to the identity of the Spirit: he and Jesus share exactly the same work. There is more. Jesus describes the Spirit as "the Spirit of Truth."[3] Jesus himself is intimately connected to truth in this Gospel. John tells us that Jesus is "full of truth" and that "truth came through Jesus Christ" (1:14, 17). Jesus calls himself "a man of truth," who tells the truth and teaches the truth (7:18; 8:31-32, 40). In fact—in this very chapter—Jesus has already named himself "the way, *the truth*, and the life" (14:6). Now, he names the Spirit "Truth" (14:17). The Spirit and Jesus share this intimate and defining characteristic.

It is what he says next, however, that forces the Twelve (and those of us who read John's testimony) to recognize Jesus isn't just *comparing* the Spirit to himself—he is *identifying* the Spirit with himself. The Spirit is Jesus in indwelling form. "The world cannot accept him, because it neither sees him nor knows him. But you know him, for he lives with you and will be in you" (John 14:17). To the world, the Spirit will be an unknown and unknowable stranger. But that's not the case with the disciples, as Jesus makes clear in this astonishing statement: "You *know* him."

How can that be? Jesus has no more than introduced them to the *Paraclete* (these are, according to John, the first words he's spoken to them about this Companion), yet he claims the disciples already know the one he's talking about.

In John's understanding, the Apostles did not, *could* not, experience the indwelling Spirit until Jesus returned to the Father. In an aside earlier in the Gospel, John explained to his readers, "Up to that time, the Spirit had not been given, since Jesus had not yet been glorified" (John 7:39). Later, in this very Discourse, Jesus will tell the Twelve, "Unless I go away, the *Paraclete* will not come to you" (John 16:7). John believed the Spirit could not be present until Jesus was absent. And yet, Jesus can tell his disciples they already "know" this *Paraclete—present tense*. They've only just heard of him . . . they have not even *met* him . . . yet Jesus can state they know him already and imply they know him intimately. How can he make such a claim?

The clue comes in what follows. "For he lives with you and will live in you." Or as the *New Living Testament* puts it: "He lives with you *now* and *later* will be in you" (emphasis added). What an odd statement! The Spirit "lives with" (or abides, dwells in the present) and the Spirit "will live in" (later on, in time to come).

It is at this point we begin to suspect that—in the mind of Jesus—the Spirit is not just *like* him, the Spirit *is* him. Jesus is living with the Apostles now as their *Paraclete*, their Truth. The Spirit will be living in the Apostles later as their *Paraclete*, their Truth. But, in some sense, it's all one and the same. Jesus is the Spirit's presence in the here-and-now just as the Spirit will be his presence in the there-and-then.[4]

Jesus has shown them the Spirit. He has revealed the Spirit by disclosing himself! Jesus is the Spirit in flesh-form. Jesus and the Spirit are living in each other; they are the same in nature and character. The Spirit—when he comes—will speak the words of Jesus and do the work of Jesus. The Son and the Spirit are *one*.

"The Spirit lives with you," states Jesus, "because *I* live with you. If you know me, you know the Spirit. Anyone who has seen me has seen the Spirit."

"He will live in you," states Jesus. "When the Spirit does come, you will recognize me in him, and welcome us into your lives."

Like Jesus and the Father, Jesus and the Spirit are one. As Jesus reveals the Father, so he reveals the Spirit. Those who have known Jesus have known both Father and Spirit.

I Will Come to You

This careful linking of the Spirit to the Christ is neither accidental nor incidental. It is foundational to understanding everything Jesus says about the Spirit in the Final Discourse: what the Spirit teaches, why the Spirit witnesses, what the Spirit accomplishes in the world and in disciples.

It is foundational to understanding what Jesus says here in the First *Paraclete* Passage. Because of this essential unity between himself and the Spirit, Jesus is able to forge a continuing and intimate link between himself and his disciples. Yes, Jesus is going away. There is a cross in his near future. And a tomb. And an ascension. Where he is going the disciples cannot come. Yet he is not abandoning the disciples. Far from it!

> [18]I will not leave you as orphans; I will come to you. [19]Before long, the world will not see me anymore, but you will see me. Because I live, you also will live. [20]On that day you will realize that I am in my Father, and you are in me, and I am in you. [21]. . . He who loves me will be loved by my Father, and I too will love him and show myself to him . . . [23]and we will come to him and make our home with him. (John 14:18-23)

"I will come to you." Is Jesus talking about the resurrection here? There are many who think so. Jesus has been discussing the *Paraclete* (in verses 16 and 17). But in this viewpoint, he makes a shift at verse 18, warning his disciples he is going away (dying), he's coming back (the resurrection), and they will see him again (the appearances).

But reading these verses like this causes real difficulties. How does the resurrection not leave the disciples as "orphans" when Jesus' resurrection appearances will be infrequent, brief, and painfully temporary?[5] Forty days past the empty tomb is the ascension, when Jesus will leave the earth for good. Are a few fleeting glimpses of a risen Christ enough to rescue the disciples from the status of "orphans"?

And what do resurrection appearances have to do with the disciples' dawning awareness that "I am in my Father, and you are in me, and I am in you" . . . or the promised experience of Jesus and the Father making a "home with" them?

Jesus is not changing the subject at verse 18. He is still talking about the *Paraclete*. Jesus is going away (leaving the flesh), but he is coming back (in the form of the Spirit) and they will "see" him again (through the Spirit's indwelling presence).[6]

The promise here is stunning. The *Paraclete* is coming soon to the disciples. They will *see* him and *know* him. He will live with them and be in them. And that Spirit will be Jesus in forever form, present with his disciples again and always. He will show himself to them. He will make his home with them. Through the indwelling Spirit.

The reason the world won't "see" Jesus (v. 19) is because unredeemed hearts are incapable of hosting the Holy Spirit. Only the disciples "see" Jesus because only they experience a Spirit who takes up residence in them and becomes Christ's tangible presence for them.[7] Along with the Spirit's indwelling, the disciples will discover a new communion with Jesus is possible ("you in me and I in you").[8]

But, Lord . . .

In this first *Paraclete* Passage, Jesus introduces the Spirit to his disciples by pointing to himself. To have the Spirit is to have Jesus. Far from abandoning them, Jesus is returning to live with them in another form . . . a forever form.

The fact that the disciples are confused by all of this is understandable. It's confusing to us! How can Jesus "go away" and "remain" at the same time? How can Jesus "leave" and "be present" simultaneously? It's enough to give disciples (then and now) a headache.[9]

That, of course, is the nature of "mystery"—something paradoxical wrapped in something perplexing, a package that is bigger than we are. But perhaps at this point, resolving the riddle is less important than celebrating the simple promise of Christ's continued presence. The disciples don't have to live without Jesus. They aren't stranded on the island of this world, cut off from their Master. Jesus will remain with them, remain in them, through the indwelling presence of the Holy Spirit.

Did they grasp all this on that final evening, when so much remained unclear and uncertain? Probably not. But they would grasp it eventually. And when they did, this promise and this presence would prove to be a source of great comfort and great power to them.

And What of Us?

These were wonderful promises for the Twelve to hear. But are they wonderful for us? Do they have any application or pertinence to our lives?

It turns out that modern disciples have much in common with ancient ones. Their fears are ours. Their needs are ours. Their situation is strikingly similar to our own. We too have made a commitment to follow Jesus. We've left behind a great deal in order to become his

---

**What we learn about the Holy Spirit
in the First *Paraclete* Passage:**

1. The Spirit is "another *Paraclete*"
2. When Jesus returns to the Father, he will ask God to send the Spirit
3. The Father will send/give the Spirit to the disciples
4. The Spirit will be with the disciples forever
5. The Spirit (like Jesus) will be "the Truth"
6. The world cannot see, know, or accept the Spirit
7. The disciples will see and know this Spirit
8. The Spirit will live "in" the disciples
9. "I will come to you . . ."; "Before long . . ."; "you will see me . . ."; "On that day . . ."; "I will show myself . . ."; "We will come to him . . ."; and "we will make our home with him . . ."–all refer to the coming of the Holy Spirit.

disciples. We've heard his words and been changed by them, and now find ourselves unfitted for ordinary living.

Like the Apostles, who will spend most of their lives ministering in a post-Easter world, we also live out our commitment to Jesus at a time and in a world from which Jesus is physically absent. Like them, we are tempted to feel abandoned, lonely, and lost. We miss our Master. We wish we could be with him. We long to "walk and talk" with the One who has turned our lives upside down.

Jesus has gone to the Father and we have been left behind—just like the Twelve. And we find ourselves very much in need of the same thing the Twelve were given to deal with a departed Jesus: the hope that there is, in fact, a continuing experience of Jesus available to us. Not just memories of him preserved in a holy book—a living presence. Not just an intrusion of miraculous signs into our ordinary world—a miraculous presence who offers personal relationship. We need *another Paraclete* as badly as they.

And so we find ourselves wondering whether the words spoken in this first *Paraclete* Passage (by Jesus to the Twelve) might extend to those who believe in Jesus through their testimony. Is this promise meant only for the original audience? Did it apply to the first readers of John's gospel, sixty years after the events of this evening? Might it be meant for us who read these words of hope two thousand years after that fateful night?

Yes. These words are for us as much as for them. The promises are ours, not just theirs. I believe that. Whether such a faith is justified, whether the promise is for *all* disciples, remains an open question we will address later in this book. For now I simply ask you to consider, "What if it *is* true?" What if this promise is for you and me?

There are several ways this opening *Paraclete* Passage has immediate impact and relevance for believers today. First, it requires us to dust off and grapple with that ancient doctrine of the Trinity. It is difficult to comprehend how we can even read John 14, much less glean the important lessons about the Spirit revealed there, without a conviction that God is one-in-three—that Father, Son, and Spirit are distinct expressions of, different forms of, a single divine nature.

We don't mind being "binitarian"—God in two persons. We can confess that Jesus reveals the Father; that he is the full expression of the

Father's character, attributes, and purposes; that he shows us the Father's heart and mind. We can confess that Jesus is God in the flesh. And so, when John asks in chapter 14, "Who is God?" we can accept the answer, "Anyone who has seen me has seen the Father."

But John uses the exact same approach to address the question, "Who is the Spirit?" The Spirit is Jesus. To know Jesus is to know the Spirit. To have the Spirit is to have Jesus, and—by extension—to have the Father as well. For John there is an essential oneness between Father, Son, and Spirit that permits Jesus to accurately and completely "make known" the other persons of the Trinity.

If the promise is for us, it means (secondly) there is an experience of the living and indwelling Spirit available for you and me today. Not just a "sign Spirit" who works and performs and operates in the world (as in Acts); an "intimate Spirit" who makes his home "in" us. Not just a Spirit who inspires holy writings that guide our lives today; a Spirit who is "resident" in us and helps us recognize God's Word in all its guises. The promise here is for a Companion, a Champion, a Helper along the way. We don't have to struggle through life on our own, under our own power, by our own bootstraps. There is a Presence who stands beside us, speaking *for* us and speaking *to* us, in every circumstance and difficulty of life.

If this promise is for us, it means (third) that the Spirit we pursue is no stranger. We aren't reaching for something unknown and unexpected. If Jesus and the Spirit are one, the Spirit we seek looks, sounds, acts, and works like Jesus. Which is a crucial step for any trustable approach to the Spirit. So long as the Spirit is unfamiliar to us, with an unknown agenda and unpredictable ways, we will always be on our guard against him or always vulnerable to something fraudulent. But when we recognize in the Spirit the face of Jesus, when we grasp that the Spirit continues the ministry and message and methods of Jesus, then we have the basis for a relationship with the Spirit we can trust.

Finally, this promise means that even we "latter day" disciples can experience—through the Spirit—the presence of Jesus. Most of us have wished (be honest now!) we could have "been there" during the days of Jesus' ministry here on earth; seen with our own eyes; walked and talked with the Living Christ. But if Jesus and the Spirit are one, Jesus walks and talks with us through the indwelling *Paraclete*. In part, the *Paraclete* makes this possible (as we will see in the next chapter) by bringing Jesus' earthly ministry to life again ("he will remind you of everything I have said"—14:26). But an indwelling Spirit also suggests the possibility of an intimate relationship with Jesus that is "beyond the sacred page." It means the same living relationship that sustained the Apostles is available to sustain us. It means a "personal relationship" with Jesus Christ is not just an Evangelical catch-phrase, but a very real, very privileged, and very necessary experience. Building this relationship between Jesus and his followers is the Spirit's prime work.

I confess to you that I want this kind of relationship with Jesus. I want it so badly, I need it so desperately, that I can no longer afford to ignore the Spirit or live a form of religion that is devoid of his presence. I want Jesus in me. I want to be in Jesus. I want to see Jesus. I want him to show himself to me. And I believe one of the principle tasks of the Holy Spirit of God is to make this intimate relationship with my Master possible.

And so I gladly welcome the Spirit into my heart and life, whatever the uncertainties and risks. For with the coming of the Spirit comes the abiding presence of Jesus Christ—in me, with me, for me, through me.

Chapter Nine

THE PROMISE OF TEACHING

(JOHN 14:25-27)

No wonder they are confused. You can almost see them scratching their heads and shrugging their shoulders at each other. What is Jesus talking about? What do all these words about a "*Paraclete*" mean?

There were so many things Jesus said and did during the course of his ministry they did not understand. Their confusion in the Upper Room on the final night is simply the latest instance of their consistent failure to keep up with their Master.

"Destroy this temple, and I will raise it again in three days" went right over their heads (John 2:19-22). Why he would speak with a Samaritan woman was beyond them (4:27). They did not comprehend the bread for the crowds (5:1-14) or the ghost on the water (6:16-21). They did not realize what had happened to Lazarus nor why Jesus was so eager to return to dangerous Judea (11:12-13). They did not see the deeper meaning in Mary's anointing (12:1-8) or the Triumphal Entry (12:12-19). They could not grasp why Jesus would wash their feet or what the dipped bread might portend (13).

That's how little they understood about events in the past. But consider what was about to take place in the fifty-day stretch between Passover and Pentecost. Think of the effort required to make sense of the cross and resurrection; the emotional whipsaw between transcendent ecstasy (in the resurrection appearances) and existential doubt (through the dark days between); the difficulty of conceiving that Jesus expected them—a ragtag band of nobodies—to change the world.

Now pour on top of this massive mix of spiritual obtuseness, stubborn misperception, and sensory overload the challenges of the next few decades: a radical redefinition of old concepts like "Messiah" and "Kingdom" and "Israel"; the unexpected shape of the "gospel" they would preach; the role of "faith" and "grace" in God's plan; the mandate of being "church" (with all its challenges and uncertainties); the inclusion of the Gentiles with all their baggage; huge, complex concepts like redemption, reconciliation, sanctification, transformation, and "becoming all things to all men."

So much to grasp. So many lessons to learn. A world to turn upside down. Lives to turn inside out. And Jesus, their Teacher, is leaving them—just when they need him most.[1]

They do not know what lies ahead, of course. And that is a mercy. For the thought of Jesus' leaving is crippling enough this night. Soon, though, they will grapple with how to continue his ministry in his absence. Even then, they won't understand that merely "continuing" isn't the issue. Compared to what lies ahead, their work so far has been child's play. They have been toddlers, terrifying themselves with swing-sets and teeter-tots, while ahead of them looms an Everest of challenge. They will throw themselves at those challenges for the next sixty years. Paul climbs this route. Peter dies on that sheer face. The Galatians will lose their way just there. The Corinthians get stuck on that false summit.

Yet climb they must. How will they find their way from the Upper Room to Judea, Samaria, and the ends of the earth? Who will show them where to go and how to act and what to say? Who can teach them what they need to know? Jesus has been their Teacher to this point. That's what they called him: "Teacher." But Jesus is leaving. He cannot take them where they need to go next. Who will be their "Teacher" now?

Peter?

John?

The Mission

In the first *Paraclete* Passage (John 14:16-23), Jesus speaks from the context of his imminent departure: "I am going away." But he washes down this bitter medicine with the promise of *another Paraclete*—his presence with them in different form.

Now, however, the emphasis shifts to the daunting prospect that there remains a mission for the Twelve to accomplish after their Master has left the building. Notice what Jesus has to say between the first *Paraclete* Passage and the second.

> 14:21Whoever has my commands and obeys them, he is the one who loves me. He who loves me will be loved by my Father, and I too will love him and show myself to him . . . 23If anyone loves me, he will obey my teaching. My Father will love him, and we will come to him and make our home with him. 24He who does not love me will not obey my teaching. These words you hear are not my own; they belong to the Father who sent me. . . 26But the Counselor, the Holy Spirit, whom the Father will send in my name, will teach you all things and will remind you of everything I have said to you.

Verses 21-24 serve as a transition between the first and second *Paraclete* Passages. On the one hand, they point back to the *Promise of Presence*: "I will show myself . . . . We will make our home . . . ." On the other hand, they point forward to the *Promise of Teaching* in the second statement—a Spirit who will help them understand what to say and do, learn their role in the work to come, and find comfort and peace in doing that work.

The "teaching" or "commands" of Jesus are mentioned repeatedly in these verses, as is the need for disciples to be "obedient." But it is obvious Jesus means something bigger by "obey" than the response of the Twelve to specific commands and individual teachings. He lumps everything together here—"my teachings," "my commands," "the Father's words"—and challenges the disciples to love him by being true to the whole. Look closely and you'll see marching orders embedded in these words.

Jesus is addressing the larger issue of *mission*.

We know that mission is on his mind because Jesus keeps returning to the subject in this Final Discourse. The disciples are "messengers" whom Jesus will send out into the world (13:16, 19-20). He anticipates they will do "what I have been doing" (14:12). He expects them to "bear much fruit" (15:2, 4, 5, 8). He knows their work will not be easy: the world will hate them because they carry Jesus' name (15:21) and his words (15:20). Still, he calls them to "testify" to what they have seen and heard (15:27).[2]

But it isn't simply context or repetition that demands we see mission in this Second *Paraclete* Passage; it is *timing* as well. Mission crops up here because passing on the mission is a top priority as Jesus prepares to leave. He has carried the mission thus far. But he is going away. Now it is time for the disciples to take up that mission and continue it in his absence.[3]

There is, however, a large sense in which describing the mission is begging the question. All well and good for Jesus to say *what* he wants the disciples to do. But *how*, oh *how*, does he expect them to do it?

A New Teacher and Guide

Every morning for three years the disciples have greeted the morning and broken fast, rolled up their blankets, kicked out the fire, and set off for the next adventure. But which way did they go? Wherever Jesus led!

Every day, in temple courts and on hillsides, the crowds gathered for words and wonders, wisdom and signs. But it was Jesus who had the words and the wonders; he was the focus, the Center. When the lame and blind cried out for healing, it was always Jesus who responded and touched them.

He set the agenda. He knew the script. He burned with the mission.

The disciples never worried themselves about such matters—they simply followed wherever Jesus led. But they need to worry now. Within hours, Jesus will leave the mission in their trembling hands. In the morning, their Master will be hanging on a cross and their world will be in tatters. He will no longer be present to order their days and guide their actions. No more will they hear him say, "Go into the city" or "Take off the grave clothes" or "Open your eyes and look at the fields"—all the specific instructions that disciples receive from a Teacher.

He is leaving; they are staying. His work is "finished"; their work has just begun. His mission is now theirs. But how should they proceed? What should they say and do? Who will show them the way into the future?

Eventually, Jesus expects his disciples to shake off the trauma of the cross and the shock of the resurrection. When they do, he expects them to continue his vital mission in the world. It will be a mission conditioned by his goals and agenda. It will also be a mission conducted in his absence.

As Paul asks decades later: "Who is equal to such a task?" (2 Cor 2:16).

Not the Twelve! They know it. And Jesus knows it. In fact, he never intended to leave the mission in their unassisted hands. From the beginning, he knew they would have a resource, to help them accomplish their mission. And so, on this final night, Jesus tells them about the *Paraclete*. "But the *Paraclete*, the Holy Spirit, whom the Father will send in my name, will teach you all things and will remind you of everything I have said to you" (John 14:26).

It's just one verse. Thirty small words. But don't let its lack of size fool you. There is an important message here about the Spirit and his role in equipping disciples for their mission.[4] That message is poured into a dense passage, packed with meaning.

Notice how careful Jesus is—again—to link the Spirit to himself. For the second time, he calls the Spirit "*Paraclete*"—reminding the disciples the Spirit continues the helping role Jesus has provided thus far. He gives this *Paraclete* a name—*Holy* Spirit—that mirrors a name Jesus himself wore: "the Holy One of God" (John 6:69). And, just as Jesus came from the Father, so the Spirit is sent from the Father. Same function; same name; same source: three points of contact between Jesus and the Spirit in the space of a dozen words.[5]

But Jesus does more than identify the Spirit with himself in this passage. For the first time, Jesus addresses the subject of the Spirit's *work*. And he does so in a way that helps the disciples see a glimmer of how they can obey Jesus' commands and continue his mission even after he is gone.

This second *Paraclete* Passage tells us of a *teaching* function for the Spirit, a function that will help the disciples hear the words of Jesus, live obediently to those words, and honor them as words from the Father. The Spirit is not just the continuing presence of Jesus for the disciples (as important as that function is). He is also the means by which Jesus continues to teach his disciples, the instrument by which the disciples keep hearing and heeding their Master. "[He] will teach you all things and will remind you of everything I have said to you."

Like Jesus, the Spirit is *Teacher*. His teaching involves, at the most basic level, a "reminder" of everything Jesus taught. The disciples, as we've already noted, were not particularly good students while Jesus was with them in the flesh. They misunderstood, distorted, forgot, or were oblivious to much of what Jesus told them. He was constantly chiding them for their hard hearts and deaf ears. So, and without doubt, they need the Spirit's reminder of "everything I have said to you."

But there is more than *remembrance* involved here; there is also an *enlightening* function to the Spirit's teaching. This is not just a promise of Spirit-improved memory—spiritual steroids to strengthen enfeebled recall. Implicit in this pledge is an assurance that what the disciples remember, they will also comprehend. Better. More completely. The Spirit will remind; but he will also explain and expound. He will deepen the disciples' understanding and give them insight. He will bestow wisdom. He will take the teachings of Jesus and apply them in relevant ways to believers' new lives and changed circumstances.[6]

This is what Jesus is getting at when he tells his disciples the Spirit will teach them "all things." Let's recognize a bit of hyperbole here. This is not a promise that disciples of Jesus, through the teaching work of the Holy Spirit, become "know-it-alls." The Spirit won't teach them quantum physics and fractal equations.

In fact, the "all things" the Spirit teaches is connected to and controlled by the phrase "everything I have said to you." The Spirit teaches everything that flows from and is a consequence of Jesus' life and ministry: the greater meaning of his words; the calling, mission, and message of disciples; what disciples' priorities should be, what their values are "in the Lord"; and everything else related to living as believers between the cross and the Second Coming.[7]

An example of this teaching role of the Spirit is provided by John himself. In the early part of his gospel, John recounts a conflict with the religious leaders. Jesus challenges them, "Destroy this temple, and I will raise it in three days" (John 2:19). In an aside (2:21-22), John admits the disciples did not realize what Jesus was talking about. Only later, after

Jesus was raised from the dead, did the disciples "recall" these words and comprehend their deeper meaning.

According to the promise of the second *Paraclete* Passage, this "recollection" was made possible by the work of the Holy Spirit. It was the Spirit who revealed what Jesus really meant by "destroy this temple . . . ." And it was the Spirit who permitted that insight to result in deeper faith: "Then they believed the Scripture and the words that Jesus had spoken" (John 2:22).

A Peek Ahead

This "teaching function" of the Spirit is very much on display in the future ministry of the Apostles. When Peter suggests they need to replace Judas and the lots are cast for Matthias (Acts 1:15ff), we are meant to understand that it is not the fisherman's managerial instincts which prompt the process; it is the Spirit who is doing his teaching/equipping work in Peter. When Peter stands on the day of Pentecost and preaches like a pro (Acts 2:14ff)—the disobedient, denying, disbelieving disappointment turned into the bold, eloquent, knowledgeable spokesman—we are meant to recognize the change is causally connected to the pouring out of the Spirit: it is the Spirit who equips Peter to play this role.

When the leaders of the Jerusalem church are confronted with a problem concerning the Grecian widows (Acts 6:1ff) and must respond with an effective solution, it requires men full of the Spirit (the Apostles) to trust the judgment of people full of the Spirit (the church as a whole) to identify servants full of the Spirit (the Seven—see vs 3) in order to reach a resolution. Here is a problem Jesus had not directly addressed (fair distribution of the church's benevolence to a marginalized group). Here is a quandary the Apostles had not yet faced (prayer and preaching or waiting tables?). And here is a process for solving problems that had never been tried (delegating a specific task to godly men who were not themselves Apostles). Was this simply evidence of apostolic creativity? Or are we meant to see in this situation an active Spirit moving aggressively to teach and equip the church for doing the mission of Christ?

When Peter swallows hard and crosses a Gentile threshold in order to preach the Gospel to Cornelius (Acts 10:1ff), the Spirit has already been hard at work preparing Peter for this moment. It was the Spirit who sent the vision to Cornelius prompting the invitation to Peter (10:3-8). It was the Spirit who sent the vision to Peter with the unclean animals and the command to "Kill and eat" (10:9-16). It was the Spirit who told Peter to go with Cornelius' men (10:20). It was the Spirit who taught Peter the meaning of his vision: "God has shown me that I should not call any man impure or unclean" (10:28). It was the Spirit who interrupted Peter's fine sermon and poured himself out on that Gentile household, astonishing Peter and all the circumcised believers with him (10:44-46). It was this evidence of Holy-Spirit-approval that gave Peter the courage to baptize the first Gentiles into Jesus—"Who was I to oppose God?" (11:17). Thus, the most significant shift in the New Testament church since the initial outpouring of the Spirit at Pentecost—the welcoming of the Gentiles into God's chosen people—was the direct result, not of Peter's insight into the true Gospel or any broadmindedness on the part of the Jewish church, but the direct teaching, leading, guiding, and equipping of the Holy Spirit. Here again, we see the Spirit acting as *Paraclete*, reminding the church of Jesus' commission and teaching these first Christians everything they needed to accomplish their Christ-given task.

In the same way, we are meant to recognize the Spirit's hand in sending Barnabas (a man full of the Spirit) to the Gentile church forming in Antioch (Acts 11:22ff), equipping him to be so effective that "a great number of people were brought to the Lord" (11:24), and prompting him to find Saul to come help with the Antioch work (11:25-26). It is the Holy Spirit who speaks to the church there, commanding that they "Set apart for me Barnabas and Saul for the work to which I have called them" (Acts 13:2) and initiating the first foray into the wider Gentile world. It is the Spirit who guides Barnabas and Saul on every step of that journey (e.g., Acts 13:4), teaches them what to say and do (13:9; 14:27), and sustains their new converts (Acts 13:52). When, in the course of time, the mission to the Gentiles was threatened ("The Gentiles must be circumcised and required to obey the law of Moses"—Acts 15:5), it was the Spirit who showed the Jerusalem Council the godly way forward ("It seemed good to the Holy Spirit and to us not to burden you with anything beyond . . ."—Acts 15:28).

How did Paul find the courage and confidence to wrestle his way through to the core Gospel (Gal 2:15-16; Rom 3:21-22)? How did he come to realize salvation is by trust in God rather than obedience and "getting it right"? What gave him the moxie to confront Peter to his face (Gal 2:11, 14) and proclaim that essential gospel in synagogues and even in Jerusalem? How did he and his fellow missionaries know about appointing elders and setting up widows' rolls; what to advise about idols and meat offered to them; how to deal with factions and immorality and heresy within the church; what to do with Judaizing teachers?

In these and a thousand other ways—large and small—we can see the *Paraclete* hard at work in his teaching function. Quite literally, the early church could not have made a move without the Spirit's instruction and practical guidance. Jesus never addressed many of the situations they encountered.[8] Their Scriptures (the Old Testament) didn't even contemplate the questions they were required to ask. And, frankly, the Apostles we know from the Gospels just weren't smart enough or wise enough to figure things out on their own. They needed a Spirit who would remind them of everything Jesus said . . . and then enlighten them as to what he really meant . . . and then help them apply those ideas to radically different circumstances and people. They needed a Spirit who could teach them everything that flowed from and was a consequence of Jesus' life and ministry; what their priorities should be and what other sacred cows could be safely sacrificed for those priorities; what was the real difference between becoming "all things to all men" and mere compromise with culture.

They needed the Spirit to teach them that. So, by the way, do we.

My Peace I Give You

It is what Jesus says next that hints at the extent of the Spirit's teaching ministry. "Peace I leave with you; my peace I give you. I do not give to you as the world gives. Do not let your hearts be troubled and do not be afraid" (John 14:27).

When Jesus speaks these words to the Twelve, their hearts *are* troubled. They *are* afraid. Jesus is leaving his mission in their hands and they know they are not up to the task. And that's why, in the context of his mission and the *Paraclete*, Jesus talks about "peace."

Are the disciples worried about tomorrow (as they certainly are in the context of the Final Discourse)? The Spirit will calm and compose them

by teaching them what to do. Are the disciples about to face difficult circumstances and a hostile world? The Spirit will build their confidence
and bolster their courage by telling them what to say. Are the disciples
tempted to discouragement and timidity and loss of hope because of the
enormity of the task and the puniness of their resources? The Spirit will
step in to encourage and embolden and strengthen their faith.

But this promise of peace highlights the fact that the Spirit intends
to teach more than just the head. Yes, the Spirit instructs their "minds,"
sharing spiritual knowledge with the disciples: a reminder of Jesus'
words; a clarity about how the principles he taught apply to their lives;
a constant awareness of their message and methods. But this same Spirit
also intends to teach their "hands" and develop spiritual skills and com-
petencies: how to preach to crowds; how to disciple Gentiles; how to lead
a church. Perhaps most importantly, the Spirit undertakes to teach their
"hearts": disciplining feelings; shaping attitudes; and keeping disciples
afloat on stormy emotional seas.

The New Testament frequently testifies to this *affective* aspect of
the Spirit's teaching in believers. When "filled with the Spirit," disciples
experienced boldness and courage (see Acts 4:8, 13, 31; 6:5-10 and 7:55;
13:9-10); they felt love and joy and hope (see Acts 13:52; Rom 5:5;
14:17; 15:13, 30; 1 Thess 1:6); they discovered fresh confidence and
renewed vigor (Acts 9:31; Rom 8:16-17; 2 Cor 1:21-22). But, above all,
the ministry of the Spirit brought "peace" to troubled disciples (Rom
8:6; 14:17; 15:13; Gal 5:22; Eph 4:3).

This is precisely the sort of "multi-faceted teaching" Jesus did, of
course. Sometimes he addressed his disciples' *thoughts*: with the principles found in the Sermon on the Mount, for example. But there were
times when he needed to burnish their skills. (I think, for instance, of the
time they were unable to cast out a demon and he had to teach them the
"technique"—"This kind can come out only by prayer"—Mark 9:29).
And there were times, many times, when he was required to address their
unruly *emotions*—fear, anger, worry, insecurity, resentment, pride, ambition—teaching them how to order their inner worlds.

In fact, within the span of the Final Discourse, Jesus does each of
these. There are things he wants his disciples to *know*: the time has come;
he is going away; the *Paraclete* is coming. There are things he wants them

to *do*: wash each other's feet; keep his commandments; bear much fruit. And there are things he wants his disciples to *feel*: love each other; do not let your hearts be troubled; don't feel abandoned; let your grief turn to joy; have peace.

In the same way, the teachings of the Spirit will be directed at the mind, the hand, and the heart. Which is exactly what you would expect *of another Paraclete*: a continuation of the same sort of teaching ministry characteristic of Jesus himself.

The promise of an empowering, equipping, teaching Spirit will, with time and experience, give the disciples the sense of confidence and courage they need to keep going. As a result of the *Paraclete's* teaching ministry, they will discover a competence for Kingdom work that results in lasting, deep, and pervasive peace.

And What of Us?

Again, these were wonderful promises for the Apostles to hear. But are they wonderful for us? Does the promise of a teaching Spirit, who instructs both mind and heart, extend to disciples who weren't in that upper room?

We certainly share the Twelve's condition. Like them, we fail to grasp much of what Jesus teaches. We too are oblivious, forgetful, and spiritually dull. Like them, we crave the practical instruction, the specific direction, the presence of Jesus could supply. We know we have a

---

What we learn about the Holy Spirit in the Second *Paraclete* Passage:

1. Besides "Paraclete," and "Spirit of truth," this Other is designated "Holy Spirit."
2. The Father will send the Paraclete to the disciples.
3. The Father will send the Paraclete "in the name" of Jesus.
4. The Spirit will teach the disciples "all things".
5. The Spirit will remind the disciples of everything Jesus said to them.
6. The result of the Spirit's presence will be peace . . . and the absence of troubled hearts and fear.

mission to accomplish, a grand calling to turn the world upside down. But, in the face of that challenge, we feel small and ill-equipped and woefully inadequate. Like them, our hearts are troubled, our fears have grown large.

In a word, we desperately need the very thing Jesus offers the Twelve on that final night: his continuing presence to lead and instruct; his direction and teaching whatever situations arise; his insight into deeper things; his wisdom about living in a fallen world. We need the confidence that comes from knowing what to do, the boldness that comes from knowing what to say, and the peace that comes from understanding what is happening.

We need a Teacher who can show us what the gospel means in the face of changing circumstances and new challenges. We need an Equipper who can train us in the ministry skills that make us effective. And we need a Comforter who can sooth our frustrations and hurts along the way.

Such a need makes us impatient with those who point so relentlessly (and exclusively) to the Bible as our sole source of spiritual instruction. Certainly there is teaching to be found there: reminders of what Jesus said and did; principles and propositions and policies. But we face situations the New Testament never addressed or imagined. A first-century book—however revered—is a far cry from the kind of intimate, personal, practical, moment-by-moment teaching offered by Jesus in the form of the *Paraclete*.

This same need also makes us impatient with those who point so obstinately (and myopically) to a Spirit who does tricks on Sundays but doesn't say much about Truth and practical daily ministry and hurting, discouraged hearts. Really, what good are prophetic utterances about the end of the world if there is no ready "reminder" of what Jesus has already taught, no equipping for effective ministry in the home and at the workplace, no bolstering of sagging spirits and fortifying of flagging faith. The momentary lift of the miraculous is wonderful—for the moment. But you and I need something more pertinent and persistent if we are to do effective work in the daily trenches of our kingdom mission.

If there is a teaching Spirit available to believers today—a Spirit who instructs the head, equips the hand, and lifts up the heart—that is good news indeed! If there is a teaching Spirit who does for us what he did for the first disciples, he can show us the difference between the true gospel and the false (a distinction desperately needed in our churches today), train us to handle problems that arise and opportunities that beckon, and bestow on us the peace that permits us to "keep our heads when all about are losing theirs and blaming it on us."[9]

We shouldn't make a move without the Spirit's guidance. Unless we think we're smart enough to figure it out on our own. Unless we believe every question, every circumstance, every challenge faced by disciples today has been sufficiently covered in a book written two thousand years ago to people who lived in a radically different world facing fundamentally different issues. Unless you never feel the crying need to walk up to Jesus, place your hand on his arm, and ask, "What did you mean when you said . . ." or "What do you think about . . ." or "How am I supposed to. . . ."

I freely confess I want and need this teaching presence. I want that kind of confidence and competence, that kind of comfort and encouragement. I want help to be obedient, wisdom to know what obedience means in these difficult times, consolation for my failures, and the discernment to know the difference between the Spirit's meat and my sacred cows. I want the *Paraclete* Jesus offers the Twelve, not just the verbal echoes of the Spirit's teaching that resonate in Scripture or the flash-and-bang of the sort of Spirit offered in revival tents and on Sunday morning television.

And so I gladly welcome the Spirit into my heart and life, whatever the uncertainties and risks. For if the Spirit comes, he comes in Jesus' name, doing Jesus' work, bearing Jesus' words, teaching the things of Jesus, enabling obedience to Jesus, shaping minds and hearts for the mission of Jesus. If that Spirit is still available to me, I want all of him I can get.

Chapter Ten

THE PROMISE OF TESTIMONY

(JOHN 15:26-27)

No wonder they are terrified. For three years, they've watched Jesus stand up for truth and speak out for God. Yet, from the beginning, he has been challenged and criticized and condemned. He tells the truth and people call him a blasphemer. He talks of God and people pick up stones. He heals the sick, yet some who witness the miracles walk away plotting to kill him.

In the hours to come, the disciples will get a crash course in the dangers of telling the truth. They will watch as Jesus is arrested, flogged, spit on, and nailed to a cross. They'll watch as leading citizens line up to revile, ridicule, and vent their venom. They'll watch as religious folk look on the dying Jesus without a shred of pity or compassion.

The disciples know their master is hated, not because he is a traitor or thief or murderer, but simply because he loves the light. What lesson could they possibly learn from all this—what has happened to Jesus in the past, what will happen to him next—other than the hard lesson that people who tell the truth about God are hated and hounded, that people who tell the truth about the sin of the world get nailed to crosses, that people who testify as powerfully as Jesus did should expect to be thanked with pain and death.

Yet, in this Final Discourse, Jesus commissions the disciples to do the same provocative work he has been doing: "And you also must testify, for you have been with me from the beginning" (John 15:27). They will be the truth-tellers from now on. In his absence, they must speak words the world does not want to hear.

Already during this long evening Jesus has said difficult things to the Twelve. He is going away—and that alarms them. He wants them to continue his mission—and that overwhelms them. Now he says they must testify. Seeing the cost of such testimony for their Master, this commissioning terrifies them. Even before Jesus announces, "If they persecuted me, they will persecute you also" (John 15:20), they know instinctively that continuing his mission will mean sharing his fate.

Perhaps for the first time in this Final Discourse, Jesus says something they understand. To be his disciple is a dangerous thing. To align themselves with him will be painful and costly. They can understand that. They are soon to understand it better.

What's Not to Like about Jesus?

It must have perplexed the disciples that the Jesus they knew and loved should be the object of such violent opposition from others.

What was not to like about him? He was kind and compassionate and wise. He taught such wonderful things: love your neighbor, love your enemy, love God. He was that rarest of treasures, a truly good man. He healed sick children, for goodness sake! How can you dislike someone who heals sick children?

And yet there were people who did not like Jesus. Nor was it a matter of simple disapproval. They hated him. They despised him. They wanted him dead. Had the disciples asked these people the reason for their enmity, they would have heard all manner of answers: "He doesn't keep the traditions; he threatens the stability of God's people; he plays fast and loose with Torah."

Jesus has a different answer to their question. It is an answer he needs the disciples to hear and understand. For this answer explains what they are soon to experience themselves.

15:21 . . . They do not know the One who sent me. 22If I had not come and spoken to them, they would not be guilty of sin. Now, however, they have no excuse for their sin. ²³He who hates me hates my Father as well. ²⁴If I had not done among them what no one else did, they would not be guilty of sin. But now they have seen these miracles, and yet they have hated both me and my Father. ²⁵But this is to fulfill what is written in their Law: 'They hated me without reason.'

The hatred directed towards Jesus isn't about religious orthodoxy or practice; it has nothing to do with traditions or interpretations of the Law, whatever rationalizations the authorities use to justify their opposition. The reason for their hatred runs far deeper. The problem, as Jesus sees it, is literally "theological"—a problem with "knowing God." He knows his Father and his opponents do not. He loves his Father and they do not. When he shows them God, they are deeply repulsed; though not by what Jesus reveals of God so much as by what that revelation says about *them*. Jesus shows them the Father and they see their own sin and brokenness and shame. They see themselves with a clarity (and a humiliation) that is unbearable. And the result? Denial. Justifications and excuses. A rationalization so vehement and violent it looks like hatred.

Not everyone reacts that way, of course. There are some who respond to this revelation with gratitude and obedience. It is the reason Jesus came preaching—to reach those few. It is the reason he commissions the disciples to testify—some will listen.

But those who don't listen, who can't hear, will hate the message and hate the messenger. And their hatred will be "without reason" (John 15:25). Their hatred will be a blind, cold, raging thing that needs no reason to sustain it.

They Will Hate You

Jesus has borne the brunt of that hatred so far. The authorities were content to direct their frustration and anger at him. Oh, they've questioned his disciples on occasion. But they've reserved the heat of their hostility for the Master himself.

Now, though, Jesus is going away. Will the heat he generated go away as well? Will the glut of violence to come satisfy the authorities?

Not at all. For Jesus intends to be the gift that keeps on giving. Now that he has come and testified, the world will never be the same. The light has come into the world (see John 1:1-4). And even if some show a marked preference for the darkness, the light will continue to shine in the lives of those who have received Jesus. The light—the hated light— will shine long after Jesus is gone.

Part of the point of this Final Discourse is that the disciples must not hide their light. They must shine with Jesus' words and work and mission. He is depending on them to keep his irritating presence alive in the world. He is counting on them to "testify" for and to him.

That means, of course, that the world's hatred is about to turn—full force—on the Twelve.

15:18If the world hates you, keep in mind that it hated me first. 19If you belonged to the world, it would love you as its own. As it is, you do not belong to the world, but I have chosen you out of the world. That is why the world hates you. 20Remember the words I spoke to you: 'No servant is greater than his master.' If they persecuted me, they will persecute you also. If they obeyed my teaching, they will obey yours also. 21They will treat you this way because of my name. . . .

16:1All this I have told you so that you will not go astray. 2They will put you out of the synagogue; in fact, a time is coming when anyone who kills you will think he is offering a service to God. 3They will do such things because they have not known the Father or me. 4I have told you this, so that when the time comes you will remember that I warned you. I did not tell you this at first because I was with you.

Jesus takes up a good portion of the Final Discourse warning the disciples about what is to come. "You must testify. But the world won't like it." He goes into graphic detail (perhaps more than the Twelve want!) about what they should expect in the future. The world will hate them. The world will persecute them. They will be turned out of the synagogue. They will be hunted and killed.

"But don't take it personally," Jesus tells them. "It's not about you. It's about me. And, ultimately, it is about my Father."

Had you been there, you could have cut the silence with a knife. The disciples don't want to hear this. Jesus is touching their greatest fear, their most persistent terror. This is the stuff that makes them want to run away, cower in some upper room, and hide from the hostile world.

You can almost hear Peter thinking, "Thanks for the encouragement, Master. Any more comforting words before we dismiss?"

The Spirit Will Testify about Me

Actually, Jesus does have something comforting to offer. They won't feel the comfort now. It will take them awhile to discover how great a comfort Jesus is about to bestow. He cannot take back their commission to witness. He cannot change the hostile and violent reactions of the world. What he can do, what he will do, is make sure they do not bear witness by themselves. "When the *Paraclete* comes, whom I will send to you from the Father, the Spirit of truth who goes out from the Father, he will testify about me. And you also must testify, for you have been with me from the beginning" (15:26-27).

This is now the third time Jesus has raised the subject of the *Paraclete* with his disciples. First, he announces he is going away; the disciples are broken-hearted; so he offers them the *Paraclete*. Then it dawns on the disciples they must make their way into the future without Jesus' tangible guidance; they are overwhelmed; so he offers them the *Paraclete*. Now Jesus tells them they must testify even at great cost; they are terrified; so, once more, he offers them the *Paraclete*.[1]

In the context of the world's hostility—as Jesus readies himself to die for the truth, as he warns the Twelve their time is coming—the whole idea of testimony becomes difficult. What can possibly overcome the world's reflexive rejection? If the world answers every witness with venom and violence, how can witness be sustained? If *Jesus* was unable to win over the world, what hope is there for the *Twelve* to do so?

With these unspoken questions, Jesus brings up the *Paraclete* once again. There is a Companion coming into the world, he assures his disciples, whose mission will be to testify to Jesus. He will speak the truth he receives from the Father about the Father's Son.

And that's important for the disciples (and us) to know for several reasons. "Testimony" (or "witness"—both are translations of the same Greek word *martureo*) is a central concept for John, occurring 31 times in his gospel. The fundamental assertion of John's gospel is that Jesus is the Christ, the Son of God. To prove that point, John brings to his story a number of "witnesses" who "testify" to Jesus: John the Baptist (1:7, 34); a woman by a well (4:39-42); the miracles (5:36; 20:30-31); Scripture (5:39); and God himself (5:32, 37; 8:18). The Spirit is simply the latest in a long list of witnesses who testify in John. Though the disciples are witnesses as well, they are not alone in their witnessing work.

Second, Jesus speaks not just to the *fact* of the Spirit's testimony but to the *content* of his testimony. The Spirit will testify about Jesus. Jesus is the light, the Christ, the Son, the One. The Spirit comes to affirm that Jesus is precisely who he claims to be.[2]

Third, notice from the context (John 15:18-25) that the *audience* for the Spirit's testimony is the *world*—the hostile, unbelieving, God-hating world. The Spirit will stand up in the very world that kills Jesus and persecutes his followers to insist that Jesus is the Son of God and that his words are true. No matter how much the world howls and threatens, it can never stifle the Spirit's witness nor still his voice. The world cannot shut this witness up or beat his witness out of him. Here is a testimony to Jesus no threat can frighten and no violence squelch. It is a "forever" testimony that cannot be blunted by the world's opposition.

Finally, there is a certain *independence* to the Spirit's testimony we should appreciate. The Spirit has his own testifying work to do, a work that doesn't depend on us. He has his own voice in this world that speaks whether we manage to witness or not. There is something awe-inspiring about imagining the Spirit—in holy counterpoint to Satan's roaring lion, seeking souls to devour (1 Pet 5:8)—ranging through the world in search of souls to save.

In the next chapter we will hear Jesus describe the Spirit as busily convicting a hard-hearted world. For now, think also of a Spirit hard at work using all of life's ups and downs—joys, tragedies, beauty, illness, mirth, griefs, regrets—to prod and poke people and pull them inexorably towards their Father. Think of a Spirit working through art and literature, music and nature, to make people conscious once again of their forgotten God and the cross-shaped truth planted at the center of life. Think of a Spirit putting Bibles in hotel rooms, moving Christian neighbors next door, using annual celebrations like Christmas and Easter, and even working through people as irritating as televangelists to get out the word that Jesus is Lord.

Is it too much to think about the Spirit testifying this directly, this intimately, when we have examples in Scripture of the Spirit working even more aggressively to testify? Think of Saul thrown from his horse on the Damascus Road and blinded, literally *forced* by the Spirit to hear his testimony to Jesus (Acts 9:1ff). Or remember Philip thrust into the path of the Ethiopian Eunuch so the Spirit would have a chance to testify through him to Jesus (Acts 8:26-39).

The Spirit testifies to Jesus. And he is not shy in doing so.

And You Also Must Testify

There is more in this third *Paraclete* Passage, however, than a promise the Holy Spirit will speak up for Jesus. There is also (pregnant within these words) the promise that the Spirit will help the disciples speak up.

It is no accident that Jesus ties the testimony of the Spirit so closely to the testimony of the disciples. Only a period separates the two ideas. "*He will testify* about me. And *you also must testify*." The testimony of the Spirit and the testimony of the disciples are linked. Both testimonies are needed, pointing to Jesus. Both witnesses are valued, knowing Jesus as well as they do. Each witness supports and enhances the other. Each witness plays his necessary part.[3]

The disciples, however, do not have permission to sit back and leave the testifying work to God's Spirit. They can't abandon that responsibility to someone who won't bleed. Yes, the Spirit testifies. But so must disciples.

What Jesus promises in these verses is that God will be at work in the world long after the cross, in places far removed from Jerusalem, through the testimony of his Spirit and through the testimony of his people. Just as the Spirit is sent out as a witness into the world, so the disciples will be sent out as witnesses. Their testimony must support his.

This careful linking of the Spirit's testimony with human testimony, however, suggests an even closer relationship between the Spirit and witnessing disciples. The Spirit does more than witness *with* . . . the Spirit witnesses *through*. He plays a vital role in nurturing the disciples' witness;

bestowing boldness, courage, power, wisdom, and (sometimes) the very words the disciples will use to testify.

Early in his ministry, Jesus had spoken to the Twelve about the role of the Spirit in their testimony: "When you are brought before synagogues, rulers and authorities, do not worry about how you will defend yourselves or what you will say, for the Holy Spirit will teach you at that time what you should say" (Luke 12:11-12).

Here, Jesus makes a direct connection between the Spirit and the witnessing work of the disciples: he gives them words to speak; he calms them as they face persecution. Later (sometime during the last week of his life), Jesus returns to this same subject and offers his disciples this bad news/good news:

> They will lay hands on you and persecute you. They will deliver you to synagogues and prisons, and you will be brought before kings and governors, and all on account of my name. This will result in your being witnesses to them. But make up your mind not to worry beforehand how you will defend yourselves. For I will give you words and wisdom that none of your adversaries will be able to resist or contradict. (Luke 21:12-15)

Here, it is Jesus himself who promises to give "words and wisdom." Since he is referring to events that take place long after his return to the Father, however, it is evident the gift will come through the work of the Spirit. In fact, based on what we've seen in the Final Discourse, there is no difference between the *Spirit* teaching disciples what to say (Luke 12) and *Jesus* giving them words to speak (Luke 21).

In the book of Acts, Luke continues this linkage between the Spirit and the testifying commission of the Apostles. He reports Jesus telling the disciples to return to Jerusalem and "wait" (Acts 1:4). There is a "gift" coming from the Father, a gift the disciples will need in order to be effective witnesses—baptism with the Holy Spirit (Acts 1:5). When the gift arrives, however: "You will receive power when the Holy Spirit comes on you; and you will be my witnesses in Jerusalem, and in all Judea and Samaria, and to the ends of the earth" (Acts 1:8).

Once again, the Spirit is connected to the witness of disciples. The Spirit will bring "power" (presumably miraculous signs and abilities, though we should not ignore the importance of Spirit-powered confidence and competence). That "power" fuels the witnessing work of the disciples. "Wait for the Spirit. He will bring power. And then you can witness."

We see examples of this Spirit-fueled testimony as the story of Acts continues to unfold. In Chapter 4, Luke tells the story of Peter and John testifying before the Sanhedrin, astonishing that council with their courage and eloquence. When Peter and John report this incident to the church, they immediately pray for "great boldness" and more "signs and wonders" (Acts 4:29-30). That prayer is answered with an outpouring of the Spirit: "After they prayed, the place where they were meeting was shaken. And they were all filled with the Holy Spirit and spoke the word of God boldly" (Acts 4:31).

In Chapter 6, Stephen is testifying to all who will listen (and some who will not). He is full of "power" and performs "great wonders and miraculous signs" (Acts 6:8). When he is opposed by certain segments of the synagogue who "argue" with him, Luke reports "they could not stand up against his wisdom or the Spirit by whom he spoke" (Acts 6:9-10).

Thus, in Scripture, the testimony of the disciples is consistently linked to and enabled by the work of the Spirit. John is not introducing a new notion by connecting Spirit and witness. He is simply reinforcing a connection we find elsewhere.

On this final night, the disciples may feel inadequate for their witnessing task. In many ways, they *are* inadequate. But Jesus assures them with this third *Paraclete* Passage that they are not alone. Every time they point their trembling fingers towards Jesus, every time they lift their quivering voices in witness, the Spirit will be speaking as well—through them—fueling their testimony with a power beyond themselves.[4]

This thought must have been a comfort to the Twelve. What a relief to learn they do not carry the testimonial burden by themselves! What a relief to know the Spirit will stand with them, adding his voice to theirs, and speak through them, amplifying their voices with his power![5]

Never the most intrepid band, the disciples must have taken courage from this promise. For, judging by what follows, they set about their witnessing task with unusual zeal in the years following Pentecost. Andrew took his testimony to Asia Minor and Greece, and was beaten half to death and then crucified in an effort to shut him up. Bartholomew witnessed in Mesopotamia, Persia, and the area around the Black Sea; he would not be silenced until flayed to death by whipping. James the brother of John preached throughout Judea and Syria, making such a nuisance of himself that finally Herod beheaded him in Jerusalem. Thaddeus and Simon (the Zealot) teamed up to carry the gospel to Syria and Persia; one was beheaded, the other sawn in half to stifle their testimony. Peter, the Denier, affirmed his Lord in Jerusalem, Syria, and Rome, culminating his witness on a cross at the order of Nero. Philip told the story of Jesus in Asia Minor and was scourged, starved, and (finally) crucified for his efforts. Thomas made it all the way to India with his testimony; he stood before a wall and was impaled with spears rather than abandon his message. Matthew witnessed in Africa and was run through with a sword somewhere in Ethiopia.[6]

Only John escaped a martyr's death, though not from lack of trying. He was as much a witness as any of them. The gospel we have from his hand is the tangible residue of his testimony (John 20:30-31). But Jesus protected him, apparently, granting him a long life and a peaceful end. "If I want him to remain alive until I return, what is that to you?" (John 21:22).

And What of Us?

Once again, we find ourselves oddly attuned to the Twelve's condition that fateful night. We know the task of testifying has been passed on to us now. We realize God is looking to us, just as he looked to them, to stand up for Jesus and speak up for truth.

We understand that, if we take our mission seriously, the hatred of the world will turn on us. Not crosses, perhaps. Not racks and thumbscrews. But something we fear as much: ridicule and rejection.

Like the Apostles, we wonder if we are adequate to our task. Will we find the courage to give voice to our convictions? Will we find the wisdom to witness effectively? Is it even possible to be an effective witness? If Jesus tried and could not break through, if the Apostles tried and could not break through, what hope is there for our feeble and fear-filled efforts?

No wonder, then, we long to believe Jesus' promise of a testifying Spirit is for us as much as for them. What if the Holy Spirit is witnessing still? What if he continues to speak to a God-deaf world: apart from us as an independent witness; partnered with us to encourage and empower our own witness? What if we are not alone? What if speaking Truth to the world is not all up to us?

In the absence of such a conviction, modern disciples are left with a severe case of evangelistic laryngitis. We have largely lost our witnessing voice. We hire ministers to speak in our stead. We wash our hands of testifying responsibility by, instead, supporting mission efforts and organizing campaign events. But that ready, steady testimony so characteristic of the early church is largely absent in our own. Their testimony turned a world upside down. Ours barely makes a dent.

If we are to recover our evangelistic voice, we must recover the evangelistic perspective of the New Testament church—a perspective founded on and conditioned by an appreciation of the Spirit's witnessing work. The Spirit witnesses (then and now) to the glory of Christ. And the Spirit can empower the witness of disciples (then and now) if only our faith will permit it.

It is in the hope of a *testifying* Spirit that I open my heart and life to the *Paraclete*, whatever the uncertainties and risks. For if that witnessing Spirit is meant to be a reality for us today, I believe he can help us do the essential work of testifying to the Christ who has given us life that is both rich and eternal.

What we learn about the Holy Spirit in the Third *Paraclete* Passage:

1. The *Paraclete* will be sent by Jesus.
2. The *Paraclete* will come from the Father.
3. The *Paraclete* is the "Spirit of Truth."
4. The Spirit goes out from the Father.
5. The Spirit will testify about Jesus.
6. The Spirit will help us to testify.

Chapter Eleven

THE PROMISE OF CONVICTION

(JOHN 16:5-11)

No wonder they feel inadequate. Just outside this upper room waits a broken world: lost and hostile. Jesus has already spoken of its enmity, its hatred, its intent to persecute and kill.

To that world, and in spite of hostility and persecution, the disciples must testify. Yes, it is terrifying to tell the truth to people who don't want to hear it. Yes, it is dangerous to tweak the beast's tail. Thankfully, theirs is not the only voice speaking up for truth—the Spirit of truth will also testify (John 15:26-27).

But it takes more than testimony to change a world. Testimony alone only makes the world angry, only increases its resistance. Testimony must be *believed* before it can be effective. The world must be *convicted* for testimony to make a difference.

The disciples can testify. They can speak truth to a hard-hearted world. But they cannot make that heart vulnerable. They cannot break the world's heart. They cannot convince and convict and make contrite. Something more powerful than the disciples' testimony is needed to accomplish that. Someone more powerful than Peter or James must do that killing work.

Lord, thy most pointed pleasure take
And stab my spirit broad awake.

Or, Lord, if too obdurate I,
Choose thou, before that spirit die,
A piercing pain, a killing sin,
And to my dead heart run them in.[1]

The Spirit and the World

John's Gospel is deeply torn about the world. On the one hand, God loves the world (3:16). He sends his Son to save the world (3:17). Jesus comes to give life and light to the world (6:33; 8:12). He preaches so the world will believe (12:46). He dies to take away the sin of the world (1:29). On the other hand, Jesus is certainly not *of* the world (8:23). The world does not recognize Jesus when he arrives (1:10) and does not rush to his light (3:19). Instead, the world hates him (7:7) and rejoices at his death (16:20). Jesus must drive out the "Prince of this world" (12:31) and "overcome" the world (16:33).

We see this same tension in John between the world and disciples. Disciples do not "belong to the world" because Jesus has chosen them out of it (15:19). They will have "trouble" in the world (16:33), be hated by the world (17:14), and need protection from the world (17:15). Jesus calls disciples to despise their life in this world (12:25).

And yet that same world is the field and focus of disciples, the sphere of their primary activity. Jesus, who calls disciples out of the world, also sends them back into the world "so that the world may believe" (17:18-23). Like their Master, disciples don't have the luxury of abandoning the world; they must lay down their lives for it.

We find (surprise, surprise) exactly the same tension between the world and the Holy Spirit. There is a sense in which the Spirit has nothing to do with the world, nor the world with the Spirit. The world does not accept the Spirit, cannot "see" or "know" the Spirit (14:17). The Spirit is for disciples, indwelling and empowering, teaching and encouraging them.

Once again, however, John insists there are two sides to every coin. The Spirit who is promised to the disciples also has a work to do in the world. Not an indwelling work. Not a sanctifying work. But an important work nonetheless.

The first hint of this world-work came in the Third *Paraclete* Passage: the Spirit *testifies*. In doing so, it is the *world* he addresses, not disciples. He stands *with* disciples in the testifying process. He gives courage *to* disciples as they testify. But his testimony (like theirs) is directed at the world.

It is in the Fourth *Paraclete* Passage, however, that the full force of the Spirit's work in the world is felt. What happens when the Spirit and disciples testify? There is a work that must take place which only the Spirit is capable of doing: cutting open the world's chest, placing his hands on the world's heart, and running into that dead heart some killing sin.

Better for You . . .

John 16:5Now I am going to him who sent me, yet none of you asks me, 'Where are you going?' 6Because I have said these things, you are filled with grief. 7But I tell you the truth: It is for your good that I am going away. Unless I go away, the *Paraclete* will not come to you; but if I go, I will send him to you.

At first blush, "It is for your good that I am going away" sounds like one of those patently untrue statements (on a par with "This is going to hurt me more than you") people sometimes make when trying to convince others of something hard to believe. The disciples are disappointed, worried, and scared out of their minds. They don't want Jesus to go. They'd give anything for him to stay. And this is the reason he gives? He's leaving "for their good"?

Even at two thousand years removed, it sounds thin.

Though the disciples may find these words hard to swallow, Jesus believes them with all his heart. He knows there is something better than him-in-the-flesh. He knows the disciples will be stronger, more effective, when he gets out of the way so the *Paraclete* can come.[2]

All the promises Jesus makes during the course of this night cannot be kept until he leaves and the Spirit comes: the Spirit who will be their "forever" Companion; the Spirit who will allow them to experience Jesus' presence whenever, wherever, and whatever; the Spirit who will teach them everything they need to know; the Spirit who will calm their troubled hearts and grant them peace; the Spirit who will testify to the world and give disciples courage to testify. It is better Jesus go so the Spirit can begin his needed work.

But it's more than that. Frankly, there are things the Spirit can do Jesus could not. There are things the Spirit can do *better* than Jesus. Jesus must go so the Spirit can do "even greater works than these" (John 14:12).

That is a hard truth to accept. It is difficult for us to believe there is anything Jesus can't do. We don't often consider that Jesus had limits during his earthly existence. In fact, we don't often use the words "Jesus" and "limits" in the same sentence. It's a little odd to imagine the One who raised the dead and calmed the storm would suffer any constraints at all.

But the fact that Jesus was "incarnate"—in the flesh—placed very real boundaries on his ministry and power. Some of those boundaries were *physical*. He couldn't be two places at one time—preaching to crowds in Jerusalem (for instance) while feeding crowds in Galilee at the same moment. He could only teach people who were in range of his voice—the Sermon on the Mount was not miraculously simulcast to listeners in other locations. He couldn't accompany his disciples everywhere, through every trial, in every challenge—there was only one of him and many of them.[3]

Some of Jesus' limits involved *time*. He lived within the boundaries of a sixty-second minute, a sixty-minute hour, a twenty four-hour day. He had limited time to accomplish his mission—little more than three years to change the world. What time he did have was cramped by his need to eat and sleep, by the hours he spent on the road, by the religious calendar, by sunset and storm.

Most of the limits Jesus lived with, however, belonged to his *listeners*. When stomachs rumbled, Jesus had to distribute bread rather than wisdom. When hearts were hard, Jesus could not break through to make people believe. When the disciples were dull and tired, he could not make them grasp what he was trying to say.[4] When faith was lacking, Jesus could not convince or work miracles.

But the promised *Paraclete* will know no such limits. He will not be bounded by flesh. He can be everywhere at once, on duty at all times.

He needs no rest, no refueling, no recovery, no recharge. Distance means nothing to him. He speaks with a voice that does not depend on air molecules and ear drums to be heard. He can enter the soul of a person, any number of persons, and reside there—a living presence in many believers at once. He lives above time—a forever presence in the lives of disciples. He can encourage without restriction, he can calm without words or touch, he can teach without hurry, he can stay with disciples forever.

And working with the limits of the human heart will be his stock-in-trade. He can soften hard hearts. He can open deaf ears. He can minister to wounded souls. He can imbue courage and hope. Most of all, as we are about to see, the Spirit knows how to prompt the kind of godly grief that leads to repentance.

Jesus is telling the truth: it really *is* for their good that he goes away. The Spirit has work to do even Jesus could not accomplish.

He Will Convict the World

[16:8]When he comes, he will convict the world of guilt in regard to sin and righteousness and judgment: [9]in regard to sin, because men do not believe in me; [10]in regard to righteousness, because I am going to the Father, where you can see me no longer; [11]and in regard to judgment, because the prince of this world now stands condemned.

What Jesus says in this *Paraclete* Passage about the Spirit's convicting work is not easy to understand. In part, that is because the language itself is difficult (as we will lament later). What is this "convicting" work? How is it accomplished? What does Jesus mean by "guilt in regard to sin and righteousness and judgment"?

But a larger part of our difficulty in understanding this teaching is not linguistic, it is philosophical. Our commonly held view of humanity is radically different from the view of Jesus. We simply don't see ourselves as Jesus sees us. Our understanding of human nature—who we are, what has gone wrong with us, how we can be "fixed"—has been shaped by the Renaissance and the Enlightenment, honed by the self-improvement and psychotherapeutic culture in which we swim, and polished by an instinct for self-justification and a love of the well-crafted excuse. We are heirs to a boundless optimism regarding human potential (or, at least, regarding ourselves) and hold a high and happy view of our species (or, at any rate, of ourselves as its representatives). If you ask us, we're likely to tell you that human beings—for all their faint flaws—are basically good at heart.

If we are broken, we are not *very* broken. If we need fixing, it shouldn't take much. A little teaching, a bit of moral fine-tuning, is all we require to find our way again. Given a choice (and the proper incentives), we'll do the right thing most every time.

Jesus begs to differ. In fact, he *died* to differ. In his view, humanity is broken and broken badly. Yes, we were created with great expectations. But we fell in love with ourselves and exchanged the truth of God for a lie. Yes, we bear the image of God. But it is an image marred, sullied, and deeply traumatized.

And, according to Jesus, we are not just broken—we are *bent*. We love the darkness and hate the light. We are clever at evil, creative in the ways of sin. We are drawn to the perverse. We deny the truth. We do not think clearly or value correctly. We have lost our spiritual compass and cannot, will not, find our way home.

So badly bent are we, according to Jesus, we cannot afford to be honest about ourselves. We must expend vast energies denying the fact, deflecting blame, constructing castles of rationalization and excuse. It is hard for us, flawed as we are, to admit any flaw at all. Our native language is self-justification. Our most urgent mission is self-protection. Our first priority is asserting our righteousness, even if the only righteousness we can claim is the sort we bestow on ourselves.

And the last thing we want is someone else telling us the truth—especially the truth about *us*. We hate people like that.

Though it may be the last thing we want, it is the one thing most needed. According to Jesus, our greatest need is the ability to see ourselves as we actually are—to see ourselves as God sees us. We need a love of truth that transcends our defensiveness. We need hearts capable of breaking over our brokenness. We need honesty about just how bent we are.

But that will mean a cure far more radical than a few rituals and the occasional attitude adjustment. It will require a Spirit audacious enough to convict us of guilt and powerful enough, then, to wash our guilt away. And this is the Spirit Jesus promises in the fourth *Paraclete* Passage: a Spirit who knows how to use killing sins to revive dead hearts.

The Spirit's Convicting Work

As true as I believe this philosophical difference is, the language of this text is still difficult and causes us problems. Attempts to decipher Jesus' words here have resulted in more than a few scholarly white-flags. For our purposes, let's make a small distinction between the details of this passage and its fundamental point.

The details have to do with the convicting work of the Spirit "in regard to sin and righteousness and judgment." It's easy enough to see how the world might need convicting about "sin." But convicting about "righteousness" and "judgment"? What does that mean?

In fact, "sin and righteousness and judgment" are important themes for the Gospel of John as a whole. They played central roles in the ministry of Jesus, not just the work of the Spirit.

Take, for example, the work of Jesus in convicting the world of sin: "If I had not come and spoken to them, they would not be guilty of sin. Now, however, they have no excuse for their sin. . . . If I had not done among them what no one else did, they would not be guilty of sin. But now they have seen these miracles, and yet they have hated both me and my Father" (John 15:22, 24).

Jesus took sin seriously. He believed it was killing humanity (John 8:24). He warned against it and begged people to stop committing it (John 5:14). He lamented a blindness to sin that kept people from penitence (John 9:41). In John 15, Jesus reminds his disciples he confronted the sin of the world so that it had "no excuse." He spoke and they had an opportunity to recognize and repent. He performed miracles and they had a chance to be convicted and confess. Instead, they denied, excused, and hated. Is Jesus telling us, in this fourth *Paraclete* Passage, the Spirit will do the same sort of work in the world? Pointing out sin? Removing any excuse?

Convicting the world of "righteousness" was also an important part of Jesus' ministry. Jesus understood there was a true righteousness (reflecting his Father and his Father's priorities) and a *shadow righteousness* that borrowed the vocabulary of righteousness but denied the idea behind it. He was the constant champion of the first sort and the constant opponent of the other. He allowed, for instance, that the Pharisees had a certain righteousness; but he warned his disciples they would have to find a *better* righteousness to enter the kingdom of heaven (Matt 5:20). He rebuked those "who were confident in their *own* righteousness" and cared nothing for God's (Luke 18:9ff). When the Pharisees sneered at such charges, Jesus responded with barely suppressed fury: "You are the ones who justify yourselves in the eyes of men, but God knows your hearts. What is highly valued among men is detestable in God's sight" (Luke 16:15). Is Jesus saying, in the fourth *Paraclete* Passage, the Spirit will take up and continue this same work—this convicting in regard to sham righteousness?

Convicting the world of judgment was also an important part of Jesus' agenda. One of the most interesting themes in John's Gospel has to do with bad judgment and twisted thinking. According to John, people in the world cannot understand the light of God (1:5), will not recognize and receive the Word of God (1:11), refuse to believe (3:32), don't properly weigh evidence (5:43; 7:21-23), will not set the right priorities (6:26-27), make superficial judgments (7:24; 8:15), and rush to wrong conclusions (e.g., 8:22). Jesus made repeated attempts to help his listeners think clearly—to hear the truth, to see the evidence, to believe his claims. But in the end he kept bumping into a world whose judgment was fatally flawed. He could plead, "Stop judging by mere appearances, and make a right judgment" (John 7:24), but it did no good. Is this the same idea Jesus is getting at when he promised the Spirit would convict the world of its judgment?

True sin. False righteousness. Bad judgment.[5] These were all things Jesus confronted during his ministry. Are these the same failings the Spirit will confront in his work with the world? Is this the convicting work the Spirit will take up and continue? When we remember that the Spirit is Jesus, his words and works are Jesus' words and works, his mission is Jesus' mission (see Chapter Eight), it is not a stretch to recognize that the convicting themes characteristic of Jesus' ministry will necessarily be characteristic of the Spirit's ministry.[6]

Enough of murky details. The point of this passage is clear: the Spirit is hard at work convicting the world of guilt on whatever front is needed.

In this fourth *Paraclete* Passage, Jesus describes a Spirit who is hounding the world, watching for every opportunity and opening, seeking fresh chances to tell the world the truth about itself. He describes a Spirit who loves the world enough to engage it and give it what it really needs: a deep awareness of guilt; a profound sorrow for brokenness; an honest confession of failings. According to Jesus, the Spirit is in the difficult business of confronting a defensive world, making it recognize its very real guilt, and then leading it to the point of godly sorrow and repentance.[7]

Jesus was in the same business. The Spirit is simply doing the work Jesus started. Only the Spirit is doing it better.

Jesus tried to show the world its brokenness; he wasn't very successful. Men loved the darkness too much and responded with denial and anger. They hated him for saying their deeds were evil (John 3:19). They killed him for it. When Jesus tried to teach true righteousness and convict his listeners of the lesser sort, he largely failed. They took offense and crucified him for his troubles. When he urged his audiences to "use right judgment," they dismissed him as demon-possessed and, in the end, murdered him to shut him up.

But killing Jesus did not stop his convicting work. In fact, it only enhanced that work. With his death, Jesus passed on the business of convicting the world to the Holy Spirit. Long after Jesus was dead and gone, the Spirit was busy poking and prodding and pointing out the world's guilt. Long after Jesus returned to the Father, the Spirit continued to hold up a mirror to the world so it could see itself honestly.

And, according to the promise of Jesus in this fourth *Paraclete* Passage, he convicts the world *better*, more effectively, than Jesus ever could. The Spirit convicts better because he does it without ceasing, for everyone, on every occasion, in every heart. He can convict here and there, him and her, then and now and in the future. And because he is present "forever," he can make his convicting attempts in our teens . . . and then again at thirty or sixty . . . and, if all else fails, he can hover close in the last moments of life and encourage a death-bed confession. He can use this struggle, that tragedy, to get our attention and show us our true selves. And if we still haven't hit bottom? The forever Spirit can wait until life finally falls on us and convinces us we are broken beyond our capacity to deny or to heal.

Even this convicting Spirit can be resisted, of course. He will not break down the fences of our hearts and do to us what we will not permit. There are many who resist the Spirit's convicting work to the death. But because the Spirit can afford to be patient and is always wise, *some* hear his voice . . . *some* are convicted . . . *some* see who they are and what they need. Whenever that happens, it is always because of the Spirit's convicting work.

In Summary

Jesus is going back to the Father. And it's a good thing. For unless Jesus goes, the *Paraclete* cannot come. Unless the *Paraclete* comes, the ultimate purposes of God cannot be accomplished. The ministry of Jesus went a long way to accomplishing God's work in the world: his teaching, his life, his death, his resurrection. But only the Spirit can complete God's work.

Key to that is the cultivation of the world's heart to hear Heaven's truth—something the Spirit is specifically sent to do. If former promises about the Spirit describe the peace, joy, and comfort the Spirit brings to the lives of believers, this promise addresses something darker the Spirit has in store for the world. The Spirit, when he comes, will trouble the world, accuse the world, disturb the world. Never again will humanity be safe from God's convicting Spirit. The Spirit loves the world too much to leave it alone.

What a relief this must have been for the disciples. In a matter of hours, Jesus is going to tear them from the womb of his protective presence and thrust them into the cold, harsh realities of life in the world. That world will be cruel to them, hateful and threatening. Still they must testify. No matter what, they must speak the truth about Jesus. As they do so, the Spirit himself will testify.

But the Spirit will do more. Like the farmer, the Spirit works to prepare the soil into which the gospel seed will fall. He harrows hearts with the plow of conviction. Not everyone responds, of course. Some hearts remain hard and shallow and choked with weeds. But a few appreciate the *Paraclete's* efforts to "stab my spirit broad awake." They are convicted. They are broken. They are penitent.

This promise of a convicting Spirit told the disciples that their work would never be in vain, their words would never come back empty. Perhaps it took the Twelve a while to tumble to this. Maybe only later, as they reflected on all Jesus said this fateful night, did they realize what this promise meant. Still, the thought of the Spirit, working before and after them to prepare the hearts of men, must have been a source of great comfort.

They knew Jesus had called them to testify. But, especially this night, they must have been profoundly aware of their inadequacies. They could speak, but they did not have the power to convict. They could tell the story, but they were not capable of cutting the heart. If all the disciples had were their words, their witness, they were doomed to futility and failure. The world would shut them up. The world would tear out their testifying tongues to silence their unwanted truth.

But if there is a convicting Spirit at work in the world, running into dead hearts a piercing pain, a killing sin, then the testimony of disciples can touch hearts made hungry; truth will meet conviction; seed may find good soil. Suddenly and miraculously, feeble words become words of life. And disciples, hand-in-hand with the Spirit, become the aroma of Christ, ministers of the new covenant, jars of clay carrying around God's treasure.

And What of Us?

Once again, we are confronted by a promise made to *them* that we hope applies to *us*. How wonderful for *them* to hear that the Spirit will be actively, aggressively preparing the world to receive the gospel. How wonderful for *them* (for instance) to see three thousand listeners "cut to the heart" (Acts 2:37) by the convicting work of the Spirit.

But is this same promise for *us*? Does this Spirit still move in the world to prepare hearts for the seed of the gospel? Is there reason to hope there might yet be partnership possible between modern-day witnesses and a still-convicting Spirit?

Let's hope so. For the convicting work of the Holy Spirit is desperately needed in these latter times. Our world still loves the darkness, still clings to the illusion of goodness, still thinks in sin-clouded ways. We believers bang our heads against these worldly walls on a daily basis. How do you convey gospel to people who are so in love with the wrong, so blind to their own brokenness, so deluded and deceived? If the task is ours alone, if it really is "up to us," there is good reason to despair.

And it's more personal than a faceless "world." Every one of us is tied by love to someone whose heart needs breaking: a son or daughter who has wandered away from faith and holiness; a spouse whose heart has been hard for years; a friend who cannot admit any need for a Savior; parents too proud to confess and repent. We love them and long for a spiritual awakening in their lives. But we know we are not capable of doing the heart-work they need. We are too limited. We do not possess that kind of power. We need something—*someone*—to do for them what we cannot do ourselves.

Jesus' promise of a convicting Spirit—actively working in this dark world—should be good news for us. It is in the hope of a convicting Spirit that I open my heart and life to the *Paraclete*, whatever the uncertainties and risks. For if that Spirit is meant to be a reality for us today, I believe he does the essential work of preparing an audience for the testimony we are commissioned to speak: convicting the world of guilt; piercing dead hearts with killing sins so new hearts can one day grow.

**What we learn about the Holy Spirit in the
Fourth *Paraclete* Passage:**

1. Unless Jesus goes away, the *Paraclete* cannot come.
2. It is for our good that Jesus goes away—so that the Spirit can come.
3. When Jesus goes away, he will send the *Paraclete* to the disciples.
4. There is a sense, however, that the Spirit is also sent to the world.
6. The Spirit's primary work in the world is convicting the world of guilt.
7. That conviction concerns the world's guilt in regard to sin, righteousness, and judgment.

Chapter Twelve

THE PROMISE OF REVELATION

(JOHN 16:12-15)

No wonder they feel as if they're drowning. Too much has happened. Too much has been said. Their heads are reeling. Their emotions are raw. They cannot take anymore.

It's been building for months. Anxieties about the Jerusalem leaders—hostile and angry and plotting. The stress of Lazarus' death, and then the shock and awe of seeing him walk from the grave. Weeks of hiding in the desert. Fighting fears on the road to Jerusalem. Jesus predicting his death. Mary anointing him for burial. Triumphal entries. Voices from heaven.

The disciples were at the end of their ropes long before they climbed the stairs to the Upper Room and sat down to their evening meal. But had they been fresh as daisies, the events of this night alone would have pushed them to the edge.

Their Master, brooding and distracted. The footwashing, witnessed in a silence of shame. Peter's proud and futile objections. Odd words about betrayal. Judas' odder exit. Talk of death and orphans. Peter, trying to make up for one folly, committing another: "I will lay down my life for you." Jesus' wistful rebuke: "You will disown me three times." More talk of leaving. Riddles and paradoxes. The hatred of the world. Someone else, some other Companion, taking Jesus' place.

Jesus sees a look on their faces that tells him he has reached their end. The blank stares. The exhausted expressions. The look of the lost and the beleaguered. They are shutting down. They have nothing left.

Though they do not know it yet, these men still have miles to go before they sleep; the worst is yet to come.

But Jesus knows it (John 16:12). And he decides to show them mercy. "I have much more to say to you." Perhaps he paused; perhaps he sighed. "But it is more than you can now bear." A nod of decision, the ghost of a smile.

A Revealing Spirit

We've reached the fifth and final *Paraclete* Passage. Jesus has one thing more to say about the Holy Spirit before he ceases teaching and commences dying. The dinner is done. The hour is late. Calvary beckons.

> 16:12I have much more to say to you, more than you can now bear. 13But when he, the Spirit of truth, comes, he will guide you into all truth. He will not speak on his own; he will speak only what he hears, and he will tell you what is yet to come. 14He will bring glory to me by taking from what is mine and making it known to you. 15All that belongs to the Father is mine. That is why I said the Spirit will take from what is mine and make it known to you.

Four times Jesus has spoken to his disciples about the Holy Spirit, telling them how the Spirit will help them in the future. Are the disciples worried about Jesus abandoning them? The Spirit will be the presence of Jesus, available to them forever (the first *Paraclete* Passage). Do they wonder how they can carry on the mission of Jesus in his absence? The Spirit will teach them everything they need to know and do (the second passage). Are they concerned about witnessing to a hostile world? The Spirit himself will testify to Jesus and give them courage to testify (the third). Do they question whether their feeble voices can possibly make a dent in a hard-hearted and sin-deadened world? The Spirit will do a convicting work in the hearts of men, revealing their guilt and their need for a Savior (the fourth).

The fifth time Jesus speaks of the Spirit, he does so in the context of their crippling fatigue. He knows anything he tells them at this point is going-in-one-ear-and-out-the-other. They cannot bear more words. They have reached their teachable limit. His time has run out. Soon, the soldiers.

Yet he has so much more to give these disciples, so much more they need to understand. The words he speaks next are a kind of surrender, a compromise for the sake of his limited men: "There is more . . . you cannot bear it . . . . I must leave the rest to the *Paraclete*."

In the final *Paraclete* Passage, Jesus promises his disciples a *revealing* Spirit, a Spirit who will say everything Jesus wants to say, would say, if only his disciples had a place to put it. This Spirit will be their guide into "all truth." He will tell them "what is yet to come." He will make known to them "all that belongs to the Father." He will give them everything Jesus has and wants them to have.[1] And he will do all this in a way these disciples—limited as they are—can "bear."

In fairness to the Apostles, part of their inability to hear what Jesus tells them this night (and to grasp so much Jesus taught through the course of his ministry) is a problem of *context*. One of the hard realities Jesus faced while in the flesh was that everything he said and did, everything he taught, took place *before* the cross and the tomb and the blaze of resurrection. Jesus ministered in a pre-Easter world. How could his disciples possibly understand many of his teachings *prior* to the events of Easter? No wonder they missed "Destroy this temple and in three days I will raise it up"; they had not yet experienced the horrors of Calvary and the joys of the empty tomb. How could they grasp the depths of God's love for the world until Jesus (God's love offering) had been "lifted up"? How could they embrace the true meaning of dying to self, the new birth, or "I am the resurrection and the life," except in the light of what was about to happen?

The cross and resurrection were still in their future. And until they knew "the rest of the story," there were some ideas, some fundamental lessons they could not "get," no matter how long or how frankly Jesus spoke.

Much of their inability to hear, however, was less a matter of *context* than of *capacity*. Though they tried, they simply could not keep up with Jesus' revelational *pace*. Too much to absorb. Too fast to understand. And, though they tried, the disciples simply lacked the ability to match Jesus' revelational *depth*. He was too profound for them. Much of the time, he was talking over their heads.

On this night, both context and capacity conspire against the disciples. They *don't know* the rest of the story. They *can't keep up* with Jesus, gushing at them because time is short. So they reach a limit. It's too much. They are full to bursting with his words. They are not big enough to contain everything he wants to give them.

Knowing that, seeing it in their faces, Jesus relents. "More. But not now. Let's wait for the *Paraclete* to reveal it all."

What Is the "much more"?

A key to understanding this fifth *Paraclete* Passage lies in defining what "more" Jesus wants to tell the disciples, what "more" the *Paraclete* will offer in his stead.

Does Jesus have more commands to give the disciples? ("Unless you make a pilgrimage to Bethlehem, you cannot be saved!") Does he have some critical secret to share with them he hasn't found the right time or occasion to disclose? Is this when Jesus planned to unveil the date of his second coming, only the disciples were too tired to hear it? (Too bad!)

The way some people read the rest of this passage, it makes you wonder if that's what they're thinking—"I have much more to say to you" must mean another command, a new teaching, a great secret. Some readers (who often happen to be preachers and writers) come to this passage and immediately jump all exegetical fences, running wildly down the road of conjecture. Apparently, they feel a compulsive need to fill in the blank of this "much more" but do not feel an equal urge to fill in the blank responsibly.

"Didn't Jesus promise the Spirit would be a guide into *all truth?* That must mean those who have the Spirit can know everything!" In one, short, exegetical leap, people who understand these words in this way elevate their views on social issues, politics, science, money, race, war, and a thousand other matters into something holier, more accurate, and more authoritative. Such views aren't just *opinion*; they are *facts* resulting from a Spirit who guides us into *all* truth. Is that what Jesus means to say? Having the Spirit gives Christians the answer to every question? A pastor's opinions about (say) a scientific theory or a political issue are more likely to be correct *because* he claims the Spirit than the opinions of experts who aren't particularly spiritual? I don't think so.

"And didn't Jesus promise the Spirit would reveal *what is yet to come*'? That must be a reference to the prophetic gift. Jesus is promising that, with the Spirit's help, we can predict the future!" Really? Does the Spirit tell me what the stock market will do next week or give me insights into future world events or show me the shape of the end times? Does having the Spirit mean I can see around the corner of tomorrow and know "what is yet to come"?

That's *not* what Jesus is talking about here. This promise is nothing more nor less than an assurance: whatever the limits and time constraints and stress levels disciples live with, whatever the immaturities and scars and inadequacies that mark them, whatever upper rooms and difficult circumstances they find themselves in—the important matters Jesus wants to share with his followers (the "much more" he has to say) will finally be heard because of the on-going ministry of the Spirit.

The "more" Jesus wants to say is not something new . . . some secret he has not yet addressed. It is "more" of what he has already been telling the Twelve and the crowds and even the Pharisees. Not more commandment. Not more predictions. More Father. More glory. More unveiling of the invisible God.

What Jesus wants to say, the much more he has to reveal, is first, last, and always about his Father. Jesus came to reveal God; to make the invisible God fully known; to shine the light of God into the world's darkness; to have God walk in his world once more and be recognized. "Now this is eternal life: that they may know you, the only true God" (John 17:3).

No theme comes closer to John's heart. From the opening words of his Gospel, and repeatedly throughout, John trumpets the truth that Jesus makes God known. Jesus is the Word, who was with God and who was God (1:1), and now shows himself to the world. He is the Light who shines in darkness (1:5), revealing (in Paul's pithy phrase) "the light of the knowledge of the glory of God in the face of Christ." He becomes flesh so we can see his glory, the glory of God himself (1:14).

"No one has ever seen God, but God the one and only, who is at the Father's side, has made him known" (1:18). Jesus is the Son of God (1:34), the Lamb of God (1:29), the Holy One of God (6:69), the Gift of God (4:10), and the bread of God (6:33); tied by every device in

John's vocabulary to the Yahweh who sent him. He is the one who came "from heaven" (3:13) and "from above" (3:31; 8:23) in order to testify to what he has seen and heard of his Father in the heavenly realms (3:11, 32). It saddens Jesus there are those who "have never heard [God's] voice nor seen his form" (5:37), but he does not count himself among that number. He has seen the Father (6:46) and knows the Father (8:55; 10:15) and exists in the flesh to make the Father known.

In fact, when the world wants to see God, Jesus simply points to himself. It is Jesus *himself* who best reveals the Father (a principle we stressed in Chapter Eight). Not his teachings. Not his miracles. His own life and character. His own priorities and relationships. Look at Jesus and you see God (12:45). Know Jesus and you know God (8:19; 14:7).

At the highest level, Jesus did not come to earth to expound Moses or set up an improved moral code or institute a new religion. He didn't come to preach the Sermon on the Mount or heal the lame man or walk around with Matthew. In the ultimate sense, he didn't even come to die on the cross.

Jesus came to reveal his Father. Everything else was a facet of that overriding mission, a means to that greatest end.

Now his time has run out, now the disciples have reached their limit, so Jesus passes on this essential work to the *Paraclete*. The responsibility of revealing the Father rests with the Spirit now. It's up to him to guide the disciples into a full understanding of the Father (that's what Jesus means by "into all truth"[2]). It's up to the Spirit to speak for Jesus and bring him glory by revealing everything about God to the disciples. It's up to the Spirit to take everything "yet to come" (think cross and resurrection and church and discipleship) and unpack it for the disciples to show how God is revealed in it.

The Spirit will do that, as we are about to see, by "taking from what is mine and making it known to you."[3]

The Revelation Chain

16:12I have much more to say to you, more than you can now bear. 13But when he, the Spirit of truth, comes, he will guide you into all truth. He will not speak on his own; he will speak only what he hears, and he will tell you what is yet to come. 14He will bring glory to me by taking from what is mine and making it known to you. ¹⁵All that belongs to the Father is mine. That is why I said the Spirit will take from what is mine and make it known to you.

In this passage, Jesus tells his disciples about a revelational chain: a revealing work passed on from Father to Son, Son to Spirit, Spirit to disciples, and (implicitly) disciples to the world.

The chain begins with the Father. The Father has a great deal that "belongs to" him (16:15): who he is and what he is about; his glory, character, and holiness; his beauty and power; his purposes and plans; his will for the world and for our lives; his love for us. When Jesus speaks here of "all that belongs to the Father," he is referring to all that is *contained* in the Father, all that is *characteristic* of the Father, all that can *be known* of the Father.

Jesus claims, in this incredible passage, that the Father has poured himself into the Son (16:15). Everything that *is* the Father, all his glory and holiness and love, has become the Son's. It all "belongs" to Jesus now. This is the basis, this is the understanding of God's revealing work, that permits Jesus to make statements like:

"I and the Father are one" (John 10:30)
"If you really knew me, you would know my Father as well."
    (John 14:7)
"Anyone who has seen me has seen the Father." (John 14:9)
"I am in the Father and the Father is in me." (John 10:38;
    14:10, 11)
"All I have is yours, and all you have is mine." (John 17:10)

It is because the Apostles *believed* Jesus when he made such claims that they would write:

"For God was pleased to have all his fullness dwell in [Jesus]."
    (Col 1:19)
"For in Christ all the fullness of the Deity dwells in bodily
    form." (Col 2:9)
"The Son is the radiance of God's glory and the exact represen-
    tation of his being . . ." (Heb 1:3)

The Father's words, the Father's work, the Father's will, the Father's character and essence—all have been given to the Son. All are contained in the Son—the second link in this revelational chain. "All that belongs to the Father is mine."

But there is more. This revelation of God was never intended to end with Jesus—a brief flash of light and glory while a worshipping world looked on. Jesus came for the specific purpose of revealing God to the world, taking all that had been given to him by the Father and making it known to humanity, pouring the fullness of God into frail men and women. He came into the world to be the light of the world and reveal the glory of the Father (the very premise of John's gospel—John 1:1-18). But the world could not bear it. Some—like the Pharisees—saw God revealed in Jesus and hated him for it. Others—like the crowds—saw that revelation, but were consumed with lesser things (e.g., their stomachs). And some—like the Apostles—saw this revelation, recognized it for what it was, but simply could not keep up. They were not fast enough to capture the revelational flow. They were not deep enough to hold the revelational ocean. They couldn't bear it, not because they resisted it or were distracted by other things, but because they were limited human beings trying to reach their arms around a revelation that was larger than they could embrace.

Perhaps a metaphor would help. Imagine, if you will, a suitcase containing all that belongs to the Father: his character and purposes, his hopes for this world, his will for our lives. That suitcase has been carefully packed by the Father. Everything needed to know him is in there.

God hands that suitcase to his Son. The Son is strong. He can do the heavy lifting of carrying that case and its contents into the world. And the Son is smart. One look inside and he understands everything packed away there. He knows it intimately, in detail. He becomes it. He incarnates it.

Jesus dresses himself in flesh to hand that suitcase on to his disciples—and forge them into the next link in this revelational chain. He intends to unpack what belongs to his Father, what has been given to him, before their very eyes. And he does that: here is the Father's glory; here is the Father's love. Only the Twelve are not as strong as the Son: they cannot bear the weight of God's glory. Nor are they as smart as the

Son: what he grasps in a moment, they require a lifetime to comprehend; what he understands intimately, they see only darkly and in part.

It is too much for them. It overwhelms them. They are thimbles trying to hold a cistern of truth. They are ninety-eight-pound-weaklings attempting to bench-press the Mystery of the Ages. What Jesus reveals is simply beyond their capacities.[4]

They drop the suitcase.

But Jesus doesn't chide them for ham-handedness. He doesn't exchange them for more capable disciples. He shows them mercy. "I have much more to say to you." Perhaps he pauses; perhaps he sighs. "But it is more than you can now bear." A nod of decision; the ghost of a smile.

Another Link

In this fifth *Paraclete* Passage, Jesus forms another link in the revelational chain—one that fits between himself and his disciples. He makes room for a Spirit who will "take from what is mine" and reveal it to limited disciples.[5] "But when he, the Spirit of truth, comes . . . he will not speak on his own; he will speak only what he hears . . . He will bring glory to me by taking from what is mine and making it known to you. All that belongs to the Father is mine. That is why I said the Spirit will take from what is mine and make it known to you" (John 16:13-15).

Notice how careful Jesus is to present this Spirit as a continuation of himself and his revealing work. The Spirit will "speak" to the disciples just as Jesus has spoken to them. But the Spirit will not be an independent voice, speaking what he wants, addressing any topic he pleases (vs 13). Rather he speaks only what is "true" and—in particular—only the truth he hears from Jesus.

Once more, the revelational chain: Jesus takes all the Father has given to him, all he intended to pour into his disciples (until it became evident they could not bear it), and pours it into the Spirit. The Spirit "hears" the truth contained in Jesus (vs 13). The Spirit "takes from" that which belongs to Jesus (vss 14-15). As a result, the Spirit receives everything the Father has poured into Jesus. All that *is* the Father, all that glory and holiness and love, has become the Son's. And now, everything that *is* the Son has become the Spirit's. It all "belongs" to the Spirit now.

Father. Son. Spirit. Links in the revelational chain. There is one link more. As Jesus makes evident in this passage, it is the responsibility of the Spirit to do for the disciples what Jesus himself could not: reveal "all that belongs to the Father" to the disciples in a way that limited humans can handle. Jesus promises the Spirit will guide the disciples into all truth, the Spirit will make known to them all he has received from Jesus and all Jesus has received from the Father. Jesus says it twice, just so the Twelve (in their befuddled state) get the point. The Spirit is going to reveal God to them in a way they can "bear."[6]

Making Revelation Manageable

Jesus tried to reveal God to his disciples, but it was too fast, too much. The disciples could not bear it. Jesus wanted them to know the Father. He showed them himself (the "fullness of deity in bodily form"— Col 2:9). But it was not enough. Rather, it was too much. They needed something other, something *less*. They needed slow, steady, consistent infusions of the knowledge of God that would reveal what they could bear as they could bear it. They needed a revelation of God that would not overwhelm or squash them. They needed a way to bridge the gap between God's greatness and their own puny capabilities.

That is, in part, what the Spirit does for disciples—he *meters the revelational flow*. Mere humans cannot take God directly and at full force. Those who see the face of God die. Even the glory of Jesus is too bright to bear at times. Disciples like the Twelve (disciples like *us*) need a revelation of God that comes in small doses and tiny words. We need a revelation delivered slowly, gradually, in chewable bites and bearable increments. God is a fire hydrant, gushing his truth at us. But we are straws, capable only of sips and dribbles.

It is precisely here the Spirit steps in. He turns down the volume, throttles back the speed, adapts God's gush to our dribble. He reveals God to us: what we can stand, when we are ready, as we are able to receive it. He makes the Father known to us without blowing our spiritual circuits. He parses out the knowledge of God slowly, taking his time with us because he has forever. When disciples cannot "bear" any more, the Spirit can pause until we are ready for another installment. When we do not understand, the Spirit will try again, another way. When sin deadens and deafens disciples to a fuller revelation of God, the Spirit will do his testifying and convicting work, preparing our hearts once again for more of God.

But the Spirit's greatest work in revealing the Father is less about slowing the *pace* of revelation than about increasing our *capacity* for revelation. No matter how slowly and carefully the Spirit pours "all that belongs to the Father" into us, thimbles can never contain oceans, Dribbles and sips may be fine as a beginning. But ultimately, the Spirit intends to make us *bigger* so we can hold more of God.

He does this by deepening us, dredging out our shallow places so more of God will fit; by maturing us, growing us up into the image of Christ. He does this by enlarging our hearts and broadening our minds and stretching our lives. He gives us eyes that see farther, see from God's perspective. He takes us where we are—as small as we are—and makes us stronger, better, truer, nobler, wiser, kinder, deeper. He turns our thimbles into buckets, our buckets into barrels, our barrels into cisterns, our cisterns into lakes, our lakes into oceans . . . always at work enlarging limited disciples so we can hold the glory of God.

Were it not for this promise of Jesus and this work of the Spirit, disciples like Peter and Paul, disciples like you and me, would never be able to hold the fullness of God. We'd blow a gasket, burst a seam, before we even came close. We're just not big enough to contain "all that belongs to the Father." But because of this promise and because of this Spirit-work, disciples as limited as the Twelve, as limited as we, can talk (with straight faces!) about reflecting "the Lord's glory" and "being transformed into his image" (2 Cor 3:18); being "transformed by the renewing" of our minds (Rom 12:2); being "conformed to the likeness of God's Son" (Rom 8:29); putting "on the new self which is being renewed in knowledge in the image of its creator" (Col 3:10); being "filled to the measure of all the fullness of God" (Eph 3:19); becoming "mature, attaining to the whole measure of the fullness of Christ" (Eph 4:13); growing up "in all things into him who is the Head, that is Christ" (Eph 4:15); and becoming "blameless and pure, children of God without fault in a crooked and depraved generation, in which you shine like stars in the universe as you hold out the word of life" (Phil 2:15-16).

Apart from the Spirit, revealing and maturing and growing us, such notions are arrogant prattle. ("With my Bible and my self-discipline, I can become a shining star!") But with the Spirit, notions like these become the defining goals of God's purposes for our lives. By taking all that belongs to the Father and making it known to us, the Spirit reveals God in all his beauty and power. By adapting God's greatness to our limited grasp, the Spirit ensures disciples hear what they can, as they are able. And while doing his revealing work, the Spirit also matures disciples, deepens disciples, so we can become people large enough to contain the fullness of God.

And What of Us?

One last time, you and I are confronted by a promise made to the original disciples that we hope, we pray, applies to us. It is wonderful for the Twelve to hear that God's revealing work is not finished, that God is not stymied by their fatigue or their immaturity or their tiny capacity as he shows himself to them. It is wonderful for Jesus to promise them a Spirit who will "take from what is mine and make it known to you."

What we learn about the Holy Spirit in the Fifth *Paraclete* Passage:

1. Jesus has much more to teach the disciples.
2. It is more than the disciples can bear.
3. The "Spirit of Truth" is coming soon.
4. He will finish Jesus' revealing work, guiding disciples into "all truth."
5. His revelation will not be original . . . it will come from Father and Son . . . an extension of their revelation.
6. He will tell the disciples "what is yet to come."
7. In the process, he will bring glory to Jesus.
8. The Father has given everything to Jesus. Jesus has given everything to the Spirit. The Spirit has given everything to the disciples.

But is this same promise for *us*? Is there still a revealing Spirit working to unpack the Father for us, to explain the Father in small words, to grow in us the capacity to bear the unbearable glory of God?

We must hope so. For when small disciples encounter a big God, something's got to give. Either we must grow larger to hold the fullness of God or God must get smaller so we can wrap our brains and lives around him.

In the absence of a living, powerful, and revealing Spirit who meters out God in ways we can bear and grows our capacity to hold more and more of God, you and I are left to our own devices. And when that happens, we will be tempted to do what others throughout history have done: reduce God to something more attuned to our limits, something *we* can manage. The Pharisees did this, finding ways to honor God with their lips while keeping their hearts at a safe distance (see Mark 7:6). We do it too, substituting church attendance and good deeds for a constant encounter with a sovereign God who will not be domesticated or diminished or depreciated and who never fails to make us feel small in comparison.

The alternative to reducing God is to embrace a revealing Spirit who, over the course of a lifetime, gives us as big a God as we can bear.

I believe there yet remains in the world a Spirit who is committed to guiding us into all truth, giving us everything that "belongs to the Father," revealing the "much more" Jesus wants us to know when we are ready to bear it. I believe there is still a Spirit who will not settle for our partial understandings and our in-the-mirror-darkly points of view and our immature approximations of spiritual realities. I believe there is still a Spirit who loves us too much to leave us alone, who helps us grow up so we can understand more, who guides us past the milk to the meat of life in God. I believe there is still a Spirit who shows us the Father and, in doing so, consistently, persistently breaks our hearts and blows our minds and enlarges our lives.

It is in the hope of this *revealing* Spirit that I open my heart and life to the *Paraclete*, whatever the uncertainties and risks. For if that Spirit is meant to be a reality for us today, I believe he will lead us, in these best of times and worst of times, to a far, far greater God than any we have known before.

THE SPIRIT, YOU, AND US

If you've made it this far, congratulations! I recognize you've had to work hard to get to this point. But it was necessary work, foundational work. We could not get to *application* without a thorough grounding in *principles*.

The Bible attests to the presence of the Spirit whenever God encountered his people in the Old Testament. Jesus—the Messiah—unleashed the Spirit into the world in an unprecedented way. Then in the Upper Room he promised his disciples a continuing experience of the Spirit that would be forever and powerful and personal. This experience of the Spirit would be necessary for their survival. The *Paraclete* would be their life-line, their sustenance.

Our focus to this point has been largely on the past. What did the Spirit do *then*? What did Jesus promise to the Twelve on that long-ago night?

Now the time has come to shift our focus. What about all the nights that followed? What about all the disciples to come? What do these promises mean for the rest of time and the rest of us? If this Spirit is available still, for you and me, what does that mean? What would that look like? What difference could that make?

Section Three is where theory becomes practice.

In Chapter Thirteen we finally answer the question, "Are these promises for us?" Yes! Unequivocally yes! And in this chapter, I give you some good reasons for thinking so.

Chapter Fourteen asks the "So what?" question. How does the Spirit act as our *Paraclete*, today, in modern times? What difference does he make in our lives? How does his power fuel our discipleship? I'll show how the promises of Jesus in the Final Discourse apply to us and, in the process, paint a portrait of a Spirit we can't live without.

Chapter Fifteen suggests practical ways we can invite the Spirit to become a greater, more influential part of our lives. We'll talk here about developing a renewed awareness of the Spirit's presence and a fresh readiness to experience his transforming power. I describe "Ten Disciplines for Seeking the Spirit" that will help you pursue a more intimate and tangible relationship with the Spirit.

Chapter Sixteen tells the tale of two churches found in the New Testament and draws a parallel to the church today. It warns against using the Spirit to cause division in Christ's body. It encourages all Christians, whatever their experience of the Spirit, to keep their eyes on the "greatest" gifts the Spirit offers. And it describes the terrible vulnerabilities facing any church that gets the Spirit wrong.

The Spirit is for us. But, like every gift, it must be accepted and enjoyed. I can show you the gift is real. It's up to you to unwrap it for your own life.

Chapter Thirteen

ARE THESE PROMISES FOR US?

There is something awful about overhearing a promise and then finding out it doesn't apply to you. Whether it's a promise as trivial as a sales promotion ("Sorry, Sir, this offer is only good for left-handed Albanians whose names begin with 'Z'") or as important as your wedding vows ("I know I promised 'til death do us part,' but I've changed my mind"), there is always disappointment and sometimes heartbreak that goes with promises you can't count on personally.

Sometimes I think it is better not to hear a promise, not to know about a promise, than to hear it and realize the promise is not for you. Better not to know someone else is getting a much better deal because they have a promise you don't. Better not to get your hopes up about a promise only to have them dashed when you discover the promise doesn't count where you're concerned.

What Jesus said about the *Paraclete* in the course of this long evening must have sounded wonderful to the Twelve. You and I get to overhear those promises as we read the Final Discourse in the Gospel of John. But are these promises wonderful for us? Are they meant only for apostolic ears? Could Jesus be speaking over the heads of his Apostles to a larger audience; an audience encompassing all believers of every age; an audience that includes us? And if he is, are we really interested in experiencing the Spirit Jesus talks about in John?

Let me give you three reasons why I believe these promises are for *all* disciples, why I'm convinced they speak to a working of the Spirit better and more vital than signs and wonders, and why we—as disciples today—desperately need the sort of Spirit Jesus offers the Apostles in the Upper Room.

1. John focused long and hard on the Final Discourse and on the *Paraclete* Jesus promised there. The fact that he did so suggests *he* believed Jesus said something, offered something, in his conversation with the Twelve that *all* disciples need to hear and experience.

2. You and I are not apostles. But we have so much in common with the Twelve *as disciples* that the promises about the *Paraclete* fit our needs just as well as theirs. If *they* could not survive and be effective without the *Paraclete*, what hope do *we* have?

3. Jesus promised the *Paraclete* and his unique work would "be with you *forever*" (John 14:16). "Forever" doesn't belong to the Apostles alone. It belongs to us as well. If the *Paraclete* is "with you forever," he is still available to us.

Why the Final Discourse?

It doesn't take a rocket scientist to figure out why Jesus had this final conversation with the Twelve. They needed these promises, and needed them desperately, to survive the difficult days ahead.

But why does John preserve this discourse, at such length and in such detail, for a group of believers who lived at the close of the apostolic era? Why would he think this conversation and these promises were important enough to report (almost verbatim) for the benefit of disciples who weren't in that Upper Room?

These are difficult questions. But they are not merely academic. They go to the heart of how we read this discourse and the sense in which these words are "for us."

I believe Jesus *made* these promises because his disciples needed them, that John *passed on* these promises because his original readers needed them, and that the Spirit *preserved* and *disseminated* John's Gospel because every subsequent believer needs these promises as well.

Consider this: John tells us not a single parable of Jesus. He does not record what Jesus said in the Sermon on the Mount. He omits any reference to Jesus' birth or the Transfiguration or the institution of the Lord's Supper. Five of the twelve Apostles (including Matthew and James) are not even named in the Gospel of John. John is very selective about what he puts into his story of Jesus. If some incident or event doesn't further his purpose for writing, John is quite willing to leave it out. Anything included in this gospel is here for a reason.

Yet John spends a great portion of his book recording the words of the Final Discourse. In fact, it dominates his gospel. He gives more space (by far) to the Final Discourse than to any other event in Jesus' ministry—more space than he devotes to all the signs combined, to the temple controversies, and even to the events of the cross and resurrection.

Think about it. The Gospel of John has twenty-one chapters. Of those, seven chapters (13-19) report the events of a single, twenty-four hour span. Four chapters (13-16) record the particulars of a single conversation. Nearly a third of all the words Jesus speaks in the entire Gospel of John are used right here.

I do the math on this point to underscore the significance John places on this conversation. Certainly, the Final Discourse is significant because of the situation: Jesus is about to die. It is significant because of the weighty themes Jesus addresses: "Love one another;" "I am the way, the truth, and the life;" "Remain in me." The emotional intensity of this conversation would alert us to its significance, if nothing else: themes of betrayal and abandonment, fear and separation, love and loss, persecution and hatred, grief and joy.

But with all that said, I still ask you to look at the numbers. Judging by how much of his Gospel John devoted to this conversation, he must have thought the Final Discourse was the most important exchange, containing the weightiest words, in all of Jesus' ministry. Important not just to the original Twelve but to believers who would read what John wrote and overhear what Jesus said in years to come.

There is no theme more central to this discourse than the *Paraclete* and Jesus' promises about him. The *Paraclete* is the "hub" of the discourse, the core to which Jesus keeps returning after brief forays into other subjects. As such, it is not a stretch to say, when John goes to such great lengths to preserve the Final Discourse, he is, in fact, preserving what Jesus says about the *Paraclete*.

The question we need to ask is, "Why?" The answer is simply that John believed this teaching on the *Paraclete* was important for a wider audience than the Twelve. He thought the readers of his gospel would be encouraged and strengthened by hearing Jesus' promises. He thought the promises about the indwelling Holy Spirit, who would work actively and supernaturally to shape disciples for God's purposes, would have significance to disciples who overheard this last conversation through his writing.

Things were critical at the time John wrote. The believers he addressed with his Gospel were in bad shape. They were suffering, discouraged, uncertain about the future, and wondering why Jesus had not returned. They were hungry for encouraging words to keep them going. John wanted to write a Gospel that, on the one hand, was true to the events of Jesus' ministry but, on the other hand, would be relevant to and beneficial for those disciples who would read what he wrote. So John focused the latter half of his Gospel on the Final Discourse and its recurring promises of the *Paraclete*; on an indwelling Spirit necessary for building the character of disciples and equipping them for ministry; on a Spirit who would grant comfort, courage, and competence; on a Spirit who would mature disciples into the image of Christ and help them bear the glory of God.

This is the first reason I offer to suggest that the *Paraclete* has wider implications for disciples that ripple far beyond the confines of the Upper Room. John focused long and hard on the *Paraclete* Jesus promised in the Final Discourse. The fact that he did so indicates he believed these promises about the *Paraclete* were as pertinent to and as necessary for disciples who read his gospel as for Apostles sixty years earlier. It intimates that the same Spirit who sustained the Twelve when Jesus left is available to sustain John's readers, whether they live in the first or the twenty-first century.

Common Ground

Most of the time, when we talk about the Apostles, we tend to focus on the *differences* between the Apostles and all other disciples. They were with Jesus from the beginning, after all. They walked and talked with him. They were set apart, specially chosen, given the keys of the kingdom. All of them had miraculous powers. Many of them wrote inspired books. Of course, Jesus would have said things to them that were not relevant to ordinary disciples like us.

True enough. The differences between the Apostles and the rest of us are real. I appreciate and respect that fact.

In the matter of the Final Discourse, however, these may be differences that don't make much of a difference. It isn't the *differences* between his Apostles and regular disciples motivating Jesus to talk about the *Paraclete*. It is, in fact, the very things *all* disciples have in common prompting Jesus to promise the *Paraclete*.

Jesus doesn't talk to the Apostles as he does on this final night because they have seen him in the flesh and witnessed his miracles and heard his voice with their own ears (which represents a very real difference between the Apostles and us). Jesus does not offer them the *Paraclete* because they've been with him up-close-and-personal. He offers them the *Paraclete* precisely because they must remain disciples *without* his up-close-and-personal. The whole point of the Final Discourse is that Jesus is going away and they must stay behind. He is leaving and they cannot follow. And if they are to survive his absence, they need the *Paraclete's* presence.

They will spend the remainder of their lives pursuing their mission with Jesus enthroned in heaven, not walking beside them on the earth. They will face a hostile world and endure its hatred without Jesus as buffer and shield. Jesus talks to them about the *Paraclete* because soon he will be dead and gone and they must find a way to muddle through without him. This is common ground between us and the Twelve. We haven't walked and talked with Jesus. But we know what it is to miss our Master. We know all about being disciples *here* while Jesus is *there*. If there is anything disciples share in common—whenever and wherever they are—it is the yearning for Jesus to be present with them, the gaping wound of his absence.

So when Jesus promises the Apostles a *Paraclete* whose presence with them will be his own continuing presence, whose dwelling in them will be better than Jesus-in-the-flesh, we should not be surprised that disciples throughout history take notice and listen harder and wonder whether this offer might be for them. It's not just Apostles who need Jesus close to hand. We need him too. And if the *Paraclete* could provide the presence of Jesus for the Apostles, we want him to do that for us also.

Nor does Jesus talk to the Apostles about the *Paraclete* on this final evening because they have been given an apostolic call. It isn't their status or role that prompts these words about the *Paraclete*; it is the fact that their hearts are troubled and they are afraid. The men Jesus addresses in these chapters aren't big, bold, brave Apostles, full of spiritual courage and wisdom, pregnant with inspired words and miraculous powers. Jesus isn't talking to haloed giants straining to turn the world upside down.

The men we meet at table this night strike us as lesser mortals who seem intimately familiar. They remind us of ourselves. Jesus talks to them of the *Paraclete* because they feel inadequate and insecure and confused. They don't understand. They don't know what to do. Their hearts are troubled. They are timid and limited and lonely. They have a mission bigger than they are. They have a calling larger than themselves.

They need the *Paraclete* not because they are special but because they are so ordinary. They will fail miserably as *disciples*—much less as *Apostles*—unless Jesus leaves behind someone to help them become the men he needs them to be.

Again, we can identify with that. You and I don't have an apostolic calling or role. We will never write an inspired book. But we certainly share the Apostles' fears and anxieties, their insufficiency and doubt, their need for transforming and equipping. Every disciple has felt this need—not just the Twelve. If there is anything disciples of all ages have in common beyond their commitment to follow Jesus, it is the certain knowledge that none of us is equal to the task.

So when Jesus promises the Twelve someone who will *make* them equal to their task, we should not be surprised that disciples through the centuries prick up their ears and crowd closer and ponder whether the promise might be for them. A *Paraclete* who can equip us and teach us and guide us is someone all of us need, common ground between Apostles of old and disciples in every age following. If the Apostles, facing new challenges and difficult situations, would not make a move without the *Paraclete's* guidance, how can we dare to do so?

This is the second reason I offer to suggest the *Paraclete* has implications for the lives of disciples that reach far beyond the confines of the Upper Room. It is the very things we have in common with the Apostles that causes Jesus to talk about the *Paraclete* in the first place. We miss our Master—like they are about to. We feel lonely and inadequate and small—just like they did on this final evening. If the *Paraclete* was Jesus' prescription for what ailed the Twelve, surely the *Paraclete* is the cure for what ails us.

Forever

"I will ask the Father, and he will give you another *Paraclete* to be with you forever—the Spirit of truth . . ." (John 14:16-17).

What does Jesus mean when he says "forever"? So long as the Apostles shall live? Until the miraculous gifts depart? Up to the moment the New Testament is written? Just long enough for us to figure out how to do this "faith" thing on our own?

The Greek word John uses here for "forever" isn't actually a word at all, it's a phrase: *into the ages* (*eis ton aiona*). John uses this expression a dozen times. And in every single case the meaning is clearly "forever," as in the rest of time, all eternity, ever-and-ever-without-end-amen.

Those who drink "living water" will never thirst again *into the ages*—ever, at any time (John 4:14). Those who eat "living bread" will live *into the ages*—eternally, without limit (6:51, 58). Those who keep Jesus' word will never die *into the ages*—death can never harm them, at any time (6:51, 52).

When Jesus promises a *Paraclete* who will be present *into the ages*, there is no time constraint involved, no statute of limitations implied. He isn't promising something for the next thirty of forty years; just until the Apostles die off; just until the New Testament is finished. He isn't suggesting a *Paraclete*-Spirit will eventually be superseded when a sign-Spirit bursts into full bloom. Jesus promises a "forever Spirit" who will remain *into the ages*. This is the third reason I offer to suggest the *Paraclete* remains in our world to touch the lives of disciples long past the circumstances of the Upper Room. He is a "forever" Spirit whose presence is not bounded by certain people or specific situations or unique times. He does a work that is not limited to particular roles or temporary needs.

He is a Spirit sent to be with us *into the ages*. And he will never cease, he will never withdraw, he will never fade for as long as the purposes of God reign.

If the *Paraclete* remains, if his vital work continues, that means the promises Jesus made this last evening still apply. That means this *Paraclete* is for us. This presence and comfort is for us. The promised guidance and teaching are for us. The courage to speak up and the partnership of conviction is for us. And a continuing revelation of the fullness of God, a persistent maturing to contain that fullness, is for us.

John tells us about this Spirit because he wants us to experience the same Presence promised to the Twelve. Disciples then, now, and at every age between are offered this Spirit because we all so desperately need him. And Jesus uses the word "forever" because he wants us to know the same Spirit sent to the Apostles is available for all disciples *into the ages*.

Chapter Fourteen

THE SPIRIT IN OUR EXPERIENCE

In the last chapter, we asked *whether* the promise of the Holy Spirit is for us and answered that question with a vigorous "Yes." In this chapter, we ask *what* the Spirit does in our lives, for modern disciples, with people like you and me.

To get at that question, allow me to return to the strange statement Jesus made to the Twelve on that final night: "Because I have said these things, you are filled with grief. But . . . it is for your good that I'm going away. Unless I go away, the *Paraclete* will not come to you; but if I go, I will send him to you" (John 16:6-7). Or as the New Century Version translates it: "It is *better for you* that I go away."

The Apostles, no doubt, had a hard time believing anything could be better than Jesus. Jesus telling them, "It is for your good that I'm going away," hardly seemed credible. But as we saw in Chapter Eleven, the *Paraclete* offered them more, could do more in them and in the world, than Jesus could. Jesus was (as always) telling them the truth, the whole truth, and nothing but the truth.

But since the promise of the *Paraclete* was never intended for the Apostles alone, since it was meant for every disciple who has followed Jesus after them, we need to consider that this "going away" was *for our good* as well.

We, of course, find that as unbelievable as they did. Better not to walk and talk with Jesus? Better not to see his face and hear his voice?

There's not a one of us who hasn't wished we lived during the times of Jesus, watched him with our own eyes, listened with our own ears. We are convinced if only we had the privilege of being with Jesus-in-the-flesh, our faith would be stronger, our lives would be straighter, and our discipleship would be sturdier.

We don't actually believe we are better off with the *Paraclete* than with a flesh-and-blood Jesus. More than a few of us would trade a lifetime with the Spirit for three years at the feet of Jesus of Nazareth. And we would make that trade absolutely convinced we were getting the better spiritual deal. We'd do the trade, even though it directly contradicts what Jesus says on the matter. We'd trade for Jesus when Jesus went to infinite trouble and pain to bring the Spirit's presence to us in place of himself![1]

He says we're better off with the Spirit, closer to him with the Spirit, better equipped by the Spirit, more competent and confident for kingdom work because of the Spirit. Jesus was eager to leave the flesh so disciples could be blessed by the Spirit's work. Jesus packed himself up and sent himself off so you and I could have an encounter with the Spirit. We, on the other hand, would send the Spirit packing for a few tangible encounters with Jesus.

What does that say about us? What does it say about our trust in our Master, about our willingness to take him at his word? And what does it say about our present experience of the Spirit—that we would trade him away so casually for a few days on a mountainside in Galilee?

Since the promise of the *Paraclete* is for us, the assurance that "it is for your good I am going away" is for us as well. And the reason it is for our good is exactly the same reason it was for the Apostles' good: only when Jesus removed himself could the Spirit come, and only when the Spirit came could disciples begin to experience something better than Jesus, something that truly was *for our good*.

The Promise of Presence

In the five *Paraclete* Passages, Jesus promised the Holy Spirit would do specific works in the lives of disciples and in the world. So what would these works look like . . . in us . . . for us?

Jesus promised, first, that the *Paraclete* would make possible a continuing experience of our Lord's presence.

Jesus has been gone for a long time now. You and I have never seen his face, nor heard his voice, nor felt his hand on our shoulder. It's hard, in the absence of such things, to sense how much he loves us, how pleased he is with us, how closely he watches over us, how attuned he is to our hurts and needs. It's hard to have meaningful relationship with the invisible man.

In fact, the easiest thing to do with this "no-longer-in-the-flesh" reality is to interpret the silence as withdrawal or lack of concern or (even) disapproval. The easiest thing is to feel the distance and wonder whether Jesus is watching or whether he cares or whether he might have given up on us.

But the Spirit makes Jesus present once more (John 14:16-23). This doesn't mean we will see his physical face or hear his actual voice. It does mean the *Paraclete* closes the distance between a departed Jesus and his left-behind disciples so we can feel the intimate relationship his face and voice once conveyed.

Remember that the writers of the New Testament were addressing people who, like us, had never seen the earthly Jesus. These people needed to know Jesus and experience his presence. What Paul and Luke and John offered the first Christians was the same thing Jesus offered the Twelve: the Spirit. Paul, for instance, didn't recount more stories about Jesus to fill in the gaps and help his readers feel closer to their Master. He offered them the Spirit, confident that a vivid experience of Jesus was possible through the Spirit's ministry.

And so he wrote about the Spirit pouring out "the love of Christ" into believers' hearts (Rom 5:5; 15:30; Eph 3:16-18); setting a seal upon Christians so they could have confidence in their salvation and in the love of the Lord who made that salvation possible (Eph 1:13; 2 Cor 1:22); letting disciples know Jesus was alive and well and continually working for their good (Rom 1:4; 8:27, 34). Paul and the other New Testament writers believed it was the Spirit who would help readers experience the person and affection and attentiveness of Jesus. It was the Spirit who would show that Jesus was in them and that they were in Jesus (John 14:20; 1 John 3:24; 4:13). It was the Spirit who would assure them they were—in fact—beloved sons and daughters, valued disciples (Gal 4:6). Those writers were confident that fellowship with the Spirit would help their converts feel united with Christ and comforted by his love (Phil 2:1); that the Spirit who long ago raised Jesus from the grave would keep working to resurrect Jesus, bringing the Crucified One back to life—over and over again—for each of them and (in times to come) every one of us.

The Spirit continues that work in your life and in mine. I believe it is the Spirit who breathes new life into too-familiar gospel stories and thus allows Jesus to live again for me. I believe I hear the voice of Jesus afresh in wise words from a brother or in the forgiveness of my wife—people the Spirit prompts and through whom he speaks. It is the Spirit who allows me to see Jesus alive in a sunset, in a wedding ceremony, in a child, and in the church.

But it's more than that—this ability of the Spirit to make Jesus present. The Spirit touches my emotions and gives me confidence in Jesus' love and approval. The Spirit touches my sense of self and convinces me of my obedience to Jesus and my secure standing before God. The Spirit reminds me that Jesus walks with me through my day, that he is beside me when others criticize (or praise!), that he is intimately aware of my motives and struggles and efforts. My fellowship with the Spirit assures me I am one with Jesus, a true disciple, a follower he loves and values.

In the morning, when I rise, I do so with the words, "Good morning, Lord," because the Spirit prompts those words. As I brush my teeth, I ask Jesus to stay close by me this day because the Spirit puts the thought in my heart and head. I feel embarrassed that Jesus overhears my curt response when I'm cut off in traffic because the Spirit reminds me my Lord is listening. I ask Jesus to give me words of comfort for a grieving family, words of wisdom for a broken couple, words of witness for a doubting soul—because the Spirit whispers constantly that I am not alone, that Jesus sits beside me as I sit with these people. I don't go certain places on the internet or on the hotel TV, not because I am above such fleshly temptations, but because the Spirit pierces me with thoughts of Jesus seeing through my eyes. I listen quietly to someone tear me apart with their brutal criticism because the Spirit helps me realize that Jesus hears what they're saying; he knows what is true of me and what is not; he knows what is in their heart and in mine. I step confidently into warring congregations because the Spirit assures me that Jesus goes with me. I open my much-broken heart yet again because the Spirit convicts me that Jesus strengthens and protects me. I pick myself up, I try again, I find the courage to risk once more, because I know the gracious, patient, powerful Jesus lives within me and will never leave me and will always help me. I know it because the Spirit tells me so.

And when, at last, I lay me down in the evening, it is with the grateful prayer, "Give me Jesus. You can have all this world, but give me Jesus." Sometimes, frankly, those words are little more than a reminder to myself—of what I value, of what I hope. Sometimes they are a desperate plea for the Father to help me keep my priorities straight. But, most of the time, it is a simple prayer to the Spirit, who makes the presence of Jesus within me of greater worth than anything the world could hope to offer.

The Promise of Teaching

He promises, next, that the *Paraclete* will "teach you all things and remind you of everything I have said to you" (John 14:26). He makes this promise in the context of passing on his mission to us. We now have kingdom business squarely in our hands. Yet there is so much we don't understand, so many ways we are inadequate to that task.

How do we continue the mission of Jesus in the twenty-first-century world? What is a faithful response to the rampant materialism of our age? What about the challenges of the Internet? What should we do with a form of modern Christianity so accommodated to culture that matters such as divorce, denominational and racial divides, and lavish lifestyles are commonplace and commonly accepted? Is God pleased by a "Christian Right" that seems more interested in building voting blocs and signing petitions than in finding fresh ways to win the world with cross-shaped living? What about the dilemmas raised by medical technology and bioethics? What is a disciple's proper response to world hunger (brought into our living rooms in hi-def horror) or the Islamic Revolution or the American Empire?

We've never had the chance to put such questions to Jesus. We've never sat on a hillside, looking first at our meager resources, then at a crowd of opportunities, and asking Jesus, "But what are they among so many?"

It's hard, in the absence of specific directions and focused teachings, to know what Jesus thinks about such contemporary challenges, what he thinks should be done about them, how he wants disciples to handle themselves in the midst of them. It's hard to discern the will of an absent Master.

The *Paraclete* equips us for our mission. The Spirit teaches us everything we need to know to do the work Jesus has given us to do. Not just about the things that never change (adultery, hatred, envy), but about those matters that pose fresh and consequential challenges to followers of Jesus.

It was the guidance of the Holy Spirit that enabled the first-century church to wade through the practical issues that constantly plagued it. What should a Jewish church do about Gentiles who wanted a piece of the gospel pie? What about the problems posed by slaves and masters together in the same local congregation? How should disciples handle matters related to idolatry and food sacrificed to idols and the central role pagan temples played in a culture like Corinth's? What was the proper stance to take about paying taxes and showing honor to a government determined to persecute and exterminate followers of the Way? When Jesus did not return again as quickly as the first Christians anticipated, should they keep working to support themselves and their families? Should they marry? What was the status of believers who died in the meantime?

Jesus, in his earthly ministry, said little or nothing about such matters. In fact, some of what he taught seemed contrary to the Spirit's eventual leading (e.g., "I was sent only to the lost sheep of Israel"—Matt 15:24). Yet, in all these ways and more, the *Paraclete* provided practical instruction for the early church and showed them the deeper meaning and wider implications of everything Jesus taught.

He does the same for us. Just because Jesus never addressed the subject of designer dresses or designer drugs doesn't mean he has no "will" about such matters. He still instructs his church about being faithful in a modern context that differs radically from the world of Jerusalem or Rome.

It is the Spirit who teaches me what to think and feel about Muslim extremists or economic melt-downs or the plight of our inner cities. It is the Spirit who shows me how to weight such matters and where they fit into kingdom priorities. Or, at least, the Spirit *could* show me such things if I ever asked him. How often do we—as individual disciples and as communities of faith—submit specific questions about contemporary issues to the judgment of the Holy Spirit . . . then wait on the Spirit and listen for his leading . . . then implement the Spirit's reply with confidence and vigor?

Listening to the Spirit in this manner means I don't always line up with current conservative positions or conventional Christian thinking. Using the Spirit's priorities renders a different "bottom line" for me than the Constitution or fiscal policies or social engineering principles. Since I am such a limited student of things spiritual, it also means positions I once held with such certainty have changed in time . . . become more nuanced . . . become (I believe) more Christ-like. I find, because of the Spirit's teaching work, that I often know more today than I did yesterday. I see things now I didn't then. I'm aware of a bigger picture, a higher priority. What once seemed so threatening to the Kingdom (say, the gay agenda) morphs into something—often concerning myself—even more threatening to the Kingdom (say, my tendency to engage people as abstractions rather than as individuals; or my preference to throw stones rather than love others in sacrificial, cross-shaped ways).

The Spirit teaches us "all things," reminds us (and *enlightens* us) about everything Jesus said, and shows us how to make our way through the quagmire of issues that continue to plague his people. And because he does that "forever" and for all disciples, we can hear a voice strong enough to pierce our stubborn deafness and convict us once again about matters that matter to God.

The Promise of Testimony

Jesus promised, also, that the *Paraclete* would be a "forever" witness to the truth and an active partner in the witness of disciples. "When the *Paraclete* comes . . . he will testify about me. And you also must testify. . . ." (John 15:26-27).

Just like the first disciples, you and I have been called to testify. We understand "Go into all the world and preach the gospel" is for every disciple who has ever followed Jesus. We cannot evade the testimonial burden even though it frightens us.

Yet evade we do. There is, perhaps, no disobedience more characteristic of the modern church than evangelistic muteness. Our chronic laryngitis when it comes to matters of faith is widely lamented and widely ignored. We are afraid of a world that does not want to hear our witness. We feel ill equipped to witness in a world that seems so much more sophisticated than in past times. And, I suspect, we feel embarrassed by compromised lives that cannot back up our testimonial words.

Since we can't say something well, we've decided it is better to say nothing at all.

Good thing we didn't live in New Testament times! The world would never have heard a witnessing peep from us. Yes, our modern world can be hostile to the Christian message, but at least they're not throwing us to the lions! And, no, we're not always "prepared to give an answer for the hope that is within us," but how much more prepared we are now than those first Christians who were "unschooled, ordinary men" (Acts 4:13). And we may not be poster children for powerful Christian living, but we know way too much about the Apostles—their stubbornness and pride and ambition—to believe it was the stellar quality of their lives that gave validity and power to their witness.

Yet they managed to be the light of the world, turning it upside down with the boldness and persistence of their testimony, while we hide our faith under the nearest bowl.

The difference in their witness and ours is not the different worlds we live in or a disparity in the knowledge we bring to the witnessing task or a discrepancy in the lives we live. The difference is that their testimony was Spirit-fueled while, too often, ours is not. They believed the Spirit was busy witnessing to a lost world about the truth of Jesus, recognizing his hand at work in the Ethiopian, Saul, Cornelius, and the Antioch church. And they understood that, when *they* witnessed, it would be by the Spirit's wisdom, with the Spirit's words, and through the Spirit's emboldening power.

That same Spirit is at work witnessing to our world today. He does it through the archaeologist's spade, the NFL coach's statement of faith, the latest discoveries of science, the harsh realities of struggle and sickness and death in every life, and the writings of the most unlikely authors. He does it in a thousand different ways for a million different people every day. He is the stubborn, constant, relentless voice speaking up for Jesus even in a world as broken as ours . . . *especially* in a world as broken as ours.

The fact that we do not hear his witnessing voice or recognize his testifying work says nothing about him and much about us. It says that, in circumstances where the first Christians would immediately see the Holy Spirit and give credit to his work, we remain oblivious, unaware, and insensible of the Spirit's activity. It's not enough for us to open our eyes and "look at the fields ripe for harvest" (John 4:35). We need eyes to see the Spirit already hard at work in those fields.

But more, the Spirit is ready, willing, and eager to do for our witness what he did for theirs: make us fearless in speaking up for Christ, give us words to say and wisdom in saying them, grant us the insight to see who is ready to hear and when the time is right. He is eager to become our partner in testimony.

We are not alone—ours is not the only voice bearing witness to the light. And we are not *alone*—when the time comes for us to speak, the Spirit will be present with us, overcoming our fears and uncertainties. His voice will speak with and in and through our voices, enhancing our timid testimony with the power of the voice that called this world into being.

The Promise of Conviction

Jesus promised, as well, that the *Paraclete* would "convict the world of guilt" (John 16:8). Being willing to tell the truth about yourself is surely one of the hardest requirements for becoming a follower of Jesus.

Yet, just as surely, it is one of the most necessary. The initial step in any Twelve Step program is to "admit we are powerless . . . that our lives have become unmanageable": recovery only begins with the truth about ourselves. The first step of discipleship is to "repent": we have to acknowledge the bad news about ourselves before we ever get to good news. When Jesus teaches that the first step toward God is to be "poor in spirit," he's saying that reaching the end of ourselves is an absolute necessity.

But "admitting," "repenting," and "reaching the end of ourselves" is a tricky business. It requires divine help. Let me give you an example.

I knew someone once who was the proud owner of a sad story. His adulteries were everyone else's fault. The wife was a nagging harpy. The job was stressful. No one really appreciated him. For years he'd denied and minimized and defended himself and his actions. He and his ex had not spoken for ages. His children wanted nothing to do with him. His friends tried to maintain contact, but he required their approval as the price of his company—something they could not afford to give.

He was alone, a solitary fortress bulwarked against any accusation of personal responsibility.

Occasionally through the years, he stopped by my office to talk, bearing Starbucks as his votive offering. In his first visits he tried to explain himself, hungry for my blessing. There was a long period when he used our time together to feel sorry for himself and complain about the tatters of his life. In later chats he was obsessed with healing the rift between himself and his children.

I well remember the day, though, when he knocked at my door with empty hands and brimming eyes. He sat on my couch and, for the first time, confessed his own sins rather than everyone else's. He wept out his guilt and remorse and sorrow. He saw what he'd done, how it had wounded the people he loved, how he was tasting the bitter ashes of a life he himself had burned to the ground.

It was a beautiful moment, the first step on a long road back to himself, to his kids, to God.

I have long forgotten *what* brought this man to a penitent place, the particular pig-pen that forced him to face himself. But I do know *who* led him there.

There is a turning point in people that happens only by the power of the Holy Spirit. It's the point where they "get it," where they see themselves and what they've done with sudden clarity, where their defenses and justifications are washed away by a flood of conviction. There is a point where people can finally tell the truth about themselves without evasion or excuse. And the only thing that brings people to this point is the Holy Spirit.

Time doesn't do it. Awful consequences won't provoke it. Piling up more evidence of personal fault doesn't seem to break through. I've tried prompting repentance in all manner of folk: cheating husbands, angry wives, rebellious children, arrogant church members, bitter septuagenarians, drunks, gluttons, and the greedy. I've confronted and cajoled and pleaded. I've used brow-beating and tears. And the hard-won lesson I've finally learned is this: people won't see the truth about themselves until they are ready; and readiness is a condition only the Spirit of God can produce.

It is the Spirit who brings people to the pig-pen and to that precious moment of self-awareness. It is the Spirit who drives people to their knees. It is the Spirit who holds up a divine mirror to broken lives and then grants people the nerve to look long and hard.

Only the Spirit can convict people of sin. Only the Spirit can bestow the courage required to confess and confront sin. Only the Spirit can lead people to that turning point when they "come to themselves" and speak those healing words: "Father, I have sinned against heaven and against you."

Jesus promises, in this fourth *Paraclete* Passage, that the convicting work of the Spirit will be necessary, will continue, forever. We see the Spirit doing that work in Jerusalem and Corinth and Galatia. And, if only we will open our eyes to it, we can see the Spirit doing that same work in people all around us—harrowing hearts with the plow of conviction so the world will be ready for the gospel seed.

The Promise of Revelation

Finally, Jesus promised the *Paraclete* would "take from what is mine—all that belongs to the Father is mine—and make it known to you" (John 16:15). Jesus came to reveal the Father but had to pass that job on to the *Paraclete* because the disciples couldn't handle his revelation. They did not have the capacity. Time was too short, the story wasn't finished, their containers were too small. So Jesus offered them the *Paraclete* who would do for them what he could not: take all the time in the world; unpack the Father in manageable portions; connect them to the Father at a rate they could handle.

The result of the Spirit's revealing ministry in the lives of the Apostles and the first Christians was a deepening awareness of God, a greater transformation of character, and a growing maturity in the Lord.

Take the cross as but one example.

It was the Spirit who revealed to the first Christians the cross was not what they feared. They thought the cross meant only death and defeat. They thought the cross was the end—for Jesus and for them. But then came resurrection and the Spirit's patient teaching that this was just what the prophets had foretold all along, that the cross was part of God's plan, that Jesus was the atoning sacrifice for a world of sin.

There was more to the cross than that, however. The cross *revealed Jesus*: the depth of his love for us, the extent of his obedience to the Father, his trust in self-giving love as an antidote to the power of sin. And the cross revealed the *Father*: his hatred of sin, his love of the world, the extent to which he would go to win us back to himself. At the cross, we meet a selfless God of boundless mercy and infinite grace. All of this the Spirit revealed to the first Christians; slowly; as they were able to absorb it.

By the day of Pentecost (judging from the sermon delivered then), this was about as much of the cross as Peter and the rest seemed to grasp. Death. Resurrection. God's purposes. The Crucified One as Lord and Christ (Acts 2:14-39).

But the Spirit was not finished unpacking the cross for these believers. By the time of Paul's first letters, the cross that once belonged to Jesus had become a cross all believers bore. It was the symbol and epitome of the selfless, sacrificial, surrendered lifestyle defining disciples of Jesus. Qualities like humility, service, and dying to self became dominant virtues in the life of the church—drawn from the teachings of Jesus, certainly, but rooted in the example of his death.

Even that did not exhaust what the Spirit had to reveal about the cross. Paul's later letters took the central dynamic of Jesus' life (cross and resurrection, death and new life) and applied it to his churches in fresh and profound ways. Now it was not just a servant lifestyle that defined cross-shaped lives; it was an aggressive, unnatural selflessness only truly mature people could demonstrate. Concepts like deferring to each other (Rom 14), limiting personal freedoms for a brother's benefit (1 Cor 8), exercising gifts "for the common good" (1 Cor 12), and suffering as a redemptive act (2 Cor, entire), became the drum Paul thumped with increasing vigor and frequency. Each of these steps was a further extension of the basic message of the cross. Each was a further application of Jesus' cross-shaped attitude to the lives and relationships of his followers. And each depended on the Holy Spirit—in his revealing, teaching role—to unpack the full meaning of the cross ("all that belonged to the Father") for disciples who would never be wise enough or good enough to figure out the cross for themselves.

I am convinced the Spirit is busily unpacking the meaning of the cross for a new generation of disciples today. And not just the cross. This same kind of revelation is taking place as people read their Bibles, as they talk in small groups and seminaries, and as they share spiritual conversations over cups of coffee: the Spirit helping us grasp the nature of God, the mind of Christ, the priorities of the kingdom, and the contours of the spiritual realm. The challenge of deepening disciples, maturing them, growing them up "into the image of Christ," increasing their capacity to know God and live like him—these are the characteristic and necessary works of the Spirit in the church and in disciples today.

We bemoan the plague of immaturity in today's church, the cancer of selfishness. But it's going to take something stronger than small groups and adult Bible classes to kill those diseases. We lament the spiritual shallowness of our people. Yet what we offer them is, "Pray more. Read more. Try harder. Make Christian friends." Our churches have become havens for people with lots of years in the Lord and little cross in them. We've given up on expecting anything better. We won't hold ourselves and others accountable to a higher standard because we're not sure there is a power capable of raising our lives to higher levels. We're stuck with people who are stuck.

But the Spirit is still present among us, doing his revealing work, creating disciples who *know* more of God, *hold* more of God, and *look* more like God. What the Spirit did in Peter and Paul, he can still do today. What the Spirit wanted to do in the Corinthians he still wants to do in us. Transformation, now as then, remains an essential work only the Spirit can accomplish.

Conclusion

This is the *Paraclete* Jesus made available to his disciples two thousand years ago. This is the *Paraclete* who has sustained the church through all the centuries since. And this is the *Paraclete* who has been promised to us, if only we will welcome him into our hearts and lives.

I'm all for reading the Bible and going to church and loving neighbors. I encourage you to pray and sing and take the Lord's Supper. These are wonderful, sustaining, nurturing spiritual activities. These are "means of grace" by which we share in the abundant life of God.

Just don't confuse these things with what Jesus offers us *in his stead*. Don't think for a minute these were what Jesus meant as being "for our good" when he went away. The church was never intended to be a replacement for Immanuel: God with us. Scripture was never imagined to be "better" for us than an ongoing relationship with our Lord. The commands (and obedience to them) are no substitute for the living, indwelling, empowering, constant, ministering *gift* Jesus had in mind for all disciples as he prepared to leave this world and return to his Father.

So by all means pray and study, give alms to the poor and fast, commit yourself to a church family, get involved with a ministry.

But don't imagine these are the things enabling us to survive and thrive as disciples in this day and time. They aren't. They were never intended to be. Jesus has something greater in store for us than this. As his disciples we are more than the beliefs we hold and the church we attend and the good deeds we do. We are more than how much Bible we've memorized or how many hours we spend in prayer or the moral code we live by.

We are the ones who have the Holy Spirit living in us. We are temples containing the *Paraclete*. We are sons and daughters of the Most High God, sealed with the guarantee of the Spirit in our hearts. We are ministers of a new covenant, made competent by the Spirit who gives life. We are those who understand the deep things of God because we have God's Spirit inside us. We are the ones being transformed into the likeness of Christ—from "glory to glory"—because of the Spirit's work within us.

Define yourself (if you must) by where you go to church, or how you choose to worship, or what you believe about this-and-that, or who your Christian friends are. Jesus defines us differently. He defines us in a way that is truly "good" for us. He defines us as people in whom the Holy Spirit has made his home.

And because (for Jesus) this is the foundational fact of our lives as disciples, it is essential (for us as disciples) to make that fact foundational in our hearts and lives. We can't afford to define our discipleship by lesser things and ignore the single truth that is the essence of discipleship. The "Spirit in us" trumps all other denominational or doctrinal or life-style cards. So long as the Spirit is in your hand, even if your other cards are weak, you can't lose.

TIM WOODROOF · 173

The "Spirit in you" is that important. As Paul puts it: "If anyone does not have the Spirit of Christ, he does not belong to Christ" (Rom 8:9).

It is this Spirit who is "for our good," the One who is better for us than Jesus himself. This is the parting gift Jesus offered to help us shine as disciples. This is the Helping Presence who lives in us and works through us forever.

He will be our constant Companion, our powerful Equipper, our Comforter and Encourager, our ever-present Partner, and our Guide into all truth. He will counter our loneliness with love and joy. He will offset our inadequacies with peace and confidence. He can take away our fears by encouraging us to be faithful in witness and gentle with words. He helps us believe we can still make a difference by granting us the courage to be patient and the wisdom to be kind. He will guide us into maturity through an ever-deepening goodness and self-control.

He will keep the promises of Jesus by pouring his fruit into our lives.

It really is "for our good" Jesus has gone away and the Spirit has come.

Chapter Fifteen

TEN DISCIPLINES FOR SEEKING THE SPIRIT

There is a world of difference between having a marriage license and having a marriage. A license gives you *permission* to make a marriage, official *sanction* for a marriage. It permits a wedding to take place.

But having a license doesn't *guarantee* you'll have a marriage; at least not a *good* one! Making a marriage requires more than having permission to do so or signing your name on the dotted line. It takes love and hard work and time to make a marriage. You have to develop certain habits, learn certain skills. It takes *discipline* to make a good, loving, intimate marriage.

In the same way, there is a world of difference between receiving the gift of the Spirit and enjoying the power and benefits of life in the Spirit. Everyone who comes to faith in Jesus Christ and gives their lives to him in repentance and baptism receives the gift of the Spirit. "Peter replied, 'Repent and be baptized, every one of you, in the name of Jesus Christ for the forgiveness of your sins. And you will receive the gift of the Holy Spirit. The promise is for you and your children and for all who are far off—for all whom the Lord our God will call'" (Acts 2:38-39).

The "gift" belongs to all believers. The "promise" is for all believers. We "receive" this Spirit-gift when we give our lives to Christ. But a public and formal declaration of faith in Christ doesn't *guarantee* you'll walk in the power and wisdom of the Spirit. Life in the Spirit requires more than

175

receiving the gift that has been promised. It takes faith and hard work and time to develop a vibrant relationship with the Spirit of God. You have to learn and practice certain habits, certain skills. It takes discipline to grow a good, loving, intimate walk with the Spirit.

Here, for your consideration, are ten suggestions for making yourself more available to the Spirit, ten "disciplines" for seeking the Spirit. For those of you with a practical bent, this is where all the hard slogging through the Spirit-theory pays off. For those who would rather stick with theory, this is where you have to face the challenge of putting theory into practice. Either way, this book won't be complete without applying the principles we've studied to our daily life.

As you read this, don't get discouraged and start thinking, "This is all too much!" Let me confess I am outlining a lifetime's agenda. You don't have to accomplish any of this today. I'm not asking you to master these disciplines by next week. I'm not suggesting we can ever wrap our minds and our lives around the whole thing.

What I am trying to do is paint a different way of looking at discipleship. I'd like you to consider the possibility that—behind all the church-going and elders' meetings and Bible-reading—there is a higher agenda, another dimension, a life-building work going on. I want you to step into the Spirit's realm and experience your life from his perspective. And then I hope to give you some practical guidance about letting the Spirit step into your life and change your perspective forever.

1. Ask for the Spirit

Relationship with the Holy Spirit begins with an invitation. "If you then, being evil, know how to give good gifts to your children, how much more will your heavenly Father give the Holy Spirit to those who ask him" (Luke 11:13).

Yes, there are times in Scripture when the Spirit falls, unasked and unexpected, on people like Cornelius. And, yes, the Spirit can do what he wants, when he wants, with whom he wants. But, as in so much of our interaction with God, the Spirit demonstrates a remarkable respect for and deference to our wills and our wishes. Just as Jesus does not come barging into our lives, demanding faith and obedience "or else," so the

Spirit will not force himself on us, taking up residence where he has not been welcomed. He wants a partner, not a puppet.

And so the Spirit waits for us to invite him inside. We can do this through baptism (a request, not just for forgiveness of sins, but for "the gift of the Holy Spirit"—Acts 2:38). We can do it through prayer (as when Peter and John prayed for Samaritan believers that "they might receive the Holy Spirit"—Acts 8:15). I personally believe we should make this request whenever we participate in communion—inviting the Spirit into our hearts through the medium of the bread and wine.

So eager is the Spirit to collaborate with us, our invitation doesn't have to be very "correct." Don't get hung up on wording or rituals. You don't need to stand on one leg, rubbing your stomach with the left hand while patting your head with the right in order to convince the Spirit of your sincerity. Just ask, in simple, heart-felt words:

> *Father, I believe you have sent the Holy Spirit—the Paraclete—to be my Companion and Comforter. I believe your Son wants me to have a close and forever relationship with the Spirit. So I open my heart and life to him. I ask you to give me the gift you have promised. I trust your Spirit because I know you. He is everything I have come to know and love about Jesus, my Lord. Let your Spirit do his transforming work in me. Make me the disciple you, your Son, and your Spirit want me to be.*

Once you ask, however, it is important that you trust God—your good Father—to give you the gift you've requested.

If you don't know what you're doing, pray to the Father. He loves to help. You'll get his help, and won't be condescended to when you ask for it. Ask boldly, believingly, without a second thought. People who "worry their prayers" are like wind-whipped waves. Don't think you're going to get anything from the Master that way, adrift at sea, keeping all your options open. (Jas 1:5-8— The Message)

So many of God's gifts are second-guessed, I fear: salvation, forgiveness of sins, reconciliation, our status as sons and daughters . . . and especially the indwelling presence of the Spirit in our lives. We may call such second-guessing "humility" or even "spiritual insecurity." The Bible calls it "lack of faith."

So when you ask God for his promised Spirit, do so with confidence that he wants to give the Spirit to you, believing that what you have asked he will accomplish, trusting that your Father will keep his promise. Ask God and then expect him to deliver, expect him to have *already* delivered.

2. Become a Spirit Student

"God has chosen to make known . . . the glorious riches of this mystery, which is Christ in you . . . (Col 1:27).

Our education about the Spirit has been sadly lacking. Some churches don't talk about him much, don't preach and teach about who he is and how he works and why he is important to discipleship today. Even in those churches where the Spirit is the subject of constant attention, the *Paraclete* we meet in John's Final Discourse, the Spirit Jesus himself talks about, is rarely discussed.

Even those of us who have walked with Jesus a long time need to go back to school when it comes to the Holy Spirit. Though asking the Father to give us his Spirit is a good start, that's all it is—a start. Now we need to devote ourselves to becoming students of the Spirit, getting to know this *Paraclete* who promises to be our Companion and Present Helper.

> *Father. I have invited your Spirit into my life. Now I need to know him. I want to learn who he is and what he does and how he acts. Teach me about your Spirit. Allow your Spirit to show me what I have the capacity to see. Let me understand his names and his nature. Teach me his ways and his work. Let him be my Companion in word and deed. Allow me to walk with him intimately, as I long to walk also with you and with your Son.*

The learning process begins by going back to Scripture and meeting the Spirit in the pages of Sacred Writing all over again. Spend some time in the surveys of the Spirit in Scripture I've provided in this book (the chapters of Section One and the Appendices included at the end). Contemplate the Spirit in the lives of Moses, David, and Paul. Memorize the Final Discourse. Immerse yourself in the eighth chapter of Romans. Think long and hard about the second chapter of 1 Corinthians ("no one knows the thoughts of God except the Spirit of God"). Learn what's really being said about the Spirit in the twelfth chapter of that book, and the loving lifestyle Paul calls (in chapter thirteen) the Spirit's "most excellent way." List out the "fruit of the Spirit" and measure yourself by that standard (Gal 5:22-23—need any help to measure up?). Linger over Paul's prayer for the Ephesians (3:14-21) and notice both the central role played by the Spirit and how much Paul's prayer speaks to our highest hopes. There is a great deal the Bible says about the Spirit we've seldom heard. So hear it now. And learn.

What begins with personal study will be enhanced by discussion. Ask a couple of friends to meet you at Starbucks one morning a week for the next few months to talk about the Spirit in Scripture, in the plan of God, and in your lives. Pray together for God to give you wisdom as you seek to know him better.

3. Develop Spirit Eyes

"So we fix our eyes not on what is seen, but on what is unseen. For what is seen is temporary, but what is unseen is eternal" (2 Cor 4:18).

Many of us do not see the Spirit at work in us and in our world. We focus squarely on "what is seen" and what is "temporary." In the meantime, an entire "unseen" sphere unfolds around us, a sphere about which we remain largely unaware.

If you and I are unable to see the Spirit at work in and around us, surely that is due to our Spirit-blindness rather than any inactivity on the Spirit's part. Like the poor man of Bethesda, we see nothing or—at best—we cannot make sense of what we see (Mark 8:22-26). We require repeated touches of the Master's hand before our spiritual sight can be restored . . . before we see more clearly.

So ask God to touch your eyes and open your heart so you can see the Spirit working. Ask him today and tomorrow and the day after. Cry out and do not allow anyone to shush you.

Father, forgive my blindness to your Spirit. Heal me so I may see. Once, it is true, I was convinced I saw everything clearly and, so, I remained blind. But now I know I need your healing touch,

opening my blind eyes and deaf ears and closed heart. Grant me the
ability to see your Spirit, Father, and—in turn—I will give you my
fixed attention.

What good are healed eyes if they won't focus on heavenly things?
Some of our blindness to the Spirit, frankly, isn't a matter of incapacity
but inattention. We walk through life with our Spirit-eyes wide shut. We
don't expect to encounter the Spirit. We don't look and so we don't see.

We need new disciplines that allow us to "fix our eyes on what is
unseen," with the operative word being "fix," as in: "fasten," "glue,"
"habitual focus," "unwavering attention." Watch for the Spirit at work
in the morning headlines, in the events of your day, in the people you
meet and the opportunities you are given. Look to see how he shows
up in times of worship, in moments of need or crisis. Pray God would
not only heal your spiritual blindness but treat your SADD—Spiritual
Attention Deficit Disorder.

4. Build a Spirit Vocabulary

"This is what we speak, not in words taught us by human wisdom
but in words taught by the Spirit, expressing spiritual truths in spiritual
words" (1 Cor 2:13).

One of the things I admire most about my charismatic brothers and
sisters is their eagerness and eloquence in witnessing to the Spirit's work
in their lives. Not only do they see his fingerprints everywhere, they talk
about the Spirit with great ease and joy. "The Spirit convicted me"; "I
haven't felt released by the Spirit"; "I've been seeking the Spirit's wisdom
on this."

Those of us who do not share that religious heritage often lack the
vocabulary to talk about the Spirit this way. Even if we found the courage
to do so, we wouldn't have the words. Speech about the Spirit might as
well be a foreign language to us. We stammer and struggle. Spirit-phrases
feel odd on our tongues. We'd much rather talk Bible or church.

Father, I confess I am "slow of tongue" when it comes to mat-
ters of the Spirit. Jesus, please touch my tongue—as you did with
the mute man—so I can "speak plainly" about the Spirit's work
within me. Forgive me for hardly understanding much less being

able to talk about spiritual truths in spiritual words. I want my speech to honor the Spirit and to be a constant testimony to his grace, goodness, and power.

So learn to use the Spirit's names in prayer and conversation. Hear the phrases used in Scripture ("live according to the Spirit"; "set your mind on what the Spirit desires"; "the mind controlled by the Spirit is life and peace"; "we are led by the Spirit of God"; "the Spirit helps us in our weakness"; "the Spirit intercedes for us"; "the fruit of the Spirit is love, joy, peace," etc.; we are "saved" and "sanctified" and "sealed" by the Spirit) and allow these Spirit-idioms to imprint onto your own mental and verbal routines. Become comfortable talking about the Spirit, giving credit to the Spirit, acknowledging the Spirit's work in your life, in your church, and in the world.

Warning: before our Spirit-speech can ever be heard, it must be *authentic*. We have permission to talk the Spirit-talk only when we walk the Spirit-walk. I've seen people who had the lingo down but lacked the life. Such speech is hypocritical and dishonest. Better to say nothing and have everyone think you a Spirit-fool than to open your mouth insincerely and remove all doubt.

5. Live in the Spirit

"Since we live by the Spirit, let us keep in step with the Spirit" (Gal 5:25).

It's all very well to accept that the Holy Spirit lives in us. It's another thing to understand that *we also live in the Spirit.* There is a sense in which the Spirit "keeps in step" with us by ministering to our particular wounds, recognizing our individual limits, and knowing our specific strengths and weaknesses. But there is also a sense in which we "keep in step" with the Spirit, learning his will and adapting to his ways.

Paul gets at this idea with phrases like: "live according to the Spirit" and be "controlled by the Spirit," "keep in step with the Spirit" and be "led by the Spirit." He believes Christians inhabit a Spirit-environment in which they "speak by the Spirit," "worship by the Spirit," "pray in the Spirit," "love in the Spirit," and bear the "fruit of the Spirit."

Everywhere we turn, everything we do, every action we take—according to Paul—is done within an environment of God's Spirit. We live, breath, and have our very being within the Spirit's realm.

John, of course (in the Final Discourse), is getting at the same idea. The *Paraclete* is our Companion, Teacher, Equipper, Partner, and Guide. He is our new reality. We live our lives in constant reference to him. The Spirit lives in us. And, because of that, we must consciously, faithfully, live in him.

This is the new perspective that shapes disciples' lives. We stepped out of Adam's world and into the realm of the Spirit when we trusted in Jesus. Now we walk in the new way, according to the new realities, of the Spirit's presence.

"Living in the Spirit" means the Spirit sets the agenda for our lives, shapes our priorities, decides our actions and attitudes. It means the Spirit's leading takes precedence over our comfort zones and preferences and traditions. It means we must make the effort to keep up with the Spirit's pace and have the courage to walk in the Spirit's direction. Don't think for a moment that will feel good. It will stretch and push and frustrate you. It will take you places, and at a speed, you don't want to go. That's what Jesus did to the Twelve. It is what the Spirit will do to us . . . if we are willing to keep in step with him.

> *Holy Father. You have promised the Paraclete will live in me and walk with me through all the highways and byways of my life. Teach me that I also live in him and walk with him. Let me devote my life to the Spirit's control and to his leading. Help me to live in Spirit-ways, according to the Spirit's wisdom and power. Let me keep in step with the Spirit, even as he walks beside me as my Companion and Guide.*

6. Pray "in the Spirit"

"But you, dear friends, build yourselves up in your most holy faith and pray in the Holy Spirit" (Jude 1:20).

Is prayer a struggle for you? Do you find your prayers becoming rote and shallow? Do you pray without much conviction your prayers are heard and answered? Do you ever find yourself at a loss to know what to pray or how to pray or even doubting your "right" to pester God with your prayers?

The alternative to tepid prayers, I suggest, is to pray "in the Spirit."

I realize some people believe "praying in the Spirit" referred to an ecstatic experience for first-century Christians, a prayer practice in which disciples were "caught up to the third heaven" (2 Cor 12:2) and spoke in prayer tongues (1 Cor 14:14-15).

But it is more likely that Jude's exhortation to "pray in the Spirit" (Jude 1:20, and Paul's similar injunction—Eph 6:18) had little to do with ecstasy and much to do with mindset. "Pray in the Spirit" most likely meant to pray *with* the Spirit, *in the context* of the Spirit, with *confidence* in the Spirit, through *the agency* of the Spirit, and *because* of the indwelling Spirit. "Pray," says Jude, "and do it with the Spirit very much in mind."

> *Father, you have given me the Paraclete to stand beside me and speak up for me. Remind me I am not alone when I pray to you, that your Spirit gives my prayers power and boldness. And help me trust your Spirit will speak up for me, he will groan and plead on my behalf. Teach me to pray in the Spirit and with the Spirit and through the Spirit . . . to pray because the Spirit is in my heart and on my mind.*

Praying "in the Spirit" would radically change the way we pray, our dependence on prayer, and what we pray for. It would allow us to pray with the confident knowledge the Spirit is in us and provides us access to the Father (Eph 2:18). This kind of praying would remind us constantly the Spirit is helping us pray, interceding for us, translating our groans into groans of his own the Father understands (Rom 8:22-27). We could pray for the Spirit to strengthen us emotionally, in our inner being, with peace, joy, hope, confidence, and love (John 14:27; Eph 3:16; Rom 8:6; 14:17; 15:13; 1 Thess 1:6). We could pray for the Spirit to equip us for effective ministry and for carrying out the mission Jesus has given us to do (1 Cor 12). We could pray for the Spirit to deepen and mature us, making us more like Christ (Rom 8:29; 2 Cor 3:18; Col 3:10).

7. Discover Your Spiritual Gifts

"A spiritual gift is given to each of us so we can help each other." (1 Cor 12:7—NLT)

Do you know what your gift is?

There are (at least) two lists of spiritual gifts found in Scripture: Romans 12:6-8 and 1 Corinthians 12:8-11. Read these lists and see if you find yourself there. You may have more than one of the gifts listed—good for you. But you have *at least* one. It's part of God's plan for you. It's part of God's plan for the church.

So what is your spiritual gift?

Father, please give me the wisdom to know what my true gift is and the courage to use it selflessly in the service of your kingdom. Forgive me when I have hidden your gift away and kept it from the Body. You, through your Spirit, have equipped me to make a difference for your people and in the world. Convict me, by your Spirit, of the need to use my gift for your glory.

You may not be comfortable with the gifts Paul lists for Corinth: messages of wisdom and knowledge, supernatural faith, healing, miraculous powers, prophecy, discerning spirits, speaking in tongues, interpretation of tongues (1 Cor 12:8-11). Okay. Go to Romans and find your gift there: service, teaching, encouragement, generosity, leadership, and showing mercy (Rom 12:6-8). Which gift has God given you "for the common good"?

What is critical is not which list your gift appears on. What's critical is not even which particular gift you've been given. No. What's critical is that you have *identified* the gift God has entrusted to you and are *using* your gift for his glory.

According to Paul (see 1 Corinthians 12), the church you attend will never be the beautiful, functional, powerful body God wants it to be unless you play your part. A gift given "for the common good" becomes—unused—a disability in the body of Christ. The church limps and gasps and blanches when it is missing vital pieces and functions.

And, according to Paul, you will never be the integral, valuable, mature, considerate, cooperative disciple God wants you to be until you put your gift to the use it was intended. You'll be constantly insecure

("The church doesn't need *me*"—12:15) or constantly self-important ("The church doesn't need *you*"—12:21). What you *won't* be is a connected part of the body, living out God's purpose for your life in the context of his church.

Yet, as critical as this matter is, many of us have no clue about our giftedness, no understanding of the important part we play in the body of Christ, and no active involvement in the life and ministries of our churches. The Spirit has given us a gift—just the gift he wanted us to have, just the gift our church needs—and (as often as not) we've buried that gift in the ground.

Inviting the Spirit into your life, becoming a student of the Spirit, learning to see with new eyes, learning to talk in new ways, living and praying in the Spirit mean you no longer have the luxury of ignoring spiritual gifts. Your growth depends on finding your gift. The people around you depend on your finding it. The church you attend needs you to find it.

8. Discern the Spirit in Others

"Brothers, choose seven men from among you who are known to be full of the Spirit and wisdom. We will turn this responsibility over to them and will give our attention to prayer and the ministry of the word" (Acts 6:3-4).

It really does take one to know one.

Who has God's Spirit in them? In whom has that Spirit grown large? Who demonstrates the Spirit's fruit in such a way that, clearly, he or she has walked "a long obedience in the same direction" with the Spirit? Which of your friends or acquaintances has experienced an authentic, transforming, character-building encounter with the Spirit you can rely on?

Questions like these sound nebulous until you consider how much of our interaction with other Christians is built on assumptions about good motive, spiritual maturity and wisdom, common commitments, and shared values and priorities. Seeing the Spirit in others, knowing he is present and active in someone else's life, helps us develop trust and confidence in each other. Failing to see that Spirit in some, or seeing him only dimly, helps us identify people we can't—for now—put much spiritual weight on.

Discerning the Spirit in others does sound vague—even judgmental!—until you recognize how much our discipleship hinges on decisions we make about who we consider wise, whose advice and teaching we seek, who we give permission to shape our thinking, who we turn to at moments of crisis, who we choose as Christian leaders, mentors, and friends. Ever chosen poorly? Ever been deeply disappointed in, deeply wounded by, someone you looked up to spiritually?

We're going to base such relational decisions on *something*. Personality. Persuasiveness. Chemistry. Common history. Demeanor. Public actions. Stated beliefs. Financial success. The Bible suggests there may be another way to make such choices and exercise discretion about other people. It involves asking the Spirit to help you discern his presence in others. It involves looking at others with spiritual eyes rather than fleshly eyes, and making decisions based on spiritual discernment rather than more surface considerations.

> Dear friends, do not believe every spirit, but test the spirits to see whether they are from God, because many false prophets have gone out into the world. This is how you can recognize the Spirit of God: Every spirit that acknowledges that Jesus Christ has come in the flesh is from God, but every spirit that does not acknowledge Jesus is not from God. (1 John 4:1-3)

Such an interesting way for John to put this: "Test the spirits." Why not just give his readers a doctrinal check list and tell them to "test the positions"?[1] Why not give them an ethical check list and tell them to "test the life"?[2] John does all that in his letter. But he does something more. He tells these Christians to "Test the spirits"—as though more is involved with spiritual discernment than assessing particular beliefs or specific lifestyles. John is not just interested in learning about a person's convictions or morality; he wants to know whether or not that person has the Spirit of God.

In fact, the first Christians did this "testing" all the time. The Apostles, for instance, asked the Jerusalem church to "choose seven men from among you who are *known to be full of the Spirit* and wisdom" (Acts 6:3ff) to be given special responsibilities within the church family. And the church responded, not with questions about what in the world "full of the Spirit" meant, but with specific nominations. When the Apostles needed to send a representative to Antioch to check out news of the first Gentile church, they chose Barnabas—the right man for the job because "he was a good man, *full of the Holy Spirit* and faith" (Acts 11:24).

The early church did not give responsibilities or leadership roles to people in whom they could not see the Spirit at work. It's easy to understand why. Only people "full of the Spirit" were equipped to understand the essential business of God's kingdom. Someone who lacked this Spirit would not be able to "accept the things that come from the Spirit of God, for they are foolishness to him, and he cannot understand them, because they are spiritually discerned" (1 Cor 2:14).

> *Father, give me Spirit eyes. Help me see the world, other people, and myself as you do. Teach me to recognize your Spirit in my brothers and sisters, to discern whether the Spirit is burning bright or dim in them. Give me compassion and patience with those who do not know your Spirit as well as I do. Give me humility and respect for those who know your Spirit better. Grant me the gift of discernment so I can know whom to lead and whom to follow.*

9. Think Trinitarian

"May the grace of the Lord Jesus Christ, and the love of God, and the fellowship of the Holy Spirit be with you all" (2 Cor 13:14).

The word "Trinity" is not found in Scripture or on the lips of Jesus and his Apostles. That doesn't mean, however, that the Bible doesn't "think Trinitarian." Indeed, in the pages of Scripture, Father/Son/Spirit are constantly linked. While this is not the place to document this statement (it has been done exhaustively by others), I do suggest that the idea of "Trinity" is foundational to Scripture, even if the word is never used. We cannot understand Jesus or the Spirit or (for that matter) the Father without resort to the notion that God is one-in-three.

God is one. Father, Son, and Spirit are one. The Father is God. The Son is God. The Spirit is God. Jesus was God incarnate. The Spirit is God in us. One God in three persons. One God in three expressions. Blessed Trinity.

I realize, of course, that some find this concept incomprehensible. For them, "Trinity" is more than mystery; it is babble, nonsense. Others are simply impatient with the idea. It's not incomprehensible so much as inconsequential. Who cares? The whole discussion is theological hair-splitting. The whole debate is "much ado about nothing."

But at the heart of the Trinitarian idea is a notion that goes to the heart of our faith. Jesus was not just a good and wise man, a man uniquely equipped to talk to us about God. Jesus was God himself, God in the flesh, God with us (Immanuel!). Jesus is not simply someone we admire; he is someone we *worship*—the "fullness of God in bodily form" (Col 2:9); the One who reveals God to the world because he *was* God (John 1:1, 18).

The list of people who have attempted to drive a wedge between the essence of God and the essence of Jesus is long and lamentable. Strip Jesus of his deity and you've just stripped Christianity of its central tenet. Demote Jesus to any status other than God and our whole structure of belief—revelation, salvation, sanctification—falls apart.

For our purposes, however, what's vital to notice is what this Trinitarian idea says about the Holy Spirit. The Holy Spirit is not just an agent of God, a tool God used to enthuse the early disciples and inspire the New Testament writings. He isn't merely a good influence and a helpful presence. He is God himself, God in other form, God *in* us. The Spirit is not simply someone we admire (or, worse, some*thing* we admire); he is someone we *worship*—the fullness of God in indwelling form; the One who continues to reveal God to the world because he *is* God (John 16:12-15).

The list of people who have attempted to drive a wedge between the essence of God and the essence of the Spirit is also long and just as lamentable. Strip the Spirit of deity and you've just stripped Christianity of its central power. Demote the Spirit to any status other than God and ideas like indwelling, transformation, revelation, and eternal-life-here-and-now lose their meaning.

It is grappling with the idea of "Trinity" that helps us understand the Spirit in you is Christ living in you—the presence of Christ, the teachings of Christ, the fullness of Christ, and the mind of Christ. The Spirit in you is God dwelling in you—bestowing the words of God, the power of God, the will of God, and the presence of God. The Spirit in you is eternal life: not heaven as yet, but what makes heaven "Heaven"—the presence of God, the life of God, a life *with* God.

Father, I know everything that belongs to you has been given to your Son. And I know everything Jesus had, he gave to the Holy Spirit. And now, I know, everything you have entrusted to the Spirit is being poured into me. I am too small to contain it all. I am weak and blind and so limited. Let your Spirit show me the fullness of your Son and the glory of yourself. I praise you and worship you and gratefully give my life to you. I pray this in the name of the Father, the Son, and the Holy Spirit.

10. Spread the Word

"We are witnesses of these things, and so is the Holy Spirit, whom God has given to those who obey him" (Acts 5:32).

Jesus changed the world with eleven men because he was able to convince them, not just to believe, but to witness. I'm thankful you have read this book. I hope it will make a difference in your life. But for this message about the Spirit to take root and grow, you must do more than nod assent and find personal benefit. You must testify.

It's good to "hear and believe." It's better to "hear, believe, and apply." Best of all, though, is to "hear, believe, apply, and tell."

Father, thank you for revealing yourself and your will and your Spirit to me. I'm eager for more. Give me the courage to share this good news with others. Give me the wisdom to share it well. And give me the compassion to love people whatever their response, however ready or not they may be. Prepare the hearts of those I love to hear my testimony to the indwelling Spirit. I trust you to open ears, to determine the time, and to anoint my conversations. May my every effort be for your glory and the good of your people.

"Telling" will help you understand the Spirit better yourself. "Telling" will encourage you to walk in the Spirit more fully, more deeply. But "telling" will also invite the people you love to a richer spiritual experience than they have known. If the ideas expressed in these pages have impacted you, please share them with others.

Chapter Sixteen

A TALE OF TWO CHURCHES

Let's travel back in time to visit two churches, long gone now, but surprisingly familiar to those of us who are acquainted with church today.

The first church was located in Asia Minor, in the city of Laodicea. It was familiar to Paul, though he did not start this congregation and had never visited personally (Col 2:1). But he'd heard about the church in this wealthy manufacturing town and wrote a letter to it (which does not survive). We know about this letter because Paul made reference to it in another letter he wrote—to the church in Colossae: "After this letter has been read to you, see that it is also read in the church of the Laodiceans and that you in turn read the letter from Laodicea" (Col 4:16).

We don't know what Paul wrote to the Laodicean church. We do know what he wrote to the Colossians, however, and can assume the Christians in Laodicea (based on Paul's instruction to read the Colossian letter there) were familiar with Paul's teachings. In particular, they knew about the Spirit. They overheard Paul commending the Colossians for their "love in the Spirit" (1:8) and must have experienced a similar Spirit-love themselves. They read about Paul praying for God to fill the Colossians with "all spiritual wisdom and understanding" (1:9), and must have known he was offering similar prayers on their behalf. And they would have understood what Paul meant when encouraging the Colossians to let "the word of Christ dwell in you richly" and sing "spiritual songs" (3:16), both activities made possible only by the Spirit's active presence. The Laodiceans, grounded in the essential gospel the Apostles preached wherever their missionary work took them, must also have been grounded in the person and work of the Spirit. To the extent that Paul's words to the Colossians were applicable to the Christians of Laodicea, there was a time when walking in the Spirit meant something to the church there.

Fast forward thirty years. We come across this church once again as John is writing his Revelation. In that book, he addresses "the seven churches of Asia Province" (Rev 1:4)—one of which happened to be the Laodicean church. Sadly, the church is in trouble when John writes:

> I know your deeds, that you are neither cold nor hot. I wish you were either one or the other! So, because you are lukewarm— neither hot nor cold—I am about to spit you out of my mouth. You say, 'I am rich; I have acquired wealth and do not need a thing.' But you do not realize that you are wretched, pitiful, poor, blind and naked. I counsel you to buy from me gold refined in the fire, so you can become rich; and white clothes to wear, so you can cover your shameful nakedness; and salve to put on your eyes, so you can see. Those whom I love I rebuke and discipline. So be earnest, and repent. (Rev 3:15-19)

This church had grown complacent, comfortable, and self-content. Wealth had inflated self-reliance and eroded the need for God. John accused these Christians of being spiritually poor, naked, and blind. Judging by their blighted spiritual condition, there does not appear to have been much Spirit in Laodicea. Little of his fruit was showing. None of his fire was evident. Apparently, the Laodiceans had found a way to do church without the Spirit's active and transforming presence.

Sounds like a few churches I know today.

The second church we should notice was located in Greece, in the city of Corinth. It also was familiar to Paul. In fact, his missionary activity began this church (Acts 18) and he spent many months with these people. He wrote at least four letters to the Christians in Corinth (only two of which—1 and 2 Corinthians—survive). He loved these believers as his own spiritual children (2 Cor 6:11-13).

Above all other churches we read about in the New Testament, the Corinthian church was gifted with *charismata*. If you wanted a poster child for miraculous powers and supernatural manifestations of the Spirit, the Corinthian church would be it. Tongues and prophecy. Healings and revelations. These Christians had it all.

And yet, Paul did not consider them "spiritual" (1 Cor 3:1). He calls them "worldly" and "mere infants in Christ." He laments that, for all their gifting, they can only digest spiritual "milk, not solid food" (1 Cor 3:2). He looks past the evidence of their powers to examine the evidence of their lives and sees little sign of the Spirit's work in their factions, quarrelling, pride, immorality, and impatience with the cross.

Apparently, this was a church experiencing enough of the Spirit to perform miraculous feats but not enough of the Spirit to be transformed into Christ-like people. They had the power to heal but not the power to change, mature, and love selflessly.

Two different churches. Two radically different experiences of the Spirit. One church where the Spirit was ignored. Another church where Spirit-gifts were eagerly celebrated. But in neither church was the Spirit's true work being accomplished. Both were filled with unspiritual, immature, wrong-headed, and misdirected members. Both churches, in spite of their differences in experiencing the Spirit, ended up in a similar, unspiritual place.

It is a terrible thing to be a church that lacks the Spirit. But it is equally terrible (and dangerous) to be a church that stops short of the Spirit's greater agenda and quenches the best work the Spirit wants to do in the lives of disciples. I wouldn't want to go to church with the Laodiceans. But neither would I want to go to church with the Corinthians.

The truth of the matter, however, is that many of us do.

Caught

I have seen church done in the absence of the Spirit of God and it is an arid, ugly thing. Powerless, self-reliant, tradition-bound, fearful of the future—the kind of church that experiences no living Spirit cannot be what God intends. It focuses on forms, on ritual, on an obsession with correctness, and is devoid of the transformative vigor that alone produces the image of God and promotes the Kingdom of God. It is a lava tube—a cold and hollow shell formed by a fire that once flowed hot and thick.

I have also seen church done with little *but* Spirit (or at least what is often confused with the Spirit) and it is a frightening, fickle thing. Visceral, abandoned, careless of both past and future—the kind of church that attends to little but signs and wonders is equally not what God intends. It is often impatient with Scripture, suspicious of any authority beyond the Spirit's personal whisperings, hungry for the sensational, and—oddly—devoid of the transformative vigor that promotes holiness and a mature relationship with Christ. It is a river in spate, a torrent breaking out of all channels, a deluge that sweeps away reason and self-control and, eventually, even the gospel itself.

I have seen churches that looked like the Laodicea of old—complacent, content, comfortable—with no expectation the Holy Spirit could break in and do some new thing today. And I have seen churches that looked like Corinth—a lot of tongues and wonders, a lot of Spirit-talk, but little comprehension of the cross or the call to maturity or the true priorities of the Spirit. Both sorts of churches are unworthy of the Name and ill-equipped to conduct God's essential Kingdom business.

Many committed Christians—disciples like you and me—find themselves caught between the rock of Spirit-oblivious church and the hard place of sign-obsessed church. We have no interest in practicing a faith that ignores the Spirit and encourages no living and active Presence within us. Nor are we willing to abandon ourselves to the merely miraculous. We long to invite the Spirit into our lives and into our churches. But that invitation is not extended so we can experience a giddiness of gifts. Rather, we long to experience a supernatural *transformation* that takes broken sinners and grows them into the "fullness of Christ" (Eph 4:13). We need the Spirit; we are hungry for the Spirit; we are eager to seek the Spirit "beyond the sacred page." We suspect there is a relationship with the Spirit more profound than anything we have yet experienced and are quite sure we will not discover it by keeping the Spirit at arm's length. But neither are we ready to stand on a spiritual precipice and leap blindly into a sensational unknown.

We don't want Christ to look at our spiritual walk and accuse us of being lukewarm—neither hot nor cold. But we also don't want Christ to accuse us of being unspiritual, perpetually immature, and lacking the

Spirit's *greatest* gifts—even though we might have the ability to speak in the tongues of men and of angels (1 Cor 13:1).

Spirit, yes. But not Spirit at any cost. Not Spirit at the expense of Scripture or the abandonment of reason or the loss of the essential gospel. Spirit, yes. But not *any* Spirit. A *discerned* Spirit . . . a *tested* Spirit . . . a *trustable* Spirit.

Is there a Spirit for Christians like us? Something, on the one hand, that is real and tangible and personal and powerful? Something, on the other hand, that avoids the dead end of the sensational and the arrogant? Something that produces real spiritual fruit, not just renewed efforts at self-improvement or the distraction of signs?

The Multi-Channeled Stream

The subject of the Holy Spirit is difficult for many of us. Truth be told, it's been a difficult subject for most people at most times, beginning with Paul's labored attempts to talk about the Spirit with the Corinthians and running all the way to modern musings about whether and how the Holy Spirit works in our lives today.

As a start, let's recognize that the relationship between church and Spirit is a multi-channeled stream. For some, the experience of the Spirit rushes full and powerful and public. For others, the experience is more restrained and personal. For still others, the experience is minimal, a trickle. Truth be told, this diverse experience of the Spirit has been a fact-of-Christian-life from the beginning. Turn to the New Testament and you will find churches that were richly charismatic and miraculously endowed: tongues, prophecies, healings, revelations—certain churches seemed to experience the mystically miraculous as a matter of course.

Judging from Paul's letters, however, this was not the case with every first-century church. Roman Christians, for example, were very aware of the Spirit and the need to be "led by the Spirit of God" (Rom 8:14). But there is no hint in Paul's letter to the Romans of the miraculous as a commonplace. No mention of tongues or healings or special wisdom. No indications of charismatic worship. The Romans were certainly con-trolled by the Spirit (Rom 8:6), indwelled by the Spirit (Rom 8:9), helped by the Spirit (Rom 8:26), given peace and joy and hope in the Spirit (Rom 14:17; 15:13). But there is no evidence of charismatic fireworks at Rome. Indeed, a quick comparison of the list of "gifts" enjoyed by the churches in Rome and Corinth makes clear the differences in their experience of the Spirit.

Paul's list of "gifts" in Corinth (1 Cor 12)	Paul's list of "gifts" in Rome (Rom 12)
Message of wisdom	Prophecy
Message of knowledge	Serving
Faith	Teaching
Healing	Encouraging
Miraculous powers	Generosity
Prophecy	Leadership
Distinguishing spirits	Showing mercy
Speaking in tongues	
Interpretation of tongues	

In Corinth the listed gifts are largely extra-normal. In Rome they seem quite ordinary.

In still other New Testament churches—judging again from the letters written to them—an experience of the Spirit is subtle and subdued. The Spirit is barely mentioned in Paul's letters to the Philippians, Timothy, and Titus, or in Peter's epistles. When he *is* mentioned, references are either to the past (what the Spirit did through the prophets or in the ministry of Jesus) or vague (e.g., "the Spirit of glory and of God rests on you"—1 Pet 4:14). James, in his letter, does not mention the Spirit at all.

So the witness of the New Testament appears to suggest that not all churches experienced the Spirit in the same way or to the same degree. The relationship between church and Spirit has been a multi-channeled stream from the beginning.

We see the same thing in the two thousand years of church history stretching between the first century and our own: movements that were radically charismatic; others that focused on unity, holiness, and assurance as the Spirit's true gifts; and yet others where the Spirit played no obvious or prominent role.

Of course, that same multi-channeled stream is evidenced in the variety of experiences of the Spirit enjoyed by various branches of God's people today: the flood of Pentecostalism, the transforming flow of movements like the Wesleyans or the Nazarenes, or the trickle that is the common experience of many mainstream Christians.

The Divide

The problem with diversity, of course, is that it leads so easily to division. There are always those who measure other Christians by the yardstick of their own experience. If one Christian's walk in the Spirit is not identical to another's, there must be something sadly lacking (or perilously excessive) in that Christian's life before God.

For this reason, the subject of the Holy Spirit has provoked division over the long history of the church and continues to do so today. Unity and peace are supposed to be the Spirit's gift to the Body (Eph 4:3). Sadly, whenever we talk about the Spirit, those qualities are often the first casualties of the debate.

There is a large segment of the church today (the "trickle" stream) that regards those whose experience of the Spirit is of the "flood" variety with great suspicion. They question the legitimacy of that experience, the veracity of reports about the Spirit's powerful work, and the credulity of brothers and sisters whose walk in the Spirit differs from their own. Such questions are not off limits. We are commanded, after all, to "test the spirits" (1 John 4:1). "For false Christs and false prophets will appear and perform great signs and miracles to deceive even the elect" (Matt 24:24).

It is only a small step, however, from asking such questions to doing something far more damaging to the cause of Christ: doubting the character and calling of fellow Christians, for example, or dismissing segments of Christ's body with a curt "I don't need you!" (1 Cor 12:21).

Sadly, non-Charismatics aren't alone in damning those whose experience of the Spirit isn't identical to their own. Those who celebrate the Spirit and his gifts often regard brothers and sisters who are not miraculously endowed with equal suspicion. Of course, it is a fatal sin to quench the Spirit of God or blaspheme against him. If that is, in fact, what non-charismatic brothers are doing, charismatically gifted Christians are right to be suspicious.

But is the absence of miraculous giftings (such as tongues) proof that the Spirit is being quenched or hampered? Some charismatics think so. There is an entire strain of Pentecostalism that would doubt the salvation of anyone who cannot speak in tongues! Never mind that the "greater" gifts of the Spirit are evident in their lives—the Spirit's character-fruit, a life of selfless love, the practice of holiness. If these people don't experience the Spirit as "we" do, they just don't measure up spiritually. How ironic that the very Spirit who intends to produce humility and gentleness in God's people becomes, so often, an excuse for pride and judgmentalism.

Both streams of Christian faith need to go back to Paul's basic teaching on the Spirit—1 Corinthians 12. There is one body, even though there are many and different kinds of gifts (vss 4-6). Each member of the body has just the manifestation, to just the degree, that God intends (vss 7-11). This diversity of gifts and experience must never destroy unity . . . indeed, it enhances unity when rightly appreciated (vss 12ff). Many gifts to cover the church's various needs. Many degrees to which those gifts are experienced (weak/strong, mature/immature, honorable/less honorable, presentable/unpresentable—vss 21ff). But still there is one body and each of us belongs to it (vs 27).

If we take these admonitions to the Corinthians seriously (admonitions, by the way, given in a context addressing the very issue of the wide variety and diversity of spiritual gifts!), we must recognize God has given "different kinds of gifts . . . for the common good" and "has arranged the parts of the body, every one of them, just as he wanted them to be" (1 Cor 12:4ff). In the end, dismissing those whose experience of the Spirit differs from our own is an indictment, not of fellow Christians, but of God's wisdom in arranging the body as he has.

Missing the Spirit's Point

Much of our wrangling about the Spirit misses the main point anyway. We seem to argue, when the subject of the Spirit comes up, about matters that are peripheral and inconsequential while ignoring entirely the larger spiritual issues at stake.

Those of us, for instance, who believe that miraculous manifestations of the Spirit ceased with the apostolic era (or, at least, have no place in the lives of disciples today) are determined to debunk the gift of tongues or healing in contemporary times. We construct whole theologies in our efforts to prove that the possibility of and our need for miraculous works of the Spirit no longer exists.

But when we've constructed our rational ramparts against any attack of the supernatural, we seem to overlook one radically important truth: there is no other way the Spirit *can* act upon us and our world *except* through the miraculous and the supernatural. So what if we doubt gifts like prophecy and miraculous powers? The larger question is: do we believe in an indwelling Spirit who changes hearts and teaches us about life and equips us for ministry and grows us into the fullness of Christ? If so, then by definition we believe in a Spirit who works outside of worldly physics, operates by different laws, and is not bound by the "normal" and "natural." How can we speak of a Spirit living in us *except* by talking about the extra-ordinary? How can we claim a Spirit who comforts and guides us, who matures and deepens us, who transforms sinners into saints *without* talking about processes and practices that are "super-natural"?

The Spirit living in us is a miracle. The Spirit operating as our *Paraclete* is a wonder. The Spirit as our "seal" and "guarantee" is a miraculous sign. The Spirit transforming us, conforming us to God's will, reshaping us into the image of Christ is a marvel of God's supernatural power as great (indeed, greater!) than strange words on our lips or healing energy in our hands.

We better hope and pray for a Spirit of the supernatural sort, capable of wonders and awe-inspiring acts. Any lesser Spirit leaves us to our own paltry powers and meager self improvements. When I look honestly at my own heart, I know I need a miracle, a great miracle, and nothing short of a miracle. In that wider context, it's difficult for me to get very excited over the question of whether the Spirit still heals bodies or inspires tongues. If the Spirit has the miraculous power to do what is needed in my heart and mind, he can do whatever he wants with my tongue and hands.

On the other hand, those of us who believe in a present experience of supernatural miracles seem just as likely to miss the main Spirit-point. Like our non-charismatic brothers, we've been equally eager to construct entire theologies and raise reasonable ramparts—only we have done so *in defense* of signs and wonders.

Having done that, however, we've often expended our time and energies defending, celebrating, and exploring the *wrong* signs and wonders . . . the *lesser* signs and wonders . . . the signs and wonders that astonish but do not, necessarily, transform. I am reminded of Samson, enabled by the Spirit to break bonds but not to tame his own lusts;[1] of Saul, empowered to prophesy by the Spirit but incapable of simple obedience to God;[2] of Judas who could cast out demons but could not control the demon in his own heart.[3]

What difference did the miraculous make in the Corinthian church? The experience of the miraculous there was a hindrance to the Spirit's best work, not a help. Their focus on signs and wonders, on the lesser gifts of tongues and healing, led not to a deeper relationship with God, but to spiritual immaturity and an addiction to fleshly things. And what difference does an experience of the miraculous make in many churches today, when carnality, pride, factions, and ignorance seem more the rule than the exception? The last thing some of our churches need is more Spirit-flash rather than more Spirit-substance. We could get along just fine without yet another example of tongue-speaking or faith-healing next Sunday. What we cannot live without, what we must not live without, is a constant and palpable experience of the transforming power of the Spirit at work to change our hearts and conform our minds.

Just as the non-charismatics among us better hope and pray for a Spirit of the supernatural sort, capable of wonders and awe-inspiring acts, so the charismatics among us better hope for a Spirit who has more to offer than out-of-body experiences and sensational, show-stopping signs. We all need a powerful Spirit, working miraculously in our lives. But we all also need a Spirit unleashed to do his greatest work in us: transforming us into the image of Christ, endowing us with the fullness of our Lord.

That is what excites me about the *Paraclete* we meet in John's Gospel. Here we find a living, active, powerful Spirit. Here is a Spirit of stunning vigor and vivacity, a Spirit working wonders in our broken world and our broken lives. Here is a Spirit whose very essence is miraculous and whose greatest work requires his greatest miracles. At the heart of Jesus' *Paraclete* is a Spirit of the supernatural sort, the very kind of Spirit we need to free us from the impossible burden of changing ourselves.

But here also is a Spirit whose miraculous powers are put to use in the service of Kingdom priorities. Here in the Final Discourse, Jesus speaks of a *Paraclete* who knows what his real business is . . . his equipping, encouraging, maturing business. Here is a Spirit dedicated to disciple development, devoted to changing hearts and lives, undistracted by lesser and secondary work. Here is a Spirit who comforts and encourages, teaches and testifies, convicts and transforms, and—ever and always—reveals to us the whole glory of God. Jesus says nothing about this Spirit and our physical health or our financial security or our ability to perform miraculous signs. He speaks, instead to this Spirit's focus on our character, our testimony, our perseverance, and our maturation. He speaks in this manner, I am convinced, not because the physical and financial and miraculous are of little concern to him or the *Paraclete*; but they are certainly not Jesus' or the Spirit's *primary* concern. There is other work, Kingdom work, to be done in the lives of disciples and it is that greatest work Jesus chooses to address in the Final Discourse.

Getting the Spirit Right

Though talking about the Holy Spirit may be difficult for us and for our churches, a discussion of the Spirit is badly needed. Any topic that involves the unity of our congregations, the transforming of our lives, the credibility of our witness, and the depth of our relationship with God is a topic God's people need to talk over long and lovingly.

It is important for us to get the Spirit right, to properly understand his ministry, and to appreciate his work in the world and in our lives. There is great danger, and great vulnerability, whenever the church gets the Spirit wrong.

Like Laodicea of old, it is possible for the modern church to misplace the Spirit and ignore his necessary work in our lives. If that happens, the results can be predicted from their sad experience: complacency, self-contentment, and concession to the merely comfortable. We will find ourselves afflicted with a kind of lukewarm-ness that mires us in apathy and leads to tepid living. No Spirit-fruit growing in our lives. No Spirit-fire blazing in our hearts. Just a spiritual numbness we salve with constant doses of poorly placed priorities and denial of our true spiritual condition. I've known churches like that. I've preached for churches like that. I've been in this "slough of spiritual despond" and I never want to live there again.

Like Corinth of old, on the other hand, it is quite possible for the modern church to mistake spiritual gifts for spirituality. An obsession with signs and wonders, a focus on *external* works of the Spirit, is just as likely to induce a blindness to the Spirit's truest and best work in our lives. If that happens to us, the results can probably be predicted by watching what happened to them: pride, misplaced priorities, factions, carnality. We will find ourselves afflicted with a debilitating immaturity that keeps us "worldly" and mires us in the sensual and the selfish. No meat, just milk. No transformation into Christ's image, just a Christian veneer covering an unchanged core. I've known churches like that. I've seen Christians like that. I've been a Christian like that and I never want to live there again.

If we get the Spirit wrong—at one extreme or the other—the Spirit cannot accomplish his true work in our lives or in our faith-communities. If we get the Spirit wrong, we are damning ourselves and our churches to perpetual immaturity, creeping unspirituality, and lives untouched by the greatest and most powerful works of the Spirit. If we get the Spirit wrong, the cost will be measured in lives wasted, souls lost, and churches destroyed.

A Place Somewhere Between

Somewhere between Spirit-famine and Spirit-excess is a Spirit for the rest of us.

Somewhere between no Spirit and only Spirit is a Spirit for the rest of us.

Somewhere between lifeless tradition and slippery slope, between quenching and disorder, between sitting on our hands and rolling in the aisles, there is a Spirit for the rest of us.

Somewhere between mind-without-Spirit and Spirit-without-mind is a Spirit the rest of us can appreciate and experience. Between the anemia of life-without-the-Spirit and the fever of possession-without-transformation there exists a place where we meet the Spirit and know the Spirit and walk in the Spirit in tangible, trustable ways.

Somewhere between the parched land of an undiscovered Spirit and the trackless swamp of abandon to the Spirit lies that slaking spiritual stream from which we drink and are revived. Between rote liturgy and riotous chaos, between the cold cathedral and the over-heated revival tent, between strict rationalism and frothy emotionalism, between conjugating Greek verbs and babbling in unknown tongues lies a territory where mind and heart find their shared home and we meet the Spirit in all his empowering, transforming, convicting, truth-giving presence.

I want to find that place. That place "somewhere between." That place God has reserved for "the rest of us." You may want to find that place too. If so, I invite you to join me on this journey.

Appendices

Appendix One

"Spirit" References in the Old Testament

Gen 1:2	Now the earth was formless and empty, darkness was over the surface of the deep, and the Spirit of God was hovering over the waters.
Gen 6:3	Then the LORD said, "My Spirit will not contend with man forever, for he is mortal; his days will be a hundred and twenty years."
Gen 41:38	So Pharaoh asked them, "Can we find anyone like this man, one in whom is the spirit of God?"
Exod 31:3	and I have filled him with the Spirit of God, with skill, ability and knowledge in all kinds of crafts
Exod 35:31	and he has filled him with the Spirit of God, with skill, ability and knowledge in all kinds of crafts
Num 11:17	I will come down and speak with you there, and I will take of the Spirit that is on you and put the Spirit on them. They will help you carry the burden of the people so that you will not have to carry it alone.
Num 11:25	Then the LORD came down in the cloud and spoke with him, and he took of the Spirit that was on him and put the Spirit on the seventy elders. When the Spirit rested on them, they prophesied, but they did not do so again.
Num 11:26	However, two men, whose names were Eldad and Medad, had remained in the camp. They were listed among the elders, but did not go out to the Tent. Yet the Spirit also rested on them, and they prophesied in the camp.
Num 11:29	But Moses replied, "Are you jealous for my sake? I wish that all the LORD's people were prophets and that the LORD would put his Spirit on them!"
Num 24:2	When Balaam looked out and saw Israel encamped tribe by tribe, the Spirit of God came upon him
Num 27:18	So the LORD said to Moses, "Take Joshua son of Nun, a man in whom is the spirit, and lay your hand on him.
Deut 34:9	Now Joshua son of Nun was filled with the spirit of wisdom because Moses had laid his hands on him. So the Israelites listened to him and did what the LORD had commanded Moses.
Judg 3:10	The Spirit of the LORD came upon him, so that he became Israel's judge and went to war. The LORD gave Cushan-Rishathaim king of Aram into the hands of Othniel, who overpowered him.

Judg 6:34	Then the Spirit of the LORD came upon Gideon, and he blew a trumpet, summoning the Abiezrites to follow him.
Judg 11:29	Then the Spirit of the LORD came upon Jephthah. He crossed Gilead and Manasseh, passed through Mizpah of Gilead, and from there he advanced against the Ammonites.
Judg 13:25	and the Spirit of the LORD began to stir him while he was in Mahaneh Dan, between Zorah and Eshtaol.
Judg 14:6	The Spirit of the LORD came upon him in power so that he tore the lion apart with his bare hands as he might have torn a young goat. But he told neither his father nor his mother what he had done.
Judg 14:19	Then the Spirit of the LORD came upon him in power. He went down to Ashkelon, struck down thirty of their men, stripped them of their belongings and gave their clothes to those who had explained the riddle. Burning with anger, he went up to his father's house.
Judg 15:14	As he approached Lehi, the Philistines came toward him shouting. The Spirit of the LORD came upon him in power. The ropes on his arms became like charred flax, and the bindings dropped from his hands.
1 Sam 10:6	The Spirit of the LORD will come upon you in power, and you will prophesy with them; and you will be changed into a different person.
1 Sam 10:10	When they arrived at Gibeah, a procession of prophets met him; the Spirit of God came upon him in power, and he joined in their prophesying.
1 Sam 11:6	When Saul heard their words, the Spirit of God came upon him in power, and he burned with anger.
1 Sam 16:13	So Samuel took the horn of oil and anointed him in the presence of his brothers, and from that day on the Spirit of the LORD came upon David in power. Samuel then went to Ramah.
1 Sam 19:20	so he sent men to capture him. But when they saw a group of prophets prophesying, with Samuel standing there as their leader, the Spirit of God came upon Saul's men and they also prophesied.
1 Sam 19:23	So Saul went to Naioth at Ramah. But the Spirit of God came even upon him, and he walked along prophesying until he came to Naioth.
2 Sam 23:2	"The Spirit of the LORD spoke through me; his word was on my tongue.
1 Kgs 18:12	I don't know where the Spirit of the LORD may carry you when I leave you. If I go and tell Ahab and he doesn't find you, he will kill me. Yet I your servant have worshiped the LORD since my youth.
2 Kgs 2:15	The company of the prophets from Jericho, who were watching, said, "The spirit of Elijah is resting on Elisha." And they went to meet him and bowed to the ground before him.

2 Kgs 2:16	"Look," they said, "we your servants have fifty able men. Let them go and look for your master. Perhaps the Spirit of the LORD has picked him up and set him down on some mountain or in some valley." "No," Elisha replied, "do not send them."
1 Chr 12:18	Then the Spirit came upon Amasai, chief of the Thirty, and he said: "We are yours, O David! We are with you, O son of Jesse! Success, success to you, and success to those who help you, for your God will help you." So David received them and made them leaders of his raiding bands.
1 Chr 28:12	He gave him the plans of all that the Spirit had put in his mind for the courts of the temple of the LORD and all the surrounding rooms, for the treasuries of the temple of God and for the treasuries for the dedicated things.
2 Chr 15:1	The Spirit of God came upon Azariah son of Oded.
2 Chr 20:14	Then the Spirit of the LORD came upon Jahaziel son of Zechariah, the son of Benaiah, the son of Jeiel, the son of Mattaniah, a Levite and descendant of Asaph, as he stood in the assembly.
2 Chr 24:20	Then the Spirit of God came upon Zechariah son of Jehoiada the priest. He stood before the people and said, "This is what God says: 'Why do you disobey the LORD's commands? You will not prosper. Because you have forsaken the LORD, he has forsaken you.'"
Neh 9:20	You gave your good Spirit to instruct them. You did not withhold your manna from their mouths, and you gave them water for their thirst.
Neh 9:30	For many years you were patient with them. By your Spirit you admonished them through your prophets. Yet they paid no attention, so you handed them over to the neighboring peoples.
Job 32:8	But it is the spirit in a man, the breath of the Almighty, that gives him understanding.
Job 32:18	For I am full of words, and the spirit within me compels me;
Job 33:4	The Spirit of God has made me; the breath of the Almighty gives me life.
Job 34:14	If it were his intention and he withdrew his spirit and breath,
Ps 51:11	Do not cast me from your presence or take your Holy Spirit from me.
Ps 104:30	When you send your Spirit, they are created, and you renew the face of the earth.
Ps 106:33	for they rebelled against the Spirit of God, and rash words came from Moses' lips.
Ps 139:7	Where can I go from your Spirit? Where can I flee from your presence?
Ps 143:10	Teach me to do your will, for you are my God; may your good Spirit lead me on level ground.

Isa 11:2	The Spirit of the LORD will rest on him— the Spirit of wisdom and of understanding, the Spirit of counsel and of power, the Spirit of knowledge and of the fear of the LORD
Isa 30:1	"Woe to the obstinate children," declares the LORD, "to those who carry out plans that are not mine, forming an alliance, but not by my Spirit, heaping sin upon sin;
Isa 32:15	till the Spirit is poured upon us from on high, and the desert becomes a fertile field, and the fertile field seems like a forest.
Isa 34:16	Look in the scroll of the LORD and read: None of these will be missing, not one will lack her mate. For it is his mouth that has given the order, and his Spirit will gather them together.
Isa 42:1	"Here is my servant, whom I uphold, my chosen one in whom I delight; I will put my Spirit on him and he will bring justice to the nations.
Isa 44:3	For I will pour water on the thirsty land, and streams on the dry ground; I will pour out my Spirit on your offspring, and my blessing on your descendants.
Isa 48:16	"Come near me and listen to this: "From the first announcement I have not spoken in secret; at the time it happens, I am there." And now the Sovereign LORD has sent me, with his Spirit.
Isa 59:21	"As for me, this is my covenant with them," says the LORD. "My Spirit, who is on you, and my words that I have put in your mouth will not depart from your mouth, or from the mouths of your children, or from the mouths of their descendants from this time on and forever," says the LORD.
Isa 61:1	The Spirit of the Sovereign LORD is on me, because the LORD has anointed me to preach good news to the poor. He has sent me to bind up the brokenhearted, to proclaim freedom for the captives and release from darkness for the prisoners,
Isa 63:10	Yet they rebelled and grieved his Holy Spirit. So he turned and became their enemy and he himself fought against them.
Isa 63:11	Then his people recalled the days of old, the days of Moses and his people— where is he who brought them through the sea, with the shepherd of his flock? Where is he who set his Holy Spirit among them,
Isa 63:14	like cattle that go down to the plain, they were given rest by the Spirit of the LORD. This is how you guided your people to make for yourself a glorious name.
Ezek 2:2	As he spoke, the Spirit came into me and raised me to my feet, and I heard him speaking to me.
Ezek 3:12	Then the Spirit lifted me up, and I heard behind me a loud rumbling sound—May the glory of the LORD be praised in his dwelling place!
Ezek 3:14	The Spirit then lifted me up and took me away, and I went in bitterness and in the anger of my spirit, with the strong hand of the LORD upon me.

Ezek 3:24	Then the Spirit came into me and raised me to my feet. He spoke to me and said: "Go, shut yourself inside your house.
Ezek 8:3	He stretched out what looked like a hand and took me by the hair of my head. The Spirit lifted me up between earth and heaven and in visions of God he took me to Jerusalem, to the entrance to the north gate of the inner court, where the idol that provokes to jealousy stood.
Ezek 11:1	Then the Spirit lifted me up and brought me to the gate of the house of the LORD that faces east. There at the entrance to the gate were twenty-five men, and I saw among them Jaazaniah son of Azzur and Pelatiah son of Benaiah, leaders of the people.
Ezek 11:5	Then the Spirit of the LORD came upon me, and he told me to say: "This is what the LORD says: That is what you are saying, O house of Israel, but I know what is going through your mind.
Ezek 11:19	I will give them an undivided heart and put a new spirit in them; I will remove from them their heart of stone and give them a heart of flesh.
Ezek 11:24	The Spirit lifted me up and brought me to the exiles in Babylonia in the vision given by the Spirit of God. Then the vision I had seen went up from me,
Ezek 18:31	Rid yourselves of all the offenses you have committed, and get a new heart and a new spirit. Why will you die, O house of Israel?
Ezek 36:26	I will give you a new heart and put a new spirit in you; I will remove from you your heart of stone and give you a heart of flesh.
Ezek 36:27	And I will put my Spirit in you and move you to follow my decrees and be careful to keep my laws.
Ezek 37:1	The hand of the LORD was upon me, and he brought me out by the Spirit of the LORD and set me in the middle of a valley; it was full of bones.
Ezek 37:14	I will put my Spirit in you and you will live, and I will settle you in your own land. Then you will know that I the LORD have spoken, and I have done it, declares the LORD.'"
Ezek 39:29	I will no longer hide my face from them, for I will pour out my Spirit on the house of Israel, declares the Sovereign LORD."
Ezek 43:5	Then the Spirit lifted me up and brought me into the inner court, and the glory of the LORD filled the temple.
Dan 4:9	I said, "Belteshazzar, chief of the magicians, I know that the spirit of the holy gods is in you, and no mystery is too difficult for you. Here is my dream; interpret it for me.
Dan 4:18	"This is the dream that I, King Nebuchadnezzar, had. Now, Belteshazzar, tell me what it means, for none of the wise men in my kingdom can interpret it for me. But you can, because the spirit of the holy gods is in you."
Dan 5:11	There is a man in your kingdom who has the spirit of the holy gods in him. In the time of your father he was found to have insight and intelligence and wisdom like that of the gods. King

Nebuchadnezzar your father—your father the king, I say— appointed him chief of the magicians, enchanters, astrologers and diviners.

Dan 5:14   I have heard that the spirit of the gods is in you and that you have insight, intelligence and outstanding wisdom.

Joel 2:28   "And afterward, I will pour out my Spirit on all people. Your sons and daughters will prophesy, your old men will dream dreams, your young men will see visions.

Joel 2:29   Even on my servants, both men and women, I will pour out my Spirit in those days.

Mic 2:7   Should it be said, O house of Jacob: "Is the Spirit of the LORD angry? Does he do such things?" "Do not my words do good to him whose ways are upright?

Mic 3:8   But as for me, I am filled with power, with the Spirit of the LORD, and with justice and might, to declare to Jacob his transgression, to Israel his sin.

Hag 2:5   'This is what I covenanted with you when you came out of Egypt. And my Spirit remains among you. Do not fear.'

Zech 4:6   So he said to me, "This is the word of the LORD to Zerubbabel: 'Not by might nor by power, but by my Spirit,' says the LORD Almighty.

Zech 6:8   Then he called to me, "Look, those going toward the north country have given my Spirit rest in the land of the north."

Zech 7:12   They made their hearts as hard as flint and would not listen to the law or to the words that the LORD Almighty had sent by his Spirit through the earlier prophets. So the LORD Almighty was very angry.

Appendix Two

"Spirit" References in the Synoptic Gospels

Matt 1:18	This is how the birth of Jesus Christ came about: His mother Mary was pledged to be married to Joseph, but before they came together, she was found to be with child through the Holy Spirit.
Matt 1:20	But after he had considered this, an angel of the Lord appeared to him in a dream and said, "Joseph son of David, do not be afraid to take Mary home as your wife, because what is conceived in her is from the Holy Spirit.
Matt 3:11	"I baptize you with water for repentance. But after me will come one who is more powerful than I, whose sandals I am not fit to carry. He will baptize you with the Holy Spirit and with fire.
Matt 3:16	As soon as Jesus was baptized, he went up out of the water. At that moment heaven was opened, and he saw the Spirit of God descending like a dove and lighting on him.
Matt 4:1	Then Jesus was led by the Spirit into the desert to be tempted by the devil.
Matt 10:1	He called his twelve disciples to him and gave them authority to drive out evil spirits and to heal every disease and sickness.
Matt 10:20	for it will not be you speaking, but the Spirit of your Father speaking through you.
Matt 12:18	"Here is my servant whom I have chosen, the one I love, in whom I delight; I will put my Spirit on him, and he will proclaim justice to the nations.
Matt 12:28	But if I drive out demons by the Spirit of God, then the kingdom of God has come upon you.
Matt 12:31	And so I tell you, every sin and blasphemy will be forgiven men, but the blasphemy against the Spirit will not be forgiven.
Matt 12:32	Anyone who speaks a word against the Son of Man will be forgiven, but anyone who speaks against the Holy Spirit will not be forgiven, either in this age or in the age to come.
Matt 22:43	He said to them, "How is it then that David, speaking by the Spirit, calls him 'Lord'? For he says,
Matt 28:19	Therefore go and make disciples of all nations, baptizing them in the name of the Father and of the Son and of the Holy Spirit,
Mark 1:8	I baptize you with water, but he will baptize you with the Holy Spirit."
Mark 1:10	As Jesus was coming up out of the water, he saw heaven being torn open and the Spirit descending on him like a dove.
Mark 1:12	At once the Spirit sent him out into the desert,
Mark 3:29	But whoever blasphemes against the Holy Spirit will never be forgiven; he is guilty of an eternal sin."
Mark 12:36	David himself, speaking by the Holy Spirit, declared: "'The Lord said to my Lord: "Sit at my right hand until I put your enemies under your feet."'

Mark 13:11	Whenever you are arrested and brought to trial, do not worry beforehand about what to say. Just say whatever is given you at the time, for it is not you speaking, but the Holy Spirit.
Luke 1:15	for he will be great in the sight of the Lord. He is never to take wine or other fermented drink, and he will be filled with the Holy Spirit even from birth.
Luke 1:35	The angel answered, "The Holy Spirit will come upon you, and the power of the Most High will overshadow you. So the holy one to be born will be called the Son of God.
Luke 1:41	When Elizabeth heard Mary's greeting, the baby leaped in her womb, and Elizabeth was filled with the Holy Spirit.
Luke 1:67	His father Zechariah was filled with the Holy Spirit and prophesied:
Luke 2:25	Now there was a man in Jerusalem called Simeon, who was righteous and devout. He was waiting for the consolation of Israel, and the Holy Spirit was upon him.
Luke 2:26	It had been revealed to him by the Holy Spirit that he would not die before he had seen the Lord's Christ.
Luke 2:27	Moved by the Spirit, he went into the temple courts. When the parents brought in the child Jesus to do for him what the custom of the Law required,
Luke 3:16	John answered them all, "I baptize you with water. But one more powerful than I will come, the thongs of whose sandals I am not worthy to untie. He will baptize you with the Holy Spirit and with fire.
Luke 3:22	and the Holy Spirit descended on him in bodily form like a dove. And a voice came from heaven: "You are my Son, whom I love; with you I am well pleased."
Luke 4:1	Jesus, full of the Holy Spirit, returned from the Jordan and was led by the Spirit in the desert,
Luke 4:14	Jesus returned to Galilee in the power of the Spirit, and news about him spread through the whole countryside.
Luke 4:18	"The Spirit of the Lord is on me, because he has anointed me to preach good news to the poor. He has sent me to proclaim freedom for the prisoners and recovery of sight for the blind, to release the oppressed,
Luke 10:21	At that time Jesus, full of joy through the Holy Spirit, said, "I praise you, Father, Lord of heaven and earth, because you have hidden these things from the wise and learned, and revealed them to little children. Yes, Father, for this was your good pleasure.
Luke 11:13	If you then, though you are evil, know how to give good gifts to your children, how much more will your Father in heaven give the Holy Spirit to those who ask him!"
Luke 12:10	And everyone who speaks a word against the Son of Man will be forgiven, but anyone who blasphemes against the Holy Spirit will not be forgiven.
Luke 12:12	for the Holy Spirit will teach you at that time what you should say."

Appendix Three

"Spirit" References in Acts

Acts 1:2	. . . until the day he was taken up to heaven, after giving instructions through the Holy Spirit to the apostles he had chosen.
Acts 1:5	For John baptized with water, but in a few days you will be baptized with the Holy Spirit.
Acts 1:8	But you will receive power when the Holy Spirit comes on you; and you will be my witnesses in Jerusalem, and in all Judea and Samaria, and to the ends of the earth.
Acts 1:16	"Brothers, the Scripture had to be fulfilled which the Holy Spirit spoke long ago through the mouth of David concerning Judas, who served as guide for those who arrested Jesus . . .
Acts 2:4	All of them were filled with the Holy Spirit and began to speak in other tongues as the Spirit enabled them.
Acts 2:17	In the last days, God says, I will pour out my Spirit on all people. Your sons and daughters will prophesy, your young men will see visions, your old men will dream dreams.
Acts 2:18	Even on my servants, both men and women, I will pour out my Spirit in those days, and they will prophesy.
Acts 2:33	Exalted to the right hand of God, he has received from the Father the promised Holy Spirit and has poured out what you now see and hear.
Acts 2:38	Peter replied, "Repent and be baptized, every one of you, in the name of Jesus Christ for the forgiveness of your sins. And you will receive the gift of the Holy Spirit."
Acts 4:8	Then Peter, filled with the Holy Spirit, said to them: "Rulers and elders of the people . . ."
Acts 4:25	You spoke by the Holy Spirit through the mouth of your servant, our father David: "'Why do the nations rage and the peoples plot in vain? . . .'"
Acts 4:31	After they prayed, the place where they were meeting was shaken. And they were all filled with the Holy Spirit and spoke the word of God boldly.
Acts 5:3	Then Peter said, "Ananias, how is it that Satan has so filled your heart that you have lied to the Holy Spirit and have kept for yourself some of the money you received for the land? . . ."
Acts 5:9	Peter said to her, "How could you agree to test the Spirit of the Lord? Look! The feet of the men who buried your husband are at the door, and they will carry you out also."
Acts 5:32	"We are witnesses of these things, and so is the Holy Spirit, whom God has given to those who obey him."
Acts 6:3	Brothers, choose seven men from among you who are known to be full of the Spirit and wisdom. We will turn this responsibility over to them

Acts 6:5	This proposal pleased the whole group. They chose Stephen, a man full of faith and of the Holy Spirit; also Philip, Procorus, Nicanor, Timon, Parmenas, and Nicolas from Antioch, a convert to Judaism.
Acts 6:10	. . . but they could not stand up against his wisdom or the Spirit by whom he spoke.
Acts 7:51	"You stiff-necked people, with uncircumcised hearts and ears! You are just like your fathers: You always resist the Holy Spirit!"
Acts 7:55	But Stephen, full of the Holy Spirit, looked up to heaven and saw the glory of God, and Jesus standing at the right hand of God.
Acts 8:15	When they arrived, they prayed for them that they might receive the Holy Spirit,
Acts 8:16	. . . because the Holy Spirit had not yet come upon any of them; they had simply been baptized into the name of the Lord Jesus.
Acts 8:17	Then Peter and John placed their hands on them, and they received the Holy Spirit.
Acts 8:18	When Simon saw that the Spirit was given at the laying on of the apostles' hands, he offered them money
Acts 8:19	and said, "Give me also this ability so that everyone on whom I lay my hands may receive the Holy Spirit."
Acts 8:29	The Spirit told Philip, "Go to that chariot and stay near it."
Acts 8:39	When they came up out of the water, the Spirit of the Lord suddenly took Philip away, and the eunuch did not see him again, but went on his way rejoicing.
Acts 9:17	Then Ananias went to the house and entered it. Placing his hands on Saul, he said, "Brother Saul, the Lord—Jesus, who appeared to you on the road as you were coming here—has sent me so that you may see again and be filled with the Holy Spirit."
Acts 9:31	Then the church throughout Judea, Galilee and Samaria enjoyed a time of peace. It was strengthened; and encouraged by the Holy Spirit, it grew in numbers, living in the fear of the Lord.
Acts 10:19	While Peter was still thinking about the vision, the Spirit said to him, "Simon, three men are looking for you. . . ."
Acts 10:38	. . . how God anointed Jesus of Nazareth with the Holy Spirit and power, and how he went around doing good and healing all who were under the power of the devil, because God was with him.
Acts 10:44	While Peter was still speaking these words, the Holy Spirit came on all who heard the message.
Acts 10:45	The circumcised believers who had come with Peter were astonished that the gift of the Holy Spirit had been poured out even on the Gentiles.
Acts 10:47	Then Peter said, "Can anyone keep these people from being baptized with water? They have received the Holy Spirit just as we have."
Acts 11:12	The Spirit told me to have no hesitation about going with them. These six brothers also went with me, and we entered the man's house.

Acts 11:15	As I began to speak, the Holy Spirit came on them as he had come on us at the beginning.
Acts 11:16	Then I remembered what the Lord had said: 'John baptized with water, but you will be baptized with the Holy Spirit.'
Acts 11:24	He was a good man, full of the Holy Spirit and faith, and a great number of people were brought to the Lord.
Acts 11:28	One of them, named Agabus, stood up and through the Spirit predicted that a severe famine would spread over the entire Roman world. (This happened during the reign of Claudius.)
Acts 13:2	While they were worshiping the Lord and fasting, the Holy Spirit said, "Set apart for me Barnabas and Saul for the work to which I have called them."
Acts 13:4	The two of them, sent on their way by the Holy Spirit, went down to Seleucia and sailed from there to Cyprus.
Acts 13:9	Then Saul, who was also called Paul, filled with the Holy Spirit, looked straight at Elymas and said . . .
Acts 13:52	And the disciples were filled with joy and with the Holy Spirit.
Acts 15:8	God, who knows the heart, showed that he accepted them by giving the Holy Spirit to them, just as he did to us.
Acts 15:28	It seemed good to the Holy Spirit and to us not to burden you with anything beyond the following requirements . . .
Acts 16:6	Paul and his companions traveled throughout the region of Phrygia and Galatia, having been kept by the Holy Spirit from preaching the word in the province of Asia.
Acts 16:7	When they came to the border of Mysia, they tried to enter Bithynia, but the Spirit of Jesus would not allow them to.
Acts 19:2	. . . and asked them, "Did you receive the Holy Spirit when you believed?" They answered, "No, we have not even heard that there is a Holy Spirit."
Acts 19:6	When Paul placed his hands on them, the Holy Spirit came on them, and they spoke in tongues and prophesied.
Acts 20:22	"And now, compelled by the Spirit, I am going to Jerusalem, not knowing what will happen to me there.
Acts 20:23	I only know that in every city the Holy Spirit warns me that prison and hardships are facing me. . . ."
Acts 20:28	Keep watch over yourselves and all the flock of which the Holy Spirit has made you overseers. Be shepherds of the church of God, which he bought with his own blood.
Acts 21:4	Finding the disciples there, we stayed with them seven days. Through the Spirit they urged Paul not to go on to Jerusalem.
Acts 21:11	Coming over to us, he took Paul's belt, tied his own hands and feet with it and said, "The Holy Spirit says, 'In this way the Jews of Jerusalem will bind the owner of this belt and will hand him over to the Gentiles.'"
Acts 28:25	They disagreed among themselves and began to leave after Paul had made this final statement: "The Holy Spirit spoke the truth to your forefathers when he said through Isaiah the prophet. . ."

Appendix Four

"Spirit" References in Paul's Writings

Rom 1:4   . . . and who through the Spirit of holiness was declared with power to be the Son of God by his resurrection from the dead: Jesus Christ our Lord.

Rom 2:29   No, a man is a Jew if he is one inwardly; and circumcision is circumcision of the heart, by the Spirit, not by the written code. Such a man's praise is not from men, but from God.

Rom 5:5   And hope does not disappoint us, because God has poured out his love into our hearts by the Holy Spirit, whom he has given us.

Rom 7:6   But now, by dying to what once bound us, we have been released from the law so that we serve in the new way of the Spirit, and not in the old way of the written code.

Rom 8:2   . . . because through Christ Jesus the law of the Spirit of life set me free from the law of sin and death.

Rom 8:4   . . . in order that the righteous requirements of the law might be fully met in us, who do not live according to the sinful nature but according to the Spirit.

Rom 8:5   Those who live according to the sinful nature have their minds set on what that nature desires; but those who live in accordance with the Spirit have their minds set on what the Spirit desires.

Rom 8:6   The mind of sinful man is death, but the mind controlled by the Spirit is life and peace. . .

Rom 8:9   You, however, are controlled not by the sinful nature but by the Spirit, if the Spirit of God lives in you. And if anyone does not have the Spirit of Christ, he does not belong to Christ.

Rom 8:11   And if the Spirit of him who raised Jesus from the dead is living in you, he who raised Christ from the dead will also give life to your mortal bodies through his Spirit, who lives in you.

Rom 8:13   For if you live according to the sinful nature, you will die; but if by the Spirit you put to death the misdeeds of the body, you will live,

Rom 8:14   because those who are led by the Spirit of God are sons of God.

Rom 8:15   For you did not receive a spirit that makes you a slave again to fear, but you received the Spirit of sonship. And by him we cry, "Abba, Father."

Rom 8:16   The Spirit himself testifies with our spirit that we are God's children.

Rom 8:23   Not only so, but we ourselves, who have the firstfruits of the Spirit, groan inwardly as we wait eagerly for our adoption as sons, the redemption of our bodies.

Rom 8:26   In the same way, the Spirit helps us in our weakness. We do not know what we ought to pray for, but the Spirit himself intercedes for us with groans that words cannot express.

Rom 8:27	And he who searches our hearts knows the mind of the Spirit, because the Spirit intercedes for the saints in accordance with God's will.
Rom 9:1	I speak the truth in Christ—I am not lying, my conscience confirms it in the Holy Spirit. . .
Rom 14:17	For the kingdom of God is not a matter of eating and drinking, but of righteousness, peace and joy in the Holy Spirit,
Rom 15:13	May the God of hope fill you with all joy and peace as you trust in him, so that you may overflow with hope by the power of the Holy Spirit.
Rom 15:16	. . . to be a minister of Christ Jesus to the Gentiles with the priestly duty of proclaiming the gospel of God, so that the Gentiles might become an offering acceptable to God, sanctified by the Holy Spirit.
Rom 15:19	. . . by the power of signs and miracles, through the power of the Spirit. So from Jerusalem all the way around to Illyricum, I have fully proclaimed the gospel of Christ.
Rom 15:30	I urge you, brothers, by our Lord Jesus Christ and by the love of the Spirit, to join me in my struggle by praying to God for me.
1 Cor 2:4	My message and my preaching were not with wise and persuasive words, but with a demonstration of the Spirit's power,
1 Cor 2:10	. . . but God has revealed it to us by his Spirit. The Spirit searches all things, even the deep things of God.
1 Cor 2:11	For who among men knows the thoughts of a man except the man's spirit within him? In the same way no one knows the thoughts of God except the Spirit of God.
1 Cor 2:12	We have not received the spirit of the world but the Spirit who is from God, that we may understand what God has freely given us.
1 Cor 2:13	This is what we speak, not in words taught us by human wisdom but in words taught by the Spirit, expressing spiritual truths in spiritual words.
1 Cor 2:14	The man without the Spirit does not accept the things that come from the Spirit of God, for they are foolishness to him, and he cannot understand them, because they are spiritually discerned.
1 Cor 3:16	Don't you know that you yourselves are God's temple and that God's Spirit lives in you?
1 Cor 6:11	And that is what some of you were. But you were washed, you were sanctified, you were justified in the name of the Lord Jesus Christ and by the Spirit of our God.
1 Cor 6:19	Do you not know that your body is a temple of the Holy Spirit, who is in you, whom you have received from God? You are not your own. . .
1 Cor 7:40	In my judgment, she is happier if she stays as she is—and I think that I too have the Spirit of God.

1 Cor 12:3	Therefore I tell you that no one who is speaking by the Spirit of God says, "Jesus be cursed," and no one can say, "Jesus is Lord," except by the Holy Spirit.
1 Cor 12:4	There are different kinds of gifts, but the same Spirit.
1 Cor 12:7	Now to each one the manifestation of the Spirit is given for the common good.
1 Cor 12:8	To one there is given through the Spirit the message of wisdom, to another the message of knowledge by means of the same Spirit,
1 Cor 12:9	to another faith by the same Spirit, to another gifts of healing by that one Spirit. . .
1 Cor 12:11	All these are the work of one and the same Spirit, and he gives them to each one, just as he determines.
1 Cor 12:13	For we were all baptized by one Spirit into one body—whether Jews or Greeks, slave or free—and we were all given the one Spirit to drink.
2 Cor 1:22	. . . set his seal of ownership on us, and put his Spirit in our hearts as a deposit, guaranteeing what is to come.
2 Cor 3:3	You show that you are a letter from Christ, the result of our ministry, written not with ink but with the Spirit of the living God, not on tablets of stone but on tablets of human hearts.
2 Cor 3:6	He has made us competent as ministers of a new covenant—not of the letter but of the Spirit; for the letter kills, but the Spirit gives life.
2 Cor 3:8	. . . will not the ministry of the Spirit be even more glorious?
2 Cor 3:17	Now the Lord is the Spirit, and where the Spirit of the Lord is, there is freedom.
2 Cor 3:18	And we, who with unveiled faces all reflect the Lord's glory, are being transformed into his likeness with ever-increasing glory, which comes from the Lord, who is the Spirit.
2 Cor 5:5	Now it is God who has made us for this very purpose and has given us the Spirit as a deposit, guaranteeing what is to come.
2 Cor 6:6	. . . in purity, understanding, patience and kindness; in the Holy Spirit and in sincere love. . .
2 Cor 11:4	For if someone comes to you and preaches a Jesus other than the Jesus we preached, or if you receive a different spirit from the one you received, or a different gospel from the one you accepted, you put up with it easily enough.
2 Cor 13:14	May the grace of the Lord Jesus Christ, and the love of God, and the fellowship of the Holy Spirit be with you all.
Gal 3:2	I would like to learn just one thing from you: Did you receive the Spirit by observing the law, or by believing what you heard?
Gal 3:3	Are you so foolish? After beginning with the Spirit, are you now trying to attain your goal by human effort?
Gal 3:5	Does God give you his Spirit and work miracles among you because you observe the law, or because you believe what you heard?

Gal 3:14	He redeemed us in order that the blessing given to Abraham might come to the Gentiles through Christ Jesus, so that by faith we might receive the promise of the Spirit.
Gal 4:6	Because you are sons, God sent the Spirit of his Son into our hearts, the Spirit who calls out, "Abba, Father."
Gal 4:29	At that time the son born in the ordinary way persecuted the son born by the power of the Spirit. It is the same now.
Gal 5:5	But by faith we eagerly await through the Spirit the righteousness for which we hope.
Gal 5:16	So I say, live by the Spirit, and you will not gratify the desires of the sinful nature.
Gal 5:17	For the sinful nature desires what is contrary to the Spirit, and the Spirit what is contrary to the sinful nature. They are in conflict with each other, so that you do not do what you want.
Gal 5:18	But if you are led by the Spirit, you are not under law.
Gal 5:22	But the fruit of the Spirit is love, joy, peace, patience, kindness, goodness, faithfulness. . .
Gal 5:25	Since we live by the Spirit, let us keep in step with the Spirit.
Gal 6:8	The one who sows to please his sinful nature, from that nature will reap destruction; the one who sows to please the Spirit, from the Spirit will reap eternal life.
Eph 1:13	And you also were included in Christ when you heard the word of truth, the gospel of your salvation. Having believed, you were marked in him with a seal, the promised Holy Spirit. . .
Eph 1:17	I keep asking that the God of our Lord Jesus Christ, the glorious Father, may give you the Spirit of wisdom and revelation, so that you may know him better.
Eph 2:18	For through him we both have access to the Father by one Spirit.
Eph 2:22	And in him you too are being built together to become a dwelling in which God lives by his Spirit.
Eph 3:5	. . . which was not made known to men in other generations as it has now been revealed by the Spirit to God's holy apostles and prophets.
Eph 3:16	I pray that out of his glorious riches he may strengthen you with power through his Spirit in your inner being. . .
Eph 4:3	Make every effort to keep the unity of the Spirit through the bond of peace.
Eph 4:4	There is one body and one Spirit—just as you were called to one hope when you were called. . .
Eph 4:30	And do not grieve the Holy Spirit of God, with whom you were sealed for the day of redemption.
Eph 5:18	Do not get drunk on wine, which leads to debauchery. Instead, be filled with the Spirit.
Eph 6:17	Take the helmet of salvation and the sword of the Spirit, which is the word of God.

Eph 6:18	And pray in the Spirit on all occasions with all kinds of prayers and requests. With this in mind, be alert and always keep on praying for all the saints.
Phil 1:19	Yes, and I will continue to rejoice, for I know that through your prayers and the help given by the Spirit of Jesus Christ, what has happened to me will turn out for my deliverance.
Phil 2:1	If you have any encouragement from being united with Christ, if any comfort from his love, if any fellowship with the Spirit, if any tenderness and compassion. . .
Phil 3:3	For it is we who are the circumcision, we who worship by the Spirit of God, who glory in Christ Jesus, and who put no confidence in the flesh. . .
Col 1:8	. . . and who also told us of your love in the Spirit.
1 Thess 1:5	. . . because our gospel came to you not simply with words, but also with power, with the Holy Spirit and with deep conviction. You know how we lived among you for your sake.
1 Thess 1:6	You became imitators of us and of the Lord; in spite of severe suffering, you welcomed the message with the joy given by the Holy Spirit.
1 Thess 4:8	Therefore, he who rejects this instruction does not reject man but God, who gives you his Holy Spirit.
1 Thess 5:19	Do not put out the Spirit's fire. . .
2 Thess 2:13	But we ought always to thank God for you, brothers loved by the Lord, because from the beginning God chose you to be saved through the sanctifying work of the Spirit and through belief in the truth.
1 Tim 3:16	Beyond all question, the mystery of godliness is great: He appeared in a body, was vindicated by the Spirit, was seen by angels, was preached among the nations, was believed on in the world, was taken up in glory.
1 Tim 4:1	The Spirit clearly says that in later times some will abandon the faith and follow deceiving spirits and things taught by demons.
2 Tim 1:14	Guard the good deposit that was entrusted to you—guard it with the help of the Holy Spirit who lives in us.
Titus 3:5	. . . he saved us, not because of righteous things we had done, but because of his mercy. He saved us through the washing of rebirth and renewal by the Holy Spirit. . .

Appendix Five

"Spirit" References in John

John 1:32	Then John gave this testimony: "I saw the Spirit come down from heaven as a dove and remain on him.
John 1:33	I would not have known him, except that the one who sent me to baptize with water told me, 'The man on whom you see the Spirit come down and remain is he who will baptize with the Holy Spirit.'
John 3:5	Jesus answered, "I tell you the truth, no one can enter the kingdom of God unless he is born of water and the Spirit.
John 3:6	Flesh gives birth to flesh, but the Spirit gives birth to spirit.
John 3:8	The wind blows wherever it pleases. You hear its sound, but you cannot tell where it comes from or where it is going. So it is with everyone born of the Spirit.
John 3:34	For the one whom God has sent speaks the words of God, for God gives the Spirit without limit.
John 4:23	Yet a time is coming and has now come when the true worshipers will worship the Father in spirit and truth, for they are the kind of worshipers the Father seeks.
John 4:24	God is spirit, and his worshipers must worship in spirit and in truth."
John 6:63	The Spirit gives life; the flesh counts for nothing. The words I have spoken to you are spirit and they are life.
John 7:39	By this he meant the Spirit, whom those who believed in him were later to receive. Up to that time the Spirit had not been given, since Jesus had not yet been glorified.
John 14:16	And I will ask the Father, and he will give you another Counselor to be with you forever—
John 14:17	the Spirit of truth. The world cannot accept him, because it neither sees him nor knows him. But you know him, for he lives with you and will be in you.
John 14:26	But the Counselor, the Holy Spirit, whom the Father will send in my name, will teach you all things and will remind you of everything I have said to you.
John 15:26	"When the Counselor comes, whom I will send to you from the Father, the Spirit of truth who goes out from the Father, he will testify about me.
John 16:7	But I tell you the truth: It is for your good that I am going away. Unless I go away, the Counselor will not come to you; but if I go, I will send him to you.
John 16:8	When he comes, he will convict the world of guilt in regard to sin and righteousness and judgment:
John 16:9	in regard to sin, because men do not believe in me;
John 16:10	in regard to righteousness, because I am going to the Father, where you can see me no longer;

John 16:11	and in regard to judgment, because the prince of this world now stands condemned.
John 16:13	But when he, the Spirit of truth, comes, he will guide you into all truth. He will not speak on his own; he will speak only what he hears, and he will tell you what is yet to come.
John 16:14	He will bring glory to me by taking from what is mine and making it known to you.
John 16:15	All that belongs to the Father is mine. That is why I said the Spirit will take from what is mine and make it known to you.
John 20:22	And with that he breathed on them and said, "Receive the Holy Spirit.

Bibliography

Commentaries on John

Beasley-Murray, George R. *John*. Word Biblical Commentary, Vol. 36. Waco: Word, 1987.

Brown, Raymond E. *The Gospel According to John XIII-XXI*. The Anchor Bible, Vol. 29a. New York: Doubleday, 1970.

Burge, Gary M. *The Anointed Community: the Holy Spirit in the Johannine Tradition*. Grand Rapids: William B. Eerdmans, 1987.

Carson, D. A. *The Gospel According to John*. The Pillar New Testament Commentary. Grand Rapids: William B. Eerdmans, 1991.

-----. *The Farewell Discourse and Final Prayer of Jesus: An Exposition of John 14-17*. Grand Rapids: Baker, 1980.

Köstenberger, Andreas J. *John*. Baker Exegetical Commentary on the New Testament. Grand Rapids: Baker Academic, 2004.

Morris, Leon. *The Gospel According to John*. The New International Commentary on the New Testament. Grand Rapids: William B. Eerdmans, 1971.

Ridderbos, Herman N. *The Gospel According to John: A Theological Commentary*. Translated by John Vriend. Grand Rapids: William B. Eerdmans, 1997.

Segovia, Fernando F. *The Farewell of the Word: The Johannine Call to Abide*. Minneapolis: Fortress, 1991.

Smith, D. Moody. *The Theology of the Gospel of John*. New Testament Theology Series. Cambridge: Cambridge University Press, 1995.

Williamson Jr., Lamar. *Preaching the Gospel of John: Proclaiming the Living Word*. Louisville: Westminster John Knox, 2004.

Works on the Holy Spirit

Boatman, Russell. *What the Bible Says about the Holy Spirit*. Joplin, MO: College Press, 1989.

Bruner, Fredrick Dale. *A Theology of the Holy Spirit*. Grand Rapids: William B. Eerdmans, 1970.

Fee, Gordon. *God's Empowering Presence: The Holy Spirit in the Letters of Paul*. Peabody, MA: Hendrickson, 1994.

-----. *Paul, the Spirit, and the People of God*. Peabody, MA: Hendrickson, 1996.

Floyd, Harvey. *Is the Holy Spirit for Me? A Search for the Meaning of the Spirit in Today's Church*. Nashville: 20th Century Christian, 1981.

Foster, Richard. *Streams of Living Water*. New York: HarperOne, 2001.

Johnson, Ashley S. *The Holy Spirit and the Human Mind*. Knoxville, TN, 1903.

Keener, Craig. *Gift and Giver: The Holy Spirit for Today*. Grand Rapids: Baker, 2001.

Nouwen, Henri. *Life of the Beloved*. New York: Crossroads, 2002.

Pinnock, Clark H. *Flame of Love: A Theology of the Holy Spirit.* Downers Grove, IL: InterVarsity, 1996.

Richardson, Robert. *A Scriptural View of the Office of the Holy Spirit.* 1872.

Works on the Trinity

Allen, C. Leonard. *Participating in God's Life: Two Crossroads for Churches of Christ.* Abilene, TX: Leafwood, 2002.

Cunningham, David. *These Three Are One: The Practice of Trinitarian Theology.* Oxford: Blackwell, 1998.

Grenz, Stanley J. *The Social God and the Relational Self: A Trinitarian Theology of the Imago Dei.* Louisville: Westminster John Knox Press, 2001.

Gunton, Colin. *Father, Son, and Holy Spirit.* London: T & T Clark, 2003.

-----. *The Promise of the Trinity.* Edinburgh: T & T Clark, 1991.

Moltmann, Jürgen. *The Trinity and the Kingdom.* Translated by Margaret Kohl. Minneapolis: Fortress Press, 1993.

Seamands, Stephen. *Ministry in the Image of God: The Trinitarian Shape of Christian Service.* Downers Grove, IL: InterVarsity Press, 2005.

Web Sites

Holy Spirit in General:
www.spirithome.com
www.carm.org/christianity/christian-doctrine/holy-spirit

Spiritual Gifts (Assessment):
http://archive.elca.org/evangelizingchurch/assessments/spiritgifts.html
www.kodachrome.org/spiritgift/
www.churchgrowth.org/cgi-cg/gifts.cgi

Spiritual Gifts (Information):
http://preceptaustin.org/spiritual_gifts_chart.htm
www.intothyword.org/pages.asp?pageid=53503
www.spirithome.com/gifts-sp.html

Endnotes

Chapter 1

1   See also John 13:36; 14:12, 30; 16:5, 16, 20, 22.
2   See also John 14:1, 21, 23; 15:4; 16:7, 16, 20.

Chapter 3

1   1500 years later, the Apostle Paul connects this "radiance" to the ministry of the Spirit (2 Cor 3:7-18). Playing with the words "face" and "glory," Paul talks about how the Spirit changes faces: God put his glory (by the Spirit?) on the face of Christ (4:6); the Spirit puts God's glory on the face of believers (3:18); and (presumably) the Spirit set God's glory on Moses' face (3:7), even though the Israelites could not bear it.

Chapter 4

1   Forgive the hyperbole. The Spirit was not *actually* irresistible. There are several instances in Acts where people lie to, test, ignore, deny, argue with, and close their hearts to the Holy Spirit (Acts 5:3, 9; 7:51; 8:18-19; 10:14; 28:25ff).

Chapter 5

1   The indwelling Spirit becomes the basis, for instance, of Paul's teaching about our being "marked" by the Spirit, who is God's brand on our lives. ("Having believed, you were marked in him with a seal, the promised Holy Spirit . . . until the redemption of those who are God's possession"—Eph 1:13-14; see also 2 Cor 1:21-22 and Gal 4:6). The indwelling Spirit is the primary reason Paul can urge his churches to live with assurance, hope, confidence, and boldness—the Spirit "in" us being a constant source of assurance about who we are and whose we are, a constant "testimony" to our status before God. ("The Spirit himself testifies with our spirit that we are God's children. Now if we are children, then we are heirs—heirs of God and co-heirs with Christ"—Rom 8:15-17; see also 2 Cor 1:22; 5:5). Paul can even speak of the Spirit "living in" the church. "You are being built together to become a dwelling in which God lives by his Spirit," he tells the Ephesians (2:22). He expresses the same idea to the Corinthians: "Don't you know that you yourselves are God's temple and that God's Spirit lives in you [plural]?" (1 Cor 3:16).

Chapter 6

1   John 2:1-11; 4:46-54; 5:1-9; 6:5-13, 19-21; 9:1-7; 11:1-44. Even the traditional seven signs do not exhaust the miraculous element in John. Jesus consistently reads the hearts and lives of people he meets in this Gospel: Nathaniel (1:48); Nicodemus (3:3); the woman at the well (4:16); and the crowds (6:43). He also,

and mysteriously, avoids being stoned to death and evades arrest—even though the authorities try their hardest. (See 5:18; 7:30-32, 45-46; 8:20, 59; 10:31-33, 39).

2   All of these statements refer to the same handful of incidents: blasphemy against the Spirit; the Spirit providing words when the disciples are arrested; David speaking by inspiration of the Spirit; etc.

3   Some translations (NIV for instance) do not capitalize the word "spirit" in this passage, unfortunately leading some readers to think that Jesus is contrasting worship in a *place* with a more interior, personalized worship. But Jesus' point here is not about *sincerity* of worship or *intensity* of worship; rather, he is introducing this woman to the idea that only when the Holy Spirit prompts worship, empowers worship, reveals a God worth worshiping and the full truth of his purposes in the world can "true worship" actually occur. In this regard, Brown comments: "His statement has nothing to do with worshiping God in the inner recesses of one's own spirit; for the Spirit is the Spirit of God, not the spirit of man, as vs. 24 makes clear." (Raymond Brown *The Gospel According to John I-XII* (New York: Doubleday and Company, Inc. 1966), 180.

4   William Shakespeare; *Romeo and Juliet*.

5   Contemporary English Version; Worldwide English Version

6   New Living Translation; New Revised Standard Version; Today's New International Version

7   King James Version; American Standard Version; Wycliffe New Testament

8   New International Version; Holman's Christian Standard Version

9   New American Standard Bible, English Standard Version; New King James Version; New Century Version

10 The Message; New International Readers Version

11 Amplified Bible

12 Amplified Bible

13 "In John 14-16 no such function of the Spirit as advocate of the disciples and defender before God is mentioned." Herman Ridderbos, *The Gospel According to John: A Theological Commentary* (Grand Rapids: William B. Eerdmans, 1997), 500. "The actual function of the Spirit-Paraclete as set forth in chapters 14-16 is not so much to represent the disciples before the divine tribunal . . . as to represent Jesus to his disciples left behind on earth." D. Moody Smith, *The Theology of the Gospel of John* (Cambridge: Cambridge University Press, 1995), 140. There *is* that statement about the *Paraclete* working to "convict the world of guilt"— John 16:8. But it is the world's own conscience, rather than a law court, where a verdict of "Guilty" is demanded. And the usual task of a *Paraclete*—even in court contexts—is *defense* rather than prosecution. Legal images certainly arise in other texts. But they should not color our understanding of the word here.

14 "The consensus is that in John 14-16 *parakletos* does not have the meaning in Greek and Hellenistic usage of advocate, professional legal adviser, defender, or representative before a court." Ridderbos, *John*, 500.

15 D. A. Carson, *The Gospel According to John* (Grand Rapids: Eerdmans, 1991), 499.

16 "For the specific use and meaning of the name "Paraclete" in John 14-16 we are dependent on the text themselves and cannot base our conclusions on representations and figures in other sources." Ridderbos, *John*, 503.

17 Ridderbos, *John*, 503.

18 Andreas Köstenberger, *John* (Grand Rapids: Baker Academic, 2004), 446.

Chapter 8

1 Herman Ridderbos, *The Gospel According to John: A Theological Commentary* (Grand Rapids: William B. Eerdmans, 1997), 503.

2 "The implication of v 16 is that Jesus has performed the role of a Paraclete during his earthly ministry, and after his departure he will ask the Father to send another Paraclete to perform a like ministry for his disciples." George Beasley-Murray *John* (Waco: Word Books, Publisher, 1987), 256. "Nevertheless 'another Paraclete' in the context of Jesus' departure implies that the disciples already have one, the one who is departing." D. A. Carson, *The Gospel According to John* (Grand Rapids: William B. Eerdmans, 1991), 500. "Clearly, therefore, John presents the Spirit-Paraclete as the successor of Jesus who carries on his revelatory work, sustaining the disciples after the rupture represented by Jesus' death." D. Moody Smith, *The Theology of the Gospel of John* (Cambridge: Cambridge University Press, 1995), 143.

3 Jesus refers to the Spirit as the "Spirit of truth" three times in this Final Discourse.

4 "Jesus' identification with the Spirit, the 'other *paracletos*,' is so strong that he can say that *he himself* will return to his followers in the person of the Spirit." Andreas Köstenberger, *John* (Grand Rapids: Baker Academic, 2004), 434. "John presents the Paraclete as the Holy Spirit in a special role, namely, as the personal presence of Jesus in the Christian while Jesus is with the Father. . . . Virtually everything that has been said about the Paraclete has been said elsewhere in the Gospel about Jesus. . . . Thus, the one whom John calls 'another Paraclete' is another Jesus. . . . the Paraclete is the presence of Jesus when Jesus is absent. Jesus' promises to dwell within his disciples are fulfilled in the Paraclete. . . . [The Paraclete is] the continued post-resurrectional presence of Jesus with his disciples. . ." Raymond Brown, *The Gospel According to John XIII-XX,* (New York: Doubleday, 1970), 1139-1141. "In the person of the Paraclete, Jesus is present within and among all believers." Lamar Williamson, Jr., *Preaching the Gospel of John: Proclaiming the Living Word* (Louisville: Westminster John Knox Press, 2004), 189. "The actual function of the Spirit-Paraclete as set forth in chapters 14-16 is not so much to represent the disciples before the divine tribunal (as in John 2:1) as to represent Jesus to his disciples left behind on earth. The Spirit-Paraclete speaks to the question of how Jesus will continue with his disciples or church during his physical absence from them." Smith, *Theology of John*, 140.

5 "It is obvious that Jesus is speaking of a more continued presence than was possible in the brief period of post-resurrectional appearances— not only the words 'I shall not leave you orphans' but the whole tone of his remarks imply permanency." Raymond Brown, *John*, 645-646.

"Though 'yet a little while' in 14:19 and 'on that day' in 14:20 at first blush may appear to refer to Jesus' resurrection appearances, Jesus' promise in 14:18 not to leave his disciples as orphans is hardly satisfied by his resurrection appearances, which were temporary in nature, and more likely refers to the permanent replacement of his presence with the Spirit." Kostenberger, *John*, 434.

6   "This understanding of the coming again of Jesus Christ transforms the meaning of the expression 'on that day' in the Fourth Gospel. . . . [John is] referring to the time when believers will live on the strength of Jesus' presence as the Paraclete." Williamson, Jr., *Preaching John*, 189.

7   Jesus "lives," but the proof of that is not his walking out of the tomb so much as his walking into disciples' lives through the ministry of the Spirit. And the disciples "live," not only because Jesus was raised from the dead but because he makes the Spirit available to them—his presence in Spirit form.

8   "It would be inaccurate to represent the Fourth Gospel as merging the resurrection of Jesus, the coming of the Spirit, and the return of Jesus into one event, for the evangelist can obviously distinguish among them. Yet the fundamental theological reality to which they point is the same, namely, Jesus' continued presence with his disciples after the death that terminates his physically mediated relationship with them." Smith, *Theology of John*, 141. "One can see that in 14:15-17 it is the Paraclete/Advocate/Spirit who will come to be with the disciples forever. In 14:18-21 it is Jesus who will come to live in the disciples and reveal himself to them. In 14:23-24 it is the Father who will come with Jesus to make a dwelling place within the disciples. All of these indwellings are thought of as accomplished through and in the Paraclete, who is the presence of Jesus while Jesus is absent . . ." Williamson, Jr., *Preaching John*, 190.

9   In fairness, we must admit that Jesus is not speaking here with mathematical precision. His language is enigmatic, riddled. He hints rather than specifies, intrigues rather than defines. Still, it is clearly the *Paraclete* he is offering his disciples . . . and *himself* in the form of the *Paraclete*.

Chapter 9

1   "The need for this among the disciples was acute, as is evident from the questions that they asked Jesus during this farewell, which prove their incomprehension." Herman Ridderbos, *The Gospel According to John: A Theological Commentary* (Grand Rapids: Eerdmans, 1997), 510.

2   In the High Priestly Prayer that immediately follows the Final Discourse (John 17), mission continues to be the point. Jesus speaks of his own mission (17:1-4) and refers repeatedly to the transfer of that mission to the Twelve: "I gave them the words you gave me and they accepted them" (17:8); "I have given them your word and the world has hated them" (17:14); "As you sent me into the world, I have sent them into the world" (17:18); "those who believe in me *through their message*" (17:20), "to let the world know" (17:23).

3   You also see evidence of this hand-off in Matthew's Great Commission: "Go and make disciples of all nations" (Matt 28:19). You hear it in Mark's version:

"Go into all the world and preach" (Mark 16:15). There are echoes of it in Luke's "Repentance and forgiveness of sins will be preached in [my] name to all nations" (Luke 24:47—where Jesus hastens to add, "You are witnesses of these things"). And, of course, there is Luke's additional memory of commissioning captured in Acts: "You will be my witnesses in Jerusalem, and in all Judea and Samaria, and to the ends of the earth" (Acts 1:8).

4   "In the NT, the experience of the Spirit is never insular. It pushes the Christian community out into the world. Therefore an important corollary of NT pneumatology is mission and witness. . . . The community did not merely enjoy tranquil reflection or the satisfaction of spiritual enthusiasm; its life was intimately involved with history. Its word of testimony became flesh and actively engaged the surrounding world." Gary Burge, *The Anointed Community: The Holy Spirit in the Johannine Tradition* (Grand Rapids: Eerdmans, 1987), 198-199.

5   "The work that the Spirit is sent out to do as the other Paraclete remains the work of Jesus; the work is being continued by the Spirit, but Jesus, in his heavenly mode of existence and position of power, is and remains the great sponsor of that work." Ridderbos, *John*, 510.

6   "In John's Gospel, the disciples are shown to fail, throughout Jesus' ministry, in their understanding of Jesus. One of the Spirit's principle tasks, after Jesus is glorified, is to remind the disciples of Jesus' teaching and thus, in the new situation after the resurrection, to help them grasp its significance and thus to teach them what it meant." D. A. Carson, *The Gospel According to John* (Grand Rapids: Eerdmans, 1991), 505. "[The Spirit] not only enables them to *recall* these things but to perceive their significance, and so he *teaches* the disciples to grasp the revelation of God brought by Jesus in its richness and profundity. Two observations accordingly are in place regarding this saying about the Paraclete: first, it is clear that the Spirit brings no new revelation; his task is to point to that which Jesus brought and to enable the disciples to understand it; second. . . his role as representative of Jesus and his task of recalling and interpreting the revelation brought by Jesus make very clear the personal nature of the Spirit." George Beasley-Murray *John* (Waco: Word, 1987), 261. "Therefore, the statement about 'teaching all things' is explained by 'and bring to your remembrance all that I have said to you,' which obviously relates not just to the disciples' capacity to remember but also to the process of learning to understand that which lay hidden, as an undiscovered treasure, in their memories and traditions concerning Jesus." Ridderbos, *John*, 510-511.

7   "Contrary to what is sometimes claimed for the 'all things' taught by the Spirit, Jesus is not suggesting that the Spirit has something to say that is new or distinct from his own teachings, or that they involve hidden revelations and secret mysteries 'that could never be imagined on the basis of Jesus' teaching during his ministry.'" D. Moody Smith, *The Theology of the Gospel of John* (Cambridge: Cambridge University Press, 1995), 141. The Spirit's teaching is not *other* than Jesus' or *different* from Jesus'. It is, rather, an *extension* of Jesus' teaching to the new world of the resurrection and the new conditions of the future.

8   In fact, if you think about it, a Gentile ministry based solely on the teachings and example of Jesus would have been difficult to justify. Eventually Jesus commanded the Apostles to "Go into all the world" (Mark 16:15) and "make disciples of all

nations" (Matt 28:19). We hear those commands through the lens of the great missionary explosion recorded in Acts and understand that—of course—Jesus meant the Gentiles to be included. But the Apostles would have heard those commands through the lens of Jesus' own example and teaching. And during his lifetime, the rule was to preach only to the Hebrews. "Do not go among the Gentiles or enter any town of the Samaritans. Go rather to the lost sheep of Israel" (Mt 10: 5-6). That's what Jesus commanded the Twelve when he first sent them out to preach. He told a Gentile woman, begging for mercy for her daughter, "I was sent only to the lost sheep of Israel" (Mt 15:24). Certainly Jesus had a soft spot for hurting people, whatever their ethnicity. He healed Gentiles and even taught a Samaritan woman. But the thrust of Jesus' ministry was to the people of Israel, not to outsiders. It's not hard to imagine the early church, left only with their memories of Jesus and without the active guidance of the Holy Spirit, deciding that, while they were commanded to go into all the world and preach the gospel, their audience was to be only Jews.

9   A paraphrase of a line in the poem "If," by Rudyard Kipling.

Chapter 10

1   "The Paraclete Passage in xv 26-27 not only looks forward to the passages that follow, but is also related to what has just been said by Jesus, for the coming of the Paraclete gives a profound explanation of why the world treats Jesus' disciples the same way it treated him. The Paraclete represents Jesus' presence among men . . . and in hating the disciples who are the dwelling place of the Paraclete, the world is striking at Jesus' continued presence on earth." Raymond Brown, *The Gospel According to John XIII-XXI* (New York: Doubleday, 1970), 698-699.

2   "The Spirit's task is to 'bear witness' concerning Jesus. . . . His witness therefore is not here conceived of as that of an advocate, speaking in defense of *the disciples*. . . nor is it that of a prosecuting attorney, giving evidence *against* the world. . . . The witness of the Spirit, conjoined with that of the disciples, is to bring to light the truth of the revelation of Jesus in his word and dead, and death and resurrection." George Beasley-Murray, *John* (Waco: Word, 1987), 276-277.

3   "[The disciples'] witness is linked with that of the Holy Spirit. It is the same Christ to whom they bear witness and it is the same salvation of which they bear witness. At the same time it is *their* witness. They cannot simply relax and leave it all to the Spirit. They have a particular function in bearing witness in that they were with Jesus from the very beginning. There is a responsibility resting on all Christians to bear their witness to the facts of saving grace. They cannot evade this." Leon Morris, *The Gospel According to John* (Grand Rapids: Eerdmans, 1971), 684.

4   "Although the Spirit may bear witness to the world apart from Christians, it would be out of step with these chapters to think that Christians are thought of as those who bear witness apart from the Spirit. Whether we think of the Spirit's help in the crisis of acute persecution. . . or in the context of sustained, faithful witness. . ., the community's witness is to be empowered by the Paraclete himself." D. A. Carson, *The Gospel According to John* (Grand Rapids: Eerdmans, 1991), 530.

5   "When, after all the negative things he has said, Jesus now promises the coming of the Paraclete as the one who will bear witness to him, this is naturally intended to reassure the disciples that in the enormous opposition they encounter in the world they will not stand alone. The Paraclete's witness to Jesus is the assistance that the Spirit will give the disciples in the great controversy between the church and the world. . ." Herman Ridderbos, *The Gospel According to John: A Theological Commentary* (Grand Rapids: Eerdmans, 1997), 526.

6   The "careers" of the various Apostles, of course, is speculative, depending on an uncertain mix of tradition, legend, and later embellishment. What is important for our purposes is not the accuracy of the details but the certainty of the Apostolic commitment to witness to the dying and rising Jesus, a commitment that led them to risk everything and (in the end) give everything to be true to their mission.

Chapter 11

1   Robert Louis Stevenson, *The Celestial Surgeon.*

2   "The thought is not that Jesus and the Holy Spirit cannot, for unarticulated metaphysical reasons, simultaneously minister to God's people, or any other such strange notion. Rather the thought is eschatological. The many biblical promises that the Spirit will characterize the age of the kingdom of God . . . breed anticipation. But this saving reign of God cannot be fully inaugurated until Jesus has died, risen from the dead, and been exalted to this Father's right hand, returned to the glory he enjoyed with the Father before the world began." D. A. Carson, *The Gospel According to John* (Grand Rapids: Eerdmans, 1991), 533-534.

3   The disciples who remained on the plain while Jesus was transfigured on the mountain, for instance, had to wait for Jesus to rejoin them before knowing what to do about a demon-possessed boy (Matt 17:1-21).

4   Matthew 15:15-20 (Compare Luke 24:45 where the resurrected Jesus has the power to "open their minds.")

5   I am indebted to D. A. Carson for his cogent and convincing work on this passage. Delving into what Jesus meant by "because men do not believe in me" or "because I am going to the Father, where you can see me no longer" or "because the prince of this world now stands condemned" is simply beyond the scope of this book. Scholarly opinion on how these comments might be connected to "sin and righteousness and judgment" is divided and, often, obfuscating.

6   "Just as Jesus forced a division in the world (15:20) by showing that what it does is evil . . ., so the Paraclete continues this work." Carson, *John*, 537. "In being the moving force behind this [convicting work] the Paraclete is simply continuing the work of Jesus who himself bore evidence against the world that what it does is evil." Raymond Brown, *The Gospel According to John XIII-XXI* (New York: Doubleday, 1970), 712.

7   "In common with other New Testament usages, [convict] means 'to convict [the world]' in the personal sense, i.e., not arguing the case of the world's objective guilt before God at the final Great Assize, but shaming the world and convincing it of its own guilt, thus calling it to repentance." Carson, *John*, 536.

Chapter 12

1   "This fifth and final Paraclete Passage (vss 12-15) is a suitable climax to the series, since it focuses on the completion of the revelation of Jesus Christ." D. A. Carson, *The Gospel According to John* (Grand Rapids: William B. Eerdmans, 1991), 539.

2   "More likely vs. 12 means that only after Jesus' resurrection will there be full understanding of what happened and was said during the ministry, a theme that is familiar in John. . . . It is unlikely that in Johannine thought there was any concept of further revelation after the ministry of Jesus, for Jesus is *the* revelation of the Father, the Word of God." Raymond Brown, *The Gospel According to John XIII-XXI* (New York: Doubleday & Company, Inc., 1970), 714. "The Paraclete's guidance along the way of all truth involves more than a deeper intellectual understanding of what Jesus has said—it involves a way of life in conformity with Jesus' teaching . . ." Brown, *John*, 715. "In any case the emphasis is on the term "all": the truth has been made known by Jesus to the disciples, but their grasp of it has been limited; the task of the Paraclete will be to lead them that they may comprehend the depths and heights of the revelation as yet unperceived by them." George Beasley-Murray, *John* (Waco: Word, 1987), 283.

3   There is a prayer at the end of this evening that closes out Jesus' ministry. It is known as the High Priestly Prayer (John 17). In it, Jesus gives his Father a final report on his mission to earth and makes a few last requests. The prayer begins: "This is eternal life: that they may know you" (17:3)—yet another reference to the primacy of his revealing work. Jesus then assures his Father that he has made that matter a priority in his ministry: "I have completed the work you gave me to do. . . . I have revealed you to those whom you gave me out of the world" (17:4, 6).

     As he finishes the prayer, however, Jesus says something that suggests he has more in mind than his own accomplishments: "I have made you known to them, and will *continue to make you known*" (17:26—emphasis mine). How can he talk about "continuing" the vital work of revealing his Father when he is leaving the world behind to go home? Jesus is pointing beyond himself and his earthly ministry to the Holy Spirit, the *Paraclete*, who is coming to continue his revealing work.

4   "Despite his words of consolation and his promise to "come back" so that they can see him again, Jesus cannot unpack for them the full meaning of these events; that would be too much for them. . . . Only the overpowering surprise of seeing him again after his resurrection will explain the riddle—partly in the light of the Scriptures (cf. 20:9) and above all through the assistance of the Spirit." Herman Ridderbos, *The Gospel According to John: A Theological Commentary* (Grand Rapids: Eerdmans, 1997), 535.

5   "We are to understand that Jesus is the nodal point of revelation, God's culminating self-disclosure, God's final self-expression, God's 'Word' (1:1, 14). . . . That does not mean he himself provides all the details his followers will need; it does mean that 'extra' bits the Holy Spirit provides after he is sent by Christ Jesus, consequent upon Jesus' death/exaltation, are nothing more than the filling out of the revelation nodally present in Jesus himself." Carson, *John*, 539.

6   Paul gets at this same idea when he prays for his churches: "I keep asking that the God of our Lord Jesus Christ, the glorious Father, may give you the Spirit of wisdom and revelation, so that you may know him better" (Eph 1:17). "I pray that out of his glorious riches [the Father] may strengthen you with power through his Spirit in your inner being, so that Christ may dwell in your hearts through faith" (Eph 3:16). "We have not stopped praying for you and asking God to fill you with the knowledge of his will through all spiritual wisdom and understanding" (Col 1:9). The "knowledge of God" is consistently linked in Paul's writings with the revelational work of the Spirit.

Chapter 14

1   "Jesus' valuation of what is for his disciples' 'good', indeed, for our good, ought to temper longings of the 'Oh-if-only-I-could-have-been-in-Galilee-when-Jesus-was-there!' sort. That same Jesus insists it is better to be alive now, after the coming of the Spirit." D. A. Carson, *The Gospel According to John* (Grand Rapids: Eerdmans, 1991), 534.

Chapter 15

1   That's what much of this letter does, by the way—point to ideas that are essential for Christian faith: Jesus came in the flesh; we have to live obediently, we have to love each other.

2   Again, personal morality is very much on John's mind in this letter: walking in darkness, confessing sin, obeying commands, living like Jesus.

Chapter 16

1   Judges 13-16

2   1 Samuel 9-15 (particularly 10:6)

3   Matthew 10:1; John 6:70

A Study Guide and Workbook for

WHAT JESUS SAID ABOUT THE HOLY SPIRIT

by Tim Woodroof

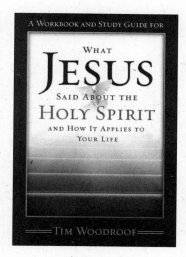

$9.99 paper
ISBN 978-0-89112-636-2

For use in classes, small groups, and personal study

WORKBOOK INCLUDES:

1. Reflection questions for each of the 16 chapters
2. Personal inductive Bible studies
3. Small group studies
4. "Disciplines" for inviting the Spirit
5. Prayers and personal devotions

LEAFWOOD
PUBLISHERS
1-877-816-4455 toll free
www.leafwoodpublishers.com